E. E. CUMMINGS
The Magic-Maker

Self-portrait, Jan. 5, 1938 (oil, 22 x 33 in., now at the Humanities Research Center, The University of Texas at Austin)

E. E. CUMMINGS,
The Magic-Maker

By Charles Norman

THE BOBBS-MERRILL COMPANY, INC.

INDIANAPOLIS · NEW YORK

The Bobbs-Merrill Company, Inc.
Publishers: Indianapolis • New York

To Nancy and Rush

Contents

Part Three

Introduction

Horace Gregory said to me one day: "Why don't you bring back *The Magic-Maker* in its original form?"

I protested that the book, long out of print, was in the present tense, since Cummings was still alive when it was published; but even as I spoke I experienced one of those rare moments when the truth is like a vision. What Mr. Gregory added was decisive.

"*The Magic-Maker* is the life of a poet," he said. He may have emphasized "life."

Perhaps he was thinking of a telegram Cummings once sent to the *Yale Literary Magazine:* "From my doubtless limited point of view the only thing to say about Dylan Thomas is that being a true poet he's alive." I know that this telegram, which appears in *The Magic-Maker,* leapt to my mind as Gregory spoke. Shortly after, I was fortunate enough to find another publisher.

I began to write this book after a friendship with E. E. Cummings which had already lasted thirty-two years. I wrote it with his approval and cooperation, and while this kind of intimate association between a biographer and his subject has certain disadvantages, there were obvious compensations.

In the first place, there had been no previous account of his early experiences and earliest work, and conversations in Patchin Place, as well as correspondence with him when he was at his farm, were the answer. His letters, in reply to my queries, were written with authority, of course, but they were also written with verve and humor; read here, they supplement in the liveliest form the recently published *Selected Letters* edited by F. W. Dupee and George Stade. And it was to the farm in New Hampshire that I went as well, to examine the accumulations of family and literary documents, which Cummings placed at my disposal. On one of these visits he drove me, in his 1929 Ford sedan, to the home of his sister, who generously lent me her manuscript account of their childhood in Cambridge, Massachusetts. Among other things, she had recorded the genesis of a famous poem: "The first and most exciting sign that spring had really come was the balloon man. First you heard his whistle in the distance. . . ."

I had, of course, followed Cummings's work and career during all the time that I knew him, and in preparation for this book I interviewed many who had known him earlier. There was also some correspondence. Alyse Gregory (Mrs. Llewelyn Powys), managing editor of *The Dial* before Marianne Moore, whose views are incorporated in the text, wrote me about an aspect of Cummings which was one of his most engaging traits—"wit at the immediate service of compassion." She also remarked on his "almost Proustian receptivity so that his understanding is practically simultaneous with one's thought and before this thought has found words." She added:

"I do not know anyone with whom conversation can take so many lively turns, and he has what one loves to think is still somehow treasured and preserved of the old America—the high standards, the reverence for things of the mind, the open sensibility and above all the grace of manners."

His wit—his conversation! Another correspondent—William Saroyan—suggested tape; but, alas, Cummings was against it. He could not see "even Freud persuading our doubtless agoraphobic nonhero to tape-talk." But over the years I managed to set down some accurate examples of his monologue manner, and several of them will be found in this book.

Although Cummings's fame rests chiefly on his poetry and *The Enormous Room*—which some critics mistakenly persist in terming a novel—an examination of his work reveals him to be, surprisingly, a modern man of letters, that is, a literary man who can write anything well. He is the author of a full-length play (prose) and several shorter ones in verse; a ballet based on *Uncle Tom's Cabin;* a travel book; fairy tales for children; poetry and art criticism; theatrical reviews, and a number of humorous and satirical articles, some under pseudonyms. As for his painting, while many writers have "also painted," Cummings had actually done more painting than writing, and I have devoted a chapter to it.

In quoting from reviews of Cummings's work I have favored reviewers who *quoted*; by doing so, I believe I have added to the variety of his range and expression so far as this book is concerned. As for the documents, there are those who do not like a great deal of this sort of thing; but let it be remembered that I was the first to offer them, and that they concern important books and events.

I am grateful to Ezra Pound for his most generous offer to let me use anything of his that would "boost . . . me nobl and dist-intissimo collega," Cummings. His monumental review of *Eimi,* which had never before been reprinted, was one of the fruits of that offer. I am also grateful to him for calling my attention to Edmondo Dodsworth's article about Cummings in *Broletto* (November, 1938). According to Pound, Dodsworth is an Italian: "name inherited from an englander, grand or gt grand father who stopped off on the way back from India." As Dodsworth's ideas seem to me to be basic for understanding poetry in our time, I give them here, in Willard R. Trask's translation:

> 1. The logical world in which the 'normal man' moves
> or thinks he moves, far from being the whole of truth, is
> only a narrow division of it, a mere system of abstractions,
> invented and maintained for reasons of practical convenience,
> whether technical or social. From the poetic point of view
> this world is by definition *the maximum of irreality.*
>
> 2. Consequently the supreme task of poetry is to destroy
> and transcend this irreality in the service of something im-
> mensely more profound and vital.

This "something," Dodsworth concludes, is *"indomitable lyrical-ness,"* in the service of which "Cummings is one of its most vital representatives."

And now, a word or two about Cummings's very personal use of typography, which has confused some and infuriated others (for examples of critical confusion and fury, see text). Even T. S. Eliot was put off by it. He wrote me in 1957: "I have a very high opinion of Mr. Cummings as a poet, in spite of my dislike of his typography." In the chapter entitled *"The Dial* and the Poet" I have devoted a great deal of space to Cummings's technique, and there some of his most beautiful poems will be found. I said: "A poem is the culmination of a poet's experience, and is itself part of that experience. Cummings communicates his experience by means of language and forms that *dramatize* it, so that the experience is still taking place so far as the reader is concerned."

But a poet's language is conveyed by means of typographical units, and he was always alert to the visual images suggested by certain of those units. An example of this will be found on page 147, where a question mark is made to glow, and in the famous mouse poem (page 169), in which the mouse, as I have pointed out, peers from a parenthesis. He is also present, I find now, in the ampersand with a comma attached, and in one other place, I think—couched in "mouse," tail down.

As for the lowercase "i," Cummings defended it by saying that English is the only language he was familiar with that capitalized the first personal pronoun. It is not much of a defense to an Englishman or an American, and when his poems are read aloud the point is elusive. He was correct about the other languages.

For his occasional separation of the parts of a word and setting a word or words between those parts, the Greek word for it is *tmesis,* and Cummings was right to complain that "the people who object to my way of writing have never read the classics. That has nothing to do with whether my work is good or bad."

As for the device, in both prose and verse, and letters, of closing up—in printers' parlance—a punctuation mark and the word that follows it, here, too, Cummings took his cue from the highest source —Shakespeare, whom he revered; not Shakespeare modernized, but the First Folio and the 1609 edition of the *Sonnets,* facsimiles of which are numerous. For the purpose of demonstration I offer Sonnet 86, the so-called "rival poet" sonnet, not because it is typographically unique—it is not; all Shakespeare's sonnets follow the same style— but because in addition to closed-up punctuation and words it has a parenthesis which appears pure Cummings:

Was it the proud full saile of his great verse,
Bound for the prize of (all-to-precious) you,
That did my ripe thoughts in my braine inhearce,
Making the tombe the wombe wherein they grew?
Was it his spirit,by spirits taught to write,
Aboue a mortall pitch,that struck me dead?
No,neither he,nor his compiers by night
Giuing him ayde,my verse astonished.
He nor that affable familiar ghost
Which nightly gulls him with intelligence,
As victors of my silence cannot boast,
I was not sick of any feare from thence.
But when your countinance fild vp his line,
Then lackt I matter,that infeebled mine.

But Cummings was also an innovator. "He was the first," I wrote, "to introduce and develop those structural elements on the printed page which act as doors and passageways to ultimate effects." Cummings modestly disclaimed all this in a letter: "From my standpoint, not EEC but EP is the authentic 'innovator'; the true trailblazer of an epoch." To this I can only say that the facade of his lines, but not their structure, may derive from Pound whose poem, "The Return," made such a profound impression on him when he read it at Harvard in 1912. Pound wrote me in 1957: "I do not think Mr. Cummings is indebted to me for any of the brilliance of his style, which is intensely personal."

Since all poets deal with the same subjects, more or less, it is only by the structure of their lines that they achieve identity. This structure, I believe, comes from the way they breathe, a point I made in a lecture about Cummings at Black Mountain College in 1939; others have since taken it up and expounded it. But, as I have stated in *The Magic-Maker*, everything Cummings wrote, including *The Enormous Room*, the play *Him*, the diary travel book *Eimi*, as well as his poems, carries the same accent, of aliveness, or in Dodsworth's phrase, "indomitable lyricalness." A poet's breathing is the measure of his intensity; it is also the source of his individuality.

Cummings died, aged sixty-seven, on September 3, 1962. His place seems secure by this simple criterion: almost half a century after the memorable *Tulips and Chimneys,* his first volume of verse, the mere mention of his name can bring entire poems to mind. It applies to all who are truly creative: an artist lives by his works of art, a poet by his poems (not by "poetry," of which there is now a great deal).

For this edition of *The Magic-Maker* I have silently corrected or emended a few passages. The crab-apple tree in Washington Square, described in Chapter One, was cut down in 1961. But the clock in Jefferson Market Court tower, also mentioned there, has long since been repaired, and the courthouse itself is now a branch of the New York Public Library.

I thank Marion Morehouse Cummings, who patiently gathered some of the material used in this book, and whose photographs of paintings and drawings appear in its pages. I thank Anne Barton Girsdansky, the poet's second wife, for her present of the enchanting photographs of Cummings as a boy with his Unitarian minister father, taken at the farm in New Hampshire around the turn of the century, and for the snapshots of herself with Cummings and Hart Crane. I thank Elizabeth Cummings Qualey for permission to quote from her manuscript. And I thank Marianne Moore—that special person.

I am particularly grateful to Dr. James Sibley Watson and his wife, Hildegarde, for their kindness to me at their home in Rochester, N.Y., where I got a first-hand account of *The Dial,* he having been one of the co-owners, and where I saw the fine, representative collection of Cummings's paintings owned by her.

I thank my friend, the Hon. Perkins Bass, former Congressman from New Hampshire, who helped me locate the State Department and Paris Embassy files on Cummings and William Slater Brown which serve as background to the chapter entitled "The Poet at War." I am also grateful to Wayne C. Grover, Archivist of the United States, who promptly supplied me with photostats of those voluminous files; to Mr. Brown ("B" in *The Enormous Room*), and to John Dos Passos, both of whom were helpful on the war period, the last-named also supplying me with information on *Eight Harvard Poets,* in the publication of which he was a prime mover. For additional information on Cummings's Harvard years, I thank S. Foster Damon, who supplied me with copious notes; I also thank him for his hospitality in Annisquam, Massachusetts.

I wish especially to thank Lola L. Szladits, curator, Berg Collection, The New York Public Library, and Mary M. Hirth, Academic Center Library, The University of Texas. I thank Dr. John H. Finley,

Master of Eliot House, and McGeorge Bundy, then Dean of the Faculty of Arts and Sciences at Harvard, for their kind reception and for letting me see—and to quote from—the interesting correspondence dealing with Cummings's appointment as Charles Eliot Norton Professor of Poetry, which occasioned the famous *Six Nonlectures*. I am also grateful to the librarians of the University, and particularly to Mrs. Marcia O'Kelly, of the Harvard Archives.

I thank the following, all connected with the memorable Provincetown Playhouse production of *Him* in 1928: Henry G. Alsberg, Zelda Dorfman, William C. Johnstone, James Light, Erin O'Brien-Moore and Lionel Stander. Gilbert Seldes I thank separately, he having been helpful in other, additional respects. I also wish to thank Arthur Pell, of the Liveright Publishing Corp.; Pascal Covici of The Viking Press; Charles A. Pearce of Duell, Sloan & Pearce; Denver Lindley and Robert Giroux, both formerly of Harcourt, Brace & Co.; the Houghton Mifflin Co. for permission to reprint two poems from *The Complete Poetical Works of Amy Lowell* and to quote from *Amy Lowell: A Chronicle* by S. Foster Damon; Little, Brown & Co. for permission to quote from *Dylan Thomas in America* by John Malcolm Brinnin, and Longmans, Green & Co., Ltd., and McGraw-Hill, for permission to quote from *The Meaning of Beauty* by Eric Newman. For this edition I have also drawn from *The Best Times,* the autobiography of John Dos Passos, published in 1966. Cummings's fugitive pieces, referred to in Chapter Nine, have been collected in *E. E. Cummings: A Miscellany,* edited by George J. Firmage. Additional book acknowledgments will be found on the copyright page.

Many names which appear in the original Introduction to *The Magic-Maker* are here omitted, without any diminution of my gratitude. But once again I acknowledge the help given me by M. R. Werner, one of Cummings's earliest friends in New York, the more so because he was the first with whom I discussed the book after clearance from above. His advice was sound, and I hope I have followed it: to write without fear or favor, if that was his phrase.

C. N.

Part One

I can not find language of sufficient energy to convey my sense of the sacredness of private integrity.

EMERSON

In accumulating property for ourselves or our posterity, in founding a family or a state, or acquiring fame even, we are mortal; but in dealing with truth we are immortal, and need fear no change nor accident.

THOREAU

It was suddenly brought home to me how much freer people were—in their emotions, in their ideas and in expressing themselves. In the twenties they could love, they could travel, they could stay up late at night as extravagantly as they pleased; they could think or say or write whatever seemed to them amusing or interesting. There was a good deal of irresponsibility, and a lot of money and energy wasted, and the artistic activities of the time suffered somewhat from its general vices, but it was a much more favorable climate for writing than the period we are in now.

EDMUND WILSON

I remember not long ago hearing Picasso and Gertrude Stein talking about various things that had happened at that time, one of them said but all that could not have happened in that one year, oh said the other, my dear you forget we were young then and we did a great deal in a year.

GERTRUDE STEIN

Chapter 1

PORTRAIT, WITH VIEWS

1

Patchin Place is a *cul-de-sac* of three-story brick houses in Greenwich Village. It has an iron gate at one end, a wooden fence and lamp-post at the other. The sidewalks are narrow; two may walk abreast if one is ready to step down. Between the sidewalks and brick walls thrust eight or nine ailanthus trees with curving trunks, giving the street a dappled shade in summer and afterwards strewing its pavement with seed-pods and wrinkled leaves. The houses are all painted alike. In them have lived a number of writers and artists, and the street is—or was before radio and TV—a quiet residential enclave with an old New York look. Across Tenth Street, on which Patchin Place abuts, stands Jefferson Market Court, no longer a court and no longer a market, and its Gothic tower clock no longer dependable.

Daily from a house on the left-hand side of Patchin Place a man emerges, bound for Washington Square. A weathered hat rides high on a head seeking to soar from squared shoulders loosely draped in an old jacket, from the left pocket of which protrudes the top of a black notebook. The face under the hat takes daylight as though it

3

and the light and air are friends. It is a face without guile. Hazel
eyes, which now seem abstracted—slight acquaintances complain of
not being recognized on the street—can in the closer proximity of a
room pierce disconcertingly or brim with laughter or mischief like a
child's. The nose is strong, the mouth full and sensual, the chin arrogant. The ears are large and seemingly tense with listening; they
belong to a born eavesdropper of human speech or a dissolving sliver
of birdsong. On rainy days the slim figure of this man strides buoy-
antly under an ancient black umbrella held aloft like a balloonman's
bouquet of balloons. He has beautiful hands.

Turning left on Tenth Street, and headed for Sixth Avenue—now
sans Elevated and officially "the Avenue of the Americas"—he passes
the florist shop on the corner where he and the proprietor, Mr.
S. Psomas, have often bowed to each other among the blossoms; for
flowers are a necessity to him, and he thinks his friends—and sometimes strangers who have been charming or kind—should have them,
too. Diagonally across Sixth Avenue from the florist shop stands the
stationery emporium of Mr. A. Schwartz, another friend. Now as he
proceeds southward on the avenue, a number of pedestrians who are
Village residents have become aware of his progress; some turn to
watch, others name him to ignorant companions, having seen him
plain. He is Edward Estlin Cummings, poet and painter; or, as he
has described himself, "an author of pictures, a draughtsman of
words."

The Village has long been aware of him. He has lived in this
quarter of New York four decades, with only occasional sojourns
abroad, and he has been celebrated virtually all that time, for he
leapt into fame with the first number of *The Dial* in January, 1920.
I have heard Villagers remark, over the years, that they had seen him
on his daily walk, and they remarked it with pleasure, as though by
this glimpse of him they had partaken of the aura which surrounds
famous men. His friends, too, have seen him, but left him to his
meditations—as a rule—by pretending blindness.

The entrance to Washington Square at Waverly Place and Macdougal Street is dominated by a towering English elm almost as
alive with sparrows as with leaves. Around it the ground lies bare
where pigeons with dusty feathers have taken over and multiplied.
A pursuing child or an eager dog can make them rise with a wind-
mill clatter, but after a brief centrifugal flight they always return—

l oo k-

pigeons fly ingand

whee(:are,spRiN,k,LiNg an in-stant with sunLight
t h e n)l-
ing all go BlacK wh-eel-ing

Buttonwoods, plane trees (which are little buttonwoods), and
gingkos—which also line the streets surrounding the park—make
small and pleasant groves. Most beautiful of all, catalpas, with heart-
shaped leaves and dangling "Indian beans," writhe into Oriental
forms which an occidental painter can admire. In the center is an
amphitheatre for young Bohemians and sprawlers in the sun; once
it was a fountain. To the north of it is Washington Arch, statues of
the first President in front and a memorable inscription across the
top in back. And behind an iron fence north of the Arch, where Fifth
Avenue begins, stands a crab-apple tree. Almost imperceptibly, on
sleety days in late February or early March, it puts forth sprinkles of
tiniest red which grow and are blossoms.

Winter or summer, Cummings sketches the Square—quickly, skilfully—in a black-bound "Record" notebook of 180 lined and numbered pages measuring 7 by 4 1/4 inches—Mr. Schwartz has named
it in his honor "the Cummings size." The sketches may range from
a disembodied head to full-length figures; one page contains a human
cross-section of the park—a fat man lolling on a bench, spectacled
intellectuals (male and female), several other pert, anonymous female faces, a girl with a doll carriage, a boy on a tricycle, a cop, two
dogs, and two pigeons in flight. Snowfalls are sure to bring him
there, he being, like Thoreau, an "inspector of snowstorms," and
I have seen him standing in the snow, with a knitted wool cap on his
head, feeding the pigeons and sparrows. For he is, after all, a coun-
tryman in the city, and many of his poems are nests for birds—the
chickadee

everywhere welcome
(but chiefly at home in
snowily nowheres
of winter his silence)

or the landscape remembered

<pre>
      at dusk
            just when
      the Light is filled with birds
</pre>

and for conclusion—

<pre>
      may my heart always be open to little
      birds who are the secret of living
      whatever they sing is better than to know
      and if men should not hear them men are old
</pre>

Shoulders squared, the handsome and arrogant head sculptured by Gaston Lachaise held proudly, Cummings at sixty-four is not much different from the young blond poet who appeared so spectacularly with his poems and drawings in *The Dial* a generation ago. He has remained an individual in the age of conformity, and the *enfant terrible* (and magic-maker) of the Twenties has stayed young doing so. The present decade has been perhaps his most active. It began with an exhibition at the Rochester Memorial Art Gallery and draws to a close with a volume of new poems, an apt parenthesis enclosing the Charles Eliot Norton lectures at Harvard, 1952-1953, and the monumental *Poems 1923-1954.* For he is still the same solitary and dedicated man he has always been, not so much aloof, as supposed, as keeping himself to himself, painting by day, writing at night, dreading company, and then entertaining the company that comes with tireless, exuberant talk. But he may suddenly rise and, taking his notebook, ascend to his top floor studio.

For he still has an inexhaustible box of tricks to astonish and delight those who are capable of being astonished and delighted—a necessary qualification in view of his history, in the course of which type-setters have quailed, book reviewers have spluttered, and letter-writers have taken pen in hand (example: "Junior could do better on his new typewriter, and he's only four, and hasn't learned to type yet").

But the very things that baffled the barbarians have made Cummings a writers' writer and, for his typographical innovations, the particular idol of the young. A famous poem in his first collection, *Tulips and Chimneys,* will illustrate:

<pre>
      Buffalo Bill's
      defunct
</pre>

who used to
ride a watersmooth-silver
stallion
and break onetwothreefourfive pigeonsjustlikethat
Jesus
he was a handsome man
and what i want to know is
how do you like your blueeyed boy
Mister Death

When Cummings went to Bennington College in Vermont to give a reading, the entire audience of girls rose as he mounted the platform and chanted this poem in unison. (He told me that he was so surprised that all he could do was to take out his handkerchief and wave it. The girls cheered.) At Bennington, as in other schools, Cummings's typographical arrangements are being studied for what they are—devices to give readers a maximum of communication and excitement.

On the subject of his technique, Cummings himself wrote: "I can express it in fifteen words, by quoting The Eternal Question And Immortal Answer of burlesk, viz. 'Would you hit a woman with a child?—No, I'd hit her with a brick.' Like the burlesk comedian, I am abnormally fond of that precision which creates movement" (from the foreword to *is* 5). His typography is sometimes a cover for his irreverences—toward other writers, patriots of the declaiming variety, politicos, and even Presidents:

the only man woman or child who wrote
a simple declarative sentence with seven grammatical
errors "is dead"
beautiful Warren Gamaliel Harding
"is" dead

It is also, occasionally, a cover for coprology.

I have mentioned Thoreau; like him, Cummings is didactic, and a teacher. It is not always agreeable to be taught. The most "modern" of the modern poets is anti-mechanistic:

(While you and i have lips and voices which
are for kissing and to sing with
who cares if some oneeyed son of a bitch
invents an instrument to measure Spring with?

He despises the radio and TV, does not have either. "Radio," he
once said, "has taken the ears away from people completely."
   He is against "progress," which he calls "regression to barbarism."

> I'd rather learn from one bird how to sing
> than teach ten thousand stars how not to dance.

Unlike most of his contemporaries, however, he is not afraid of
sentiment. He is the foremost celebrant of love among the poets of
our time—

> be of love(a little)
> More careful
> Than of everything

—and "we're wonderful one times one" are reiterated themes.
He has great admiration for the individual—

> any man is wonderful
> and a formula
> a bit of tobacco and gladness
> plus little derricks of gesture

—and his work is full of tender as well as savage portraits. In a time
when it is seemingly fashionable to hate one's parents, he is re-
freshing. While his mother was still alive he wrote a poem in praise
of her; and in recent years, at every reading he has given, he has
included a long elegy on his father, the late Rev. Edward Cummings,
a Unitarian minister and sometime teacher at Harvard.

2

   In their ground floor apartment, thronged with books, hung
with pictures, where herds of miniature elephants trek over book-
cases and mantel, Cummings and his wife entertain their friends at
tea, occasionally dinner. Cummings likes to sit with crossed arms in
a straight-backed chair, which he sometimes tilts against the wall.
Crumpled bills, coins and his notebook lie on a table where he
dropped them when he returned from his walk, perhaps after an
"assignation" with the crab-apple tree on the Square. He is an intense listener, and an eager talker. His tongue is sharp, and he talks

occasionally at a rapid rate, out of the side of his mouth, with a mimic's art and the insistence of a barker. He is also earnest:

"Pound once wrote a magnificent thing. 'What matters is not the idea a man holds, but the depth at which he holds it.'

"The only way I can define art is in a negative way: a poem is something that can't be translated. To define a thing is to limit it and a poem is infinite. I'll tell you what else I believe: the importance of intensity in art, which is what Pound was saying. I'd say 90 percent of the human race believes that two readers make a poem better than one reader, and that a hundred readers make it still better. And all that palaver has nothing to do with art. It isn't just one plus one plus one. A poem, a painting, lives in itself.

"A man who lives intensely really lives, but a man who lives to be 120 doesn't necessarily live at all.

"Today so-called writers are completely unaware of the thing which makes art what it is. You can call it nobility or spirituality, but I should call it intensity. Sordid is the opposite. Shakespeare is never sordid. His poetry was the most intense. Take the Prospero lines in The Tempest: 'To do me business in the veins of the earth / When they are baked with frost.' Words which in prose would be nonsense. But these lines happen to be poetry and the greatest poetry" (from an interview by Harvey Breit, *Times Book Review*, Dec. 31, 1950).

Cummings is against organized groups of every kind including, apparently, organized readers. He was against "black shirt and brown," and is against the "kumrads" who dance when "moscow pipes." But like the Left, the Right can find small comfort in his views. He told me:

"The difference between a business man and an artist is this: the business man lives in a world which is completely outside him. That's his reality. When that world collapses, he collapses. But the artist never turns a hair. Why? Because the artist's country is inside him.

"The business man is still secretly despised. Ask rich people how they made their money, and you will see by their reactions what I mean. I always ask them."

At the core of his position is his belief that only by doing or making things one's self can one be fulfilled, or at least grow:

"If a poet is anybody, he is somebody to whom things made matter very little—somebody who is obsessed by Making. Like all obsessions, the Making obsession has disadvantages; for instance, my only interest in making money would be to make it. Fortunately, however, I should prefer to make almost anything else, including locomotives and roses. It is with roses and locomotives (not to mention acrobats Spring electricity Coney Island the 4th of July the eyes of mice and Niagara Falls) that my 'poems' are competing.

"They are also competing with each other, with elephants, and with El Greco" (foreword to *is* 5).

To make things one's self means silence and solitude, a concept utterly at odds with the present epoch of sound which pours its waves over individual and community alike to shut out the present moment, in which alone a poet lives. He said at Harvard: "How could anyone want to be now, when anyone can go whening all over creation at the twist of a knob? What could induce anyone anywhere to desire aloneness, when billions of soi-disant dollars are mercifully squandered by a good and great government lest anyone anywhere should ever for a single instant be alone? As for being yourself—why on earth should you be yourself; when instead of being yourself you can be a hundred, or a thousand, or a hundred thousand thousand, other people? The very thought of being oneself in an epoch of interchangeable selves must appear supremely ridiculous" (Nonlecture Two). His own choice was made long ago:

> i will cultivate within
> me scrupulously the Inimitable which
> is loneliness . . .

Marion Cummings admires her husband's work, painting as well as poetry, and her "private" little collection of his oils and watercolors shows a delighted and discerning eye. She is an omnivorous reader, in French and Spanish as well as English, and has her own views about contemporary writers, particularly poets. A few years ago she took up photography as a hobby; now her first floor studio is full of portraits of famous visitors to Patchin Place. Her camera portraits of Cummings are familiar to readers of his books. She is a tall, handsome woman and, as Marion Morehouse, was famous in her own right. Edward Steichen, "the greatest of living fashion photographers," termed her "the best fashion model I ever worked with." She was probably also the most beautiful, as her pictures in *Vogue* and other magazines indicate. She appeared in two films, and I have heard that whenever she arrived on location, in a Long Island studio, spectators and technicians ceased watching the stars to watch her. When she married Cummings she put her career behind her.

Being the wife of a famous man can have its drawbacks, but she handles with efficiency as well as charm the problems that arise. For many years Cummings did not make carbon copies of his business letters; she finally persuaded him to make and file them. He does not answer the telephone, and the brunt of requests, permissions, and invitations is borne by her. She is also his agent-in-residence. One day an anthologist telephoned to persuade Cummings to lower his uptown agent's price on certain poems. When she reported the conversation, Cummings merely smiled and said, "Tell him not to use them." She told. (The anthologist used them.)

Poems 1923-1954 is dedicated to her, and of the many poems addressed to her I choose from his latest book:

> your birthday comes to tell me this
>
> —each luckiest of lucky days
> i've loved,shall love,do love you,was
>
> and will be and my birthday is

They spend their summers in New Hampshire, on a farm which Cummings inherited from his mother. Every May—the first week if the weather is warm, the second warm or cold—Cummings and his wife journey there, going by plane to Boston, from Boston by train. Their sojourn at the farm is never under four months; often it is closer to five. Until 1957 there was no electricity in the house, and reading was done by kerosene lamps. Despite the wiring, there is no radio, no TV.

For trips to the nearby village Cummings drives a 1929 Ford sedan, upholstered and roomy as an old-fashioned Pullman. It rides high over the narrow, winding dirt roads; cars of later design, he says, are too low-slung to be of use. Besides, he explains—smiling—should his car get stuck in a rut, only three pairs of hands could lift it out. On his farm, particularly in overalls doing chores, he looks a bit more the Yankee he is.

There are more than three hundred acres of woodland which, despite the blandishments of regional lumbermen, have been left strictly alone. So have the grass and bushes around the house, with

the result that thrushes are more numerous than chickadees or sparrows. Hummingbirds sip from vials of sugared water outside the
screen porch where Cummings and his wife take their meals. The
stone floor of the porch is strewn with empty shells from peanuts in
a cookie jar where chipmunks come three times a day, beginning
with the first sound in the kitchen in the morning. There is also
water for them in a glass dish.

Cummings had assured me that the hummingbirds "bow good-by"
to him when they are ready to take off for their long flight to the
Caribbean at summer's end; and I hereby testify that it is so. On the
last day of August, 1957, as we were sitting on the porch, which faces
the mountains of the Sandwich Range, he called my attention to
two hummingbirds outside the screen.

"They are bowing good-by," he said.

Like tiniest helicopters the hummingbirds rose straight up to the
top of the screen, then descended, five or six times, turned and
were gone.

Chapter 2

"CONCEIVE A MAN . . ."

1

conceive a man,should he have anything
would give a little more than it away

(his autumn's winter being summer's spring
who moved by standing in november's may)
from whose(if loud most howish time derange

the silent whys of such a deathlessness)
remembrance might no patient mind unstrange
learn(nor could all earth's rotting scholars guess
that life shall not for living find the rule)

and dark beginnings are his luminous ends
who far less lonely than a fire is cool
took bedfellows for moons mountains for friends

—open your thighs to fate and(if you can
withholding nothing)World,conceive a man

Cummings does not believe in "the hyperscientific doctrine that
heredity is nothing because everything is environment." But it is

clear—from conversations with him; from his autobiographical lectures at Harvard, from which the above sentence is quoted; and from a manuscript account by his sister of their childhood—that his environment might have made a poet out of a foundling.

Consider his father and mother.

Replying to his friend Paul Rosenfeld, the music critic of *The Dial,* who asked him for information about his father, Cummings wrote:

> He was a New Hampshire man, 6 foot 2, a crack shot & a famous fly-fisherman & a firstrate sailor (his sloop was named The Actress) & a woodsman who could find his way through forests primeval without a compass & a canoeist who'd stillpaddle you up to a deer without ruffling the surface of a pond & an ornithologist & taxidermist & (when he gave up hunting) an expert photographer (the best I've ever seen) & an actor who portrayed Julius Caesar in Sanders Theatre & a painter (both in oils & watercolours) & a better carpenter than any professional & an architect who designed his own houses before building them & (when he liked) a plumber who just for the fun of it installed all his own waterworks & (while at Harvard) a teacher with small use for professors—by whom (Royce, Lanman, Taussig, etc.) we were literally surrounded (but not defeated)—& later (at Doctor Hale's socalled South Congregational really Unitarian church) a preacher who announced, during the last war, that the Gott Mit Uns boys were in error since the only thing which mattered was for man to be on God's side (& one beautiful Sunday in Spring remarked from the pulpit that he couldn't understand why anyone had come to hear him on such a day) & horribly shocked his pewholders by crying "the Kingdom of Heaven is no spiritual roofgarden: it's inside you."

Another Cambridge neighbor and professor was William James, who introduced Cummings's father and mother to each other.

Edward Cummings, Harvard (*magna cum laude,* in philosophy) 1883, and after graduation a student of divinity, was the first holder of the Robert Treat Paine fellowship in social science. He studied abroad with the Reverend Samuel A. Barnett at Toynbee Hall and Professor Estlin Carpenter at Oxford, in honor of whom he named his son. On returning to this country Mr. Cummings was an instructor at Harvard in English, political economy and sociology for one year each, and, from 1893 to 1900, assistant professor of sociology in the Department of Economics. Of this period of his life the *Dictionary of American Biography* says: "As a teacher at Harvard he was human, alert, and stimulating."

In October, 1900, he was ordained minister of the South Congregational Society, Unitarian, of Boston, and became the colleague of the Reverend Edward Everett Hale, a distinguished clergyman and author of the nineteenth century classic, *The Man Without a Country*. Dr. Cummings succeeded Dr. Hale in 1909, and remained the pastor of the South Congregational church until 1925, when it merged with the First Church of Boston.

A number of Dr. Cummings's sermons, as well as treatises on trade unionism and industrial arbitration, were published in his lifetime. A sermon, "The Layman's Answer," was chosen by the Unitarian Layman's League "as one of the three best sermons preached, June, 1919, on the general subject, 'Unitarianism, what it means and what it can do under existing conditions for the help of mankind.'" It was published by G. H. Ellis, Boston, 1919. From a wide selection, I have chosen the following passage from "Lincoln, A Sermon," delivered by Dr. Cummings to his parishioners in 1909:

"If the great volume of Lincoln literature is significant, the great number of readers is still more significant, and the kind of readers is most significant of all. For the readers of Lincoln literature are not confined to any fastidious or specially educated class. Lincoln, fortunately, is the idol of what we sometimes call the common people. And by the common people I do not mean exclusively people of our older American stock, or even our native-born citizens. He is also, happily, the idol and the ideal of many of our newest, foreign-born recruits. It is one of the encouraging signs of the times that many of the most enthusiastic admirers of Lincoln are to be found among the so-called aliens who are flocking to our shores from every part of the old world. These immigrants, foreigners, refugees and their children, who are sometimes regarded as a menace to our democratic institutions, are also enthusiastic admirers of this American of Americans, this democrat of democrats. And I know of no better evidence of their right to come here than this ability which they and their children show to recognize and choose the best. And I know of no greater or more important service than this which Lincoln is rendering his country today,—leavening all the diverse and incoherent elements of our population with the pervasive, democratic leaven of his own personality; binding all parts of the nation together in one organic, living whole, in spite of all the differences of races, language, religion and tradition."

But even with his father's precepts to guide him, Cummings can be very disconcerting. His friends are familiar with the way in which he triggers a shot; for whenever, in a pause in a discussion, he remarks, "Want to know what *I* think?" they have learned to look around for shelter. One night—it was just after World War II—he remarked to a guest: "Know what *I* think? I think the only real Americans are those descended from the original stock that settled the Atlantic seaboard." His guest, who was not descended from that original stock, but was still in uniform, did not pursue the subject.

Of his mother, the former Rebecca Haswell Clarke, of Roxbury, Massachusetts, Cummings said in his first Harvard lecture: "Whereas my father had created his Unitarianism (his own father being a Christian of the hellfire variety) she had inherited hers; it was an integral part of herself, she expressed it as she breathed and as she smiled. The two indispensable factors in life, my mother always maintained, were 'health and a sense of humor.'" He also said: "never have I encountered anyone more joyous, anyone healthier in body and mind, anyone so quite incapable of remembering a wrong, or anyone so completely and humanly and unaffectedly generous." This is the poem he wrote:

if there are any heavens my mother will(all by herself)have
one.   It will not be a pansy heaven nor
a fragile heaven of lilies-of-the-valley but
it will be a heaven of blackred roses

my father will be(deep like a rose
tall like a rose)

standing near my

(swaying over her
silent)
with eyes which are really petals and see

nothing with the face of a poet really which
is a flower and not a face with
hands
which whisper
This is my beloved my

                              (suddenly in sunlight
he will bow,

& the whole garden will bow)

2

Consider his birthplace.

Edward Estlin Cummings was born "at home," October 14, 1894, at 104 Irving Street, Cambridge, Massachusetts (astrologically: in Libra, the House of Marriage, his planet being Venus). The house is still standing, and looks today probably as it always did—a large, roomy, three-story house half-hidden by foliage in a quiet street of similar, amply spaced houses behind their iron or wooden fences. Its entrance is flanked by double pillars, and there is a verandah on one side facing a large oval garden ringed with a white-pine hedge and bounded on the outside by three curving streets: Farrar, Scott and Irving.

"The third story," Cummings's sister Elizabeth, now the wife of Professor Carlton Qualey, has recalled, "had two very good places to play. One was a big room under the roof. It had a skylight at one end, and steps leading up onto the flat of the roof. We could go up onto the flat roof if we were careful and walked softly. It was made of copper and had a railing all around it. If we ran or jumped, it was bad for the copper and might cause leaks. My brother made a box kite and a windlass for it, and used to take it up on the flat roof and fly it there. He let me help him turn the windlass. It was hard work, but very exciting. . . .

"The tool room was another good place to play. It was an un-finished room with a skylight, just off the landing, before you got to the third floor. Part of the room was fixed up with shades, a sink, and red and blue light bulbs. That was where my father developed and printed the pictures he took with his camera. Part of the room

was used for storing things like extra bedding and trunks. There was
a long tool bench with a vise and a rack full of tools and, of course,
wood to make things of, and all sorts of nails and screws. I couldn't
use the tools, but I loved to help my father and brother. I could blow
sawdust away so that they could see the pencil line they were trying
to saw along. I could pedal the big old grindstone, too, so they could
sharpen tools."

A camera fan. The inhabitants of 104 Irving were progressive; the
first telephone in Cambridge was installed there.

There was something progressive, as well, about the inhabitants'
attitude toward children. The oval garden, which could have been
a show place, was allowed to become, instead, a play place. There
were about ten or twelve boys and girls in the neighborhood, and they
all played in the Cummings "yard." Mrs. Qualey wrote: "Some people
worried about children spoiling their lawns. My father liked to have us
play in our yard, and used to say he was raising children and not
grass. We could call and shout, but we were forbidden to scream
unless we were hurt. My father did a lot of his work at home in his
study. He said that happy noises, even loud ones, never disturbed
him."

There was a swing, a bar, hanging rings, a sandpile, and "several
good climbing trees." On one of these her father and brother built
a tree house. "It was a sturdy little house, and cozy, too. You climbed
up to the door by a strong ladder with wide rungs. There was a little
stove with a real stove pipe, and a bunk big enough for my brother
to sleep on, and a real window with a wooden shutter. There was
room for at least six people [little people?] inside the house, and
there was a small porch, with a railing around it, facing the street.
We spent a lot of time in the tree house in all kinds of weather. The
stove kept it warm in cold weather and, though it was a heating stove
and not a cook stove, we could make toast, and cocoa, and pop corn
on it. My brother used to go to the tree house to be alone, and sometimes spent the night there."

"Just in front of the house itself stood two huge apple-trees," Cummings told his audience at Harvard; "and faithfully, every spring,
these giants lifted their worlds of fragrance toward the room where
I breathed and dreamed. Under one window of this room flourished
(in early summer) a garden of magnificent roses."

In her catalogue of the games played in the garden—football, ten-

nis, "scrub" baseball, tag, hopscotch, jump rope, jacks and marbles—
Mrs. Qualey quotes this verse which her mother had learned as a
little girl:

> Inty, minty, kuty, corn,
> Apple seed and apple thorn.
> Wire, briar, limber lock.
> Five geese in a flock.
> Sit and sing
> By the spring.
> O-U-T spells out goes he (she).

She also reveals the genesis of one of her brother's best-loved poems:
"The first and most exciting sign that spring had really come was
the balloon man. First you heard his whistle in the distance; then he
would come walking down the street, carrying a basket full of balloons
of all colors tugging at their strings." Cummings wrote:

> in Just-
> spring   when the world is mud-
> luscious the little
> lame balloonman
>
> whistles   far   and wee
>
> and eddieandbill come
> running from marbles and
> piracies and it's
> spring
>
> when the world is puddle-wonderful
>
> the queer
> old balloonman whistles
> far   and   wee
> and bettyandisbel come dancing
>
> from hop-scotch and jump-rope and
>
> it's
> spring
> and

                              the

                          goat-footed

        balloonMan   whistles
        far
        and
        wee

The Cummings children and their friends also played in "Norton's Woods," where Charles Eliot Norton had his residence. "Here, as a very little child," Cummings said in his second lecture, "I first encountered the mystery who is Nature."

Mrs. Qualey also has an account of the circus which came, like the balloon man, every spring "and pitched a huge tent in an open space outside the city of Boston. Before I was old enough to go to the circus, I had heard my brother tell about going with my father, and had seen the pictures he had made of the animals and the acrobats."

In a *Vanity Fair* article about the circus in 1925 Cummings wrote: "Although it was only once, and twenty-odd years ago, that my eyes had the extraordinary honour to behold a slight young man whose first name was DANGER DERIDING DEATH DEFYING DESPERATE DARE-DEVIL DIAVOLO LOOPS THE LOOP ON A BICYCLE (his last name being, if I am not mistaken, PORTHOS: LEAPS THE GAP OVER FIVE ELE-PHANTS), I have not forgotten this person and shall never forget him, simply because he was a great artist—who, like Paul Cézanne, died the most fortunate and illustrious of deaths: died at the *motif,* and in the execution of his art."

As for the elephants, he drew them over and over, and used to astonish dinner companions by drawing them on the tablecloth up-side-down—that is, legs outward. In the article just mentioned he suggested that everyone has a specially liked animal and confessed that "my own totem is the elephant." As a child, he had a toy ele-phant which his father often mended, and at Harvard he wrote a story entitled "The King," which was really a tribute to his unforgotten toy.

When Estlin and Elizabeth came down with measles, they were put in the "big room" shared, usually, by their grandmother and an aunt. Elizabeth wrote:

"My brother was great fun to be with. He could draw pictures, and tell stories, and imitate people and animals, and invent games, and could make you laugh, even when you thought you felt very miserable. I think that we were in that room for several weeks, but I had a wonderful time. It must have been then that my brother arranged with his make-believe friend (Kingston) to take me and my make-believe friend (Frimmon) up in Kingston's new flying-machine. You are so used to airplanes that going up in a make-believe one doesn't sound very exciting to you, probably. But my brother and I had never seen an airplane. There was talk about some men who were trying to invent a flying-machine, and we had seen a picture of the one they were working on, but nobody really expected that flying-machines would amount to much."

Alas, they were mistaken. Her account continues:

"When we had the whooping cough we were sick for weeks and weeks. After we got over the worst we didn't have to stay in bed, and could even play in the yard on nice days. But we still coughed like anything at times. About half the children in the neighborhood had the whooping cough, or had been exposed to it. My brother formed a club called the 'Whooper Club.' Anyone could belong who had whooping cough or who expected to come down with it. My brother was president, and editor of the 'Whooper Club' paper, which he typed on mother's old Hammond typewriter. Every member of the 'Whooper Club' had to write or dictate a story for the paper. We had badges and a motto, too, and we all played together and had so much fun that children tried to get exposed to the whooping cough so they could join.

"My brother used to make different kinds of drawings, too, sometimes ones (a little like the ones in the funny papers) that he mounted on strips of cardboard. They told stories about us, our animals, and all sorts of other things."

3

Consider the other inhabitants.

At the time Elizabeth Cummings was born, 104 Irving was occupied by her father, mother, brother; a grandmother and an aunt, and Uncle George, her mother's brother. Later there was another "aunt," a dear friend of her mother's. There were also Julia, the cook, and Sandy, "who did a little of everything." And there were two dogs, a cat, goldfish, and rabbits in a pen in the back yard.

"After myself and my father and mother," Cummings told a Harvard audience, "I loved most dearly my mother's brother George. He was by profession a lawyer, by inclination a bon vivant, and by nature a joyous human being. When this joyous human being wasn't toiling in his office, or hobnobbing with socalled swells at the Brookline country club, he always became my playfellow."

Of the two aunts, it may not be necessary to say more than that they kept an eye on their nephew. This collective eye was directed not so much to deportment as to neatness. In this, we may suppose Elizabeth Cummings to have been a little angel, as all little girls once were, and possibly are still. It was—and is—different with boys; and so it chanced with Estlin. Boys of a half century ago wore knickerbockers, and not long trousers, an item of apparel which even graces the tender legs of toddlers today, the times being more enlightened. Knickerbocker trouser legs are fastened below-knee, and do not always stay fastened; sometimes one, sometimes both, will slip down and dangle, carrying a stocking along. Aunt Jane, and afterwards Aunt Emma, were insistent that they stay up. In time, by a domestic application of "divide and conquer," each assumed for herself the responsibility for one of the trouser legs; so that it was not unusual in that household, when Estlin hove in view, to hear one aunt say to the other: "There goes your leg."

Of the grandmother, I have heard from more than one visitor to 104 Irving Street her oft-repeated remark about the entire household: "I never feel easy until they are all safely in bed."

And now I should like to say something collective about the inhabitants; or rather, since he has said it better than I can, I shall quote Cummings, who told his Harvard audience: "I here devoutly thank a beneficent Providence for allowing me to live my childhood and my boyhood and even my youth without ever once glimpsing that typical item of an era of at least penultimate confusion—the uncomic nonbook. No paltry supermen, no shadowy space-cadets, no trifling hyperjunglequeens and pantless pantherwomen insulted my virginal imagination. I read or was read, at an early age, the most immemorial myths, the wildest wild animal stories, lots of Scott and quantities of Dickens (including the immortal *Pickwick Papers*), *Robinson Crusoe* and *The Swiss Family Robinson, Gulliver's Travels, Twenty Thousand Leagues Under the Sea,* poetry galore, *The Holy Bible,* and *The Arabian Nights.* One city winter I floated through chivalry with

Mallory and Froissart: the following country summer—we had by then acquired a farm—I dressed as a Red Indian, slept in a teepee, and almost punctured our best Jersey cow with a random arrow; in emulation of the rightful inhabitants of my wrongful native land."

Elsewhere he adds *Lorna Doone* ("with whom I fell sublimely in love") and *Treasure Island* to his juvenile reading.

He was read to; he read *books*; the grandmother and the aunts sang and played the piano; his father painted, his mother "loved poetry; and copied most of the poems she loved best into a little book which was never far from her."

When does a poet emerge, if poet there is to be? All children utter and write lines of primeval brightness and beauty. The organ of speech and the hand that scrawls at the mind's bidding are discoveries fraught with tremendous excitement.

Of Cummings's earliest verse, there exists a couplet whose survival we owe to his mother; it might not have won a contest in *St. Nicholas,* but it is a good start, nothing clever in it, only observation and delight, as good ingredients for a poem as the most finicky critic could ask:

> O,the pretty birdie,O;
> with his little toe,toe,toe!

(It is always the hopping that does it.)

Cummings has told, in his second Harvard lecture, about the poetic periods through which he passed. The first he illustrated by the poem just quoted. The second, for which no example exists, except in his memory, had over it the sombre cast of social-consciousness: "A good poem was a poem which did good, and a bad poem was a poem which didn't: Julia Ward Howe's Battle Hymn Of The Republic being a good poem because it helped free the slaves. Armed with this ethical immutability, I composed canticles of comfort on behalf of the griefstricken relatives of persons recently deceased; I implored healthy Christians to assist poor-whites afflicted with The Curse Of The Worm (short for hookworm); and I exhorted right-minded patriots to abstain from dangerous fireworks on the 4th of July. Thus, it will be seen that, by the year 1900, one growing American boy had reached exactly that stage of 'intellectual development' beyond which every ungrowing Marxist adult of today is strictly forbidden, on pain of physical disappearance, ever to pass."

The third poetic period began with a present from his Uncle George. It was *The Rhymester* which, Cummings recalls, "diverted my eager energies from what to how: from substance to structure. I learned that there are all kinds of intriguing verse-forms, chiefly French; and that each of these forms can and does exist in and of itself, apart from the use to which you or I may not or may put it."

I take, from the lecture referred to, a chance meeting on Irving Street "one ever memorable day" when Cummings and Professor Josiah Royce came face to face. Royce was the man on whom "the mantle of philosophical authority had fallen at Harvard" and of whom Santayana was to write: "even without knowing that he had already produced a new proof of the existence of God, merely to look at him you would have felt he was a philosopher; his great head seemed too heavy for his small body, and his portentous brow, crowned with thick red hair, seemed to crush the lower part of his face."

" 'Estlin' his courteous and gentle voice hazarded 'I understand that you write poetry.' I blushed. 'Are you perhaps' he inquired, regarding a particular leaf of a particular tree 'acquainted with the sonnets of Dante Gabriel Rossetti?' I blushed a different blush and shook an ignorant head. 'Have you a moment?' he shyly suggested, less than half looking at me; and just perceptibly appended 'I rather imagine you might enjoy them.' Shortly thereafter, sage and ignoramus were sitting opposite each other in a diminutive study (marvelously smelling of tobacco and cluttered with student notebooks of a menacing bluish shade)—the ignoramus listening, enthralled; the sage intoning, lovingly and beautifully, his favorite poems. And very possibly (although I don't, as usual, know) that is the reason—or more likely the unreason—I've been writing sonnets ever since."

Cummings has written a great many sonnets; and it is apparent from their variety that he can do anything he wishes with the sonnet form. Although he told me, "I did not decide to become a poet—I was always writing poetry," it was not until Harvard, the Harvard of his undergraduate days, that he became—in Johnson's sublime phrase —"irrecoverably a poet."

4

Perhaps, as the Bible says, there is a time to be born. For a future rebel, Cummings could not have been born at a better time

or place. The world of his infancy and youth had still a moral atmosphere, and that atmosphere was rather heavily laden with certain
values and virtues seemingly made to be rejected:

> the Cambridge ladies who live in furnished souls
> are unbeautiful and have comfortable minds
> (also, with the church's protestant blessings
> daughters, unscented shapeless spirited)
> they believe in Christ and Longfellow, both dead. . . .

It was also a world which was completely male-dominated, and in
which the *paterfamilias* was the master of his house. Cummings has
not forgotten the effect on everyone at 104 Irving Street the first
time his father appeared as an ordained minister, however quickly
the old cheerfulness broke through to reign as before.

Before Elizabeth was born, Dr. and Mrs. Cummings bought a farm
in New Hampshire. It was called "the Joy Farm," after its owner,
Ephraim Joy, "but it earned the name on its own account," as Mrs.
Qualey afterwards wrote. There was a little frame house and an immense barn. "Some farmers think that it spoils the hay to let children
play in it," she wrote. "Our horses and cows seemed to like our hay,
though we did play a lot in the haymow." As was the case on Irving
Street, neighbors' children came to Joy Farm to play.

The original house was plastered inside to keep out the cold and
had floor boards ranging in width from eight inches to a couple of
feet. A brick fireplace with two openings, like a primitive Moloch
with two mouths, stood awkwardly, but efficiently, in the main room.
Mount Chocorua was visible in the distance, but it was necessary to
step outside to see it; Dr. Cummings put in windows from which
the mountain could be seen, and added extensions and another story
to the house, as well as a flat roof on the extension from which the
sunset and stars could be observed. Here Cummings has painted many
of his oil landscapes and watercolor sunsets.

"My father was always building something, or repairing something, or doing something special, and of course all of us wanted
to help," Mrs. Qualey wrote. "He built a study at the edge of the
woods. It was a very unusual one because it had so many sides that
it was almost round. It had a big fireplace with a sunken hearth, and
on each side of the fireplace were cement steps leading to a little
room upstairs. Outside the upstairs windows was a wide walk that

went all the way around the study and was like a sort of balcony. There were beds there, and downstairs my father built himself a desk where he could work during the day when he needed to be undisturbed.

"He built a little place for my brother to study, too. It was under a tree about half way from the house to my father's study. It was not a real building. There was a long plank the right height for a desk and about long enough for three people to sit at it at once. There was another long plank the right height for a bench. There was a wall at the back with a window in it, and walls at each end with cupboards and cubbyholes for books and things. Instead of an ordinary roof and door, there was a hinged roof that could be raised so as to stand out straight and give shade to the desk and the bench. It could be lowered to make the study into a sort of rain-tight box. My brother used the study a lot, and I used to use it sometimes when I did my lessons. I can remember learning my multiplication tables at that study."

The Cummings children were taught self-reliance. Both were given compasses to carry when they went exploring in the woods, and Estlin had the additional honor and responsibility of carrying matches. If they were really lost, he was to build a small fire—"on a rock where it could not spread"—and someone at the house would see the smoke. But peril came to the children, not in the woods, but on the water.

On the shore of the lake Dr. Cummings built, chiefly with his own hands, an immense, roomy, rambling summer house with a flat-topped roof from which the surrounding countryside, its mountains mirrored in the lake, could be scanned. On a summer day in 1911, when Estlin was sixteen and Elizabeth ten, they went out in a canvas boat which was guaranteed by its makers to be unsinkable, taking Rex, a bull terrier, with them. In the middle of the lake, where the water was forty feet deep, a sudden lunge of the dog tipped the boat over. It sank at once, leaving only paddles, floor boards and two box seats floating. Rex started for the shore, and brother and sister held on to the boxes, managing to stay afloat despite their heavy clothes and shoes. Mrs. Qualey says they did not try to take them off, and could not have managed it if they had tried.

"It did not occur to me to be afraid," she wrote, "because my brother was cheerful and I had perfect confidence in him.

"Suddenly we realized that Rex had given up swimming for the shore and was swimming back toward us. He was thrashing around in a frightened way. He must have felt himself at the end of his strength and, hearing our familiar voices, turned back to us for help. My brother raised himself out of the water enough to shout loudly to Rex to go back. But Rex did not understand, and swam all the more frantically toward the voice he knew he could trust. By the time he got to me, he was in a panic and splashing so he could hardly see where he was going. He must have seen something that looked solid and have thought that he could climb out of the water onto it. I felt his weight on my shoulders; then lost hold of my box and went under water. I came up, spluttering, and got hold of the box again. Again Rex tried to climb on, and again I lost hold and went under water. My brother was swimming toward us and calling to Rex. The next thing I knew, Rex and my brother were struggling in the water; then I didn't see Rex any more. I could only guess how my brother must feel. I knew he would have done almost anything to save Rex, but he could not let Rex keep forcing me under water."

Back in the summer house, the rest of the family had been watching the sunset, when Dr. Cummings suggested a ride in the motor boat. Everyone went, including the grandmother, "who wasn't crazy about boats." Aunt Jane steered. Suddenly Dr. Cummings shouted to Aunt Jane: "Steer for those two heads in the water!"

"He explained to my mother, who was sitting next to him, that he could see two people swimming a long way from shore and was going to tell them it was dangerous, even if they were annoyed and thought it was none of his business. When the boat came close to the two heads in the water, the family could hardly believe their eyes. My brother's voice, telling them to pick me up first, sounded natural, but actually he was chilled and almost exhausted.

"For years my father insisted on keeping the two boxes we had hung onto. 'I keep them to remind me whenever things seem to me to be bad,' he said."

With advancing years one tends to remember who one is, and whence one sprang. To this father, the son has paid tribute in a long poem which is now a fixed piece in his public readings. The poem ends:

> though dull were all we taste as bright,
> bitter all utterly things sweet,
> maggoty minus and dumb death
> all we inherit, all bequeath

and nothing quite so least as truth
—i say though hate were why men breathe—
because my father lived his soul
love is the whole and more than all

On November 2, 1926, Dr. and Mrs. Cummings left Cambridge
for Joy Farm in a newly purchased automobile. Mrs. Cummings
was at the wheel. In the region of the Ossippee mountains snow
fell, and they stopped to wipe the windshield. A few minutes later,
in a blinding snowstorm, the car came to a railroad crossing; a loco-
motive sheared the car in two, killing Dr. Cummings instantly and
seriously injuring Mrs. Cummings. They were found by two brake-
men from the train.

"These men took my sixty-six year old mother by the arms and
tried to lead her toward a nearby farmhouse," Cummings said at
Harvard; "but she threw them off, strode straight to my father's
body, and directed a group of scared spectators to cover him. When
this had been done (and only then) she let them lead her away.

"A day later, my sister and I entered a small darkened room in a
country hospital. She was still alive—why, the head-doctor couldn't
imagine. She wanted only one thing: to join the person she loved
most. He was very near her, but she could not quite reach him. We
spoke, and she recognized our voices. Gradually her own voice began to understand what its death would mean to these living children
of hers; and very gradually a miracle happened. She decided to live."

I had the pleasure of meeting her at Patchin Place, a cheerful,
informed, motherly woman enjoying the company of her son, his
wife and their friends. She had worked for a while, after her recovery,
as a volunteer with the Travelers Aid in Grand Central Station; now
she had her own apartment on Washington Square, where she continued to paste into scrapbooks any and every item that mentioned
E. E. Cummings, a labor of love which has saved me many labors.
Cummings once told me that, after reading the reviews of *The Enormous Room,* he decided he would never read another. It is probable
that he did not read most of them; I know, however, that he read one
in 1953 which upset him (portions of it will be found in the last
chapter).

Chapter 3

HARVARD

1

Cummings, of course, was destined for Harvard. "As a baby," he has recounted, "I sported a white sweater, on which my mother had embroidered a red H." He first attended a private school in Cambridge where, he says, he learned nothing and "burst into tears and nosebleeds." Then came three public schools, the most important of which was the Cambridge High and Latin School, on Trowbridge Street, where he prepared for Harvard. One of the public schools had for principal a Negress "blessed with a delicious voice, charming manners, and a deep understanding of children." In his letter to Paul Rosenfeld, previously quoted, Cummings says his father sent him to that particular school because of her. Her name was Maria Baldwin. Cummings also pays tribute to a Mr. Cecil Derry, "one of those blessing and blessed spirits who deserve the name of teacher: predicates who are utterly in love with their subject; and who, because they would gladly die for it, are living for it gladly. From him I learned (and am still learning) that gladness is next to godliness. He taught me Greek." From Irving Street, it was a short walk cross-lots to Trowbridge, through the little park where the Cambridge

Public Library stands today, and which must have been more like a little wood at the beginning of the century.

Cummings entered Harvard in the fall of 1911. A member of the graduating class of that year was a diminutive—five feet four—bespectacled student named Joseph Ferdinand Gould, who will reappear in my narrative as "Little Joe Gould, the last of the Bohemians," after his translation to Greenwich Village.

Speaking to me of his memorable first year, Cummings related how he spent a rapturous afternoon and evening in the Harvard Union library reading his own discovery—Marlowe (probably in the great edition, Oxford University Press, 1910, of Professor Tucker Brooke). Forty-five years later he was still able to recite passages from *Hero and Leander* and the *Amores*. He told me that, as the evening wore on, the librarian began to appear more and more frequently to observe the phenomenon of a lone student actually reading for pleasure and unaware of the time; and he added, smiling, how surprised that librarian would have been had he known that Marlowe's and (through Marlowe) Ovid's eroticism were as titillating to the seventeen-year-old as the grandeur of the verse.

"Officially," Cummings said in Nonlecture Three, "Harvard presented me with a smattering of languages and sciences; with a glimpse of Homer, a more than glimpse of Aeschylus Sophocles Euripides and Aristophanes, and a deep glance at Dante and Shakespeare."

By the end of his first year, Cummings was a contributor to the Harvard *Monthly*. He continued to contribute to it through his postgraduate year, 1916. He also appeared, though much less frequently, in the Harvard *Advocate*. At least one of his poems was signed "E. Estlin Cummings," but chiefly the signature was the familiar one of later years. The first of his poems to appear in the *Monthly* was entitled "Vision," and its inspiration was, not surprisingly, Harvard. It is in the heroic vein, and I give it here because it is the first of his poems to reach an audience in the great world, and also because it is itself not without interest for its structure and phrasing:

> The dim deep of a yellow evening slides
> Across the green, and mingles with the elms.
> A faint beam totters feebly in the west,
> Trembles, and all the earth is wild with light,
> Stumbles, and all the world is in the dark.

The huge black sleeps above;—lo, two white stars.

Harvard, your shadow-walls, and ghost-toned tower,
Dim, ancient-moulded, vague, and faint, and far,
Is gone! And through the flesh I see the soul:
Coloring iron in red leaping flame,
The thunder-strokes of mighty, sweating men,
Furious hammers of clashing fierce and high,—
And in a corner of the smithy coiled,
Black, brutal, massive-linked, the toil-wrought chain
Which is to bind God's right hand to the world.

It appears to be a sonnet, but lacks rhyme and has an extra line. Afterwards, there were sonnets in profusion, perfect enough to please the most academic eyes, and something besides: past the striving for fresh images, fresh images—

Great carnal mountains crouching in the cloud.

The influence of Rossetti and of the whole pre-Raphaelite brother-hood—"the fleshly school," as it was called—is apparent in many of the poems, with their ballad subjects and archaic language. "Ballade," published in the *Advocate,* a poem of six stanzas, ends:

White stretched the north-land, white the south . . .
She was gone like a spark from the ash that chars;
    And "After her!" he sware . . .
They found the maid. And her eyes were stars,
A starry smile was upon her mouth,
    And the snow-flowers in her hair.

Also in the *Advocate* was an eight-line poem entitled "Summer Silence," an exercise in the Spenserian stanza, as its sub-title announces; but it is less Spenser than Cummings, and more Procrustean than either:

Eruptive lightnings flutter to and fro
Above the heights of immemorial hills;
Thirst-stricken air, dumb-throated, in its woe
Limply down-sagging, its limp body spills
Upon the earth. A panting silence fills
The empty vault of Night with shimmering bars

Of sullen silver, where the lake distils
Its misered bounty.—Hark! No whisper mars
The utter silence of the untranslated stars.

Undergraduate verse reveals, better than anything else can, what discipline is needed to make an art of verse-writing. It was a cynic who said "Poets are born, not made"—a born poet has to make himself. There are enough Cummings poems in the Harvard *Monthly* and *Advocate* to make a book; but it would not be a good book. What is useful about this particular piece of knowledge is that Cummings was writing a great deal, while paying enough attention to his studies to graduate with honors.

By 1915 the phrases which are peculiarly "Cummings" begin to leap out from the published poems—

Bluer are they than ponds of dream—

from "Ballad of Love," and

A great, red, fearsome flower

from "Longing." There is also, in the refrain of "Ballade of Soul," a beginning awareness of the world outside the sheltering walls of Harvard and the warm family life in Irving Street:

But are there Souls in winter garmentless,
Be with them, God! and pity also me.

Of almost equal significance as his poems in the *Monthly* were the men he met in its office on the dusty third floor of the Harvard Union. A glance through the issues of this magazine, with its Fatima ad on the inside cover, reveals the following editors, Cummings among them, during his undergraduate years: J. Donald Adams, R. S. Mitchell, J. S. Watson, Gilbert Vivian Seldes, Robert Gruntal Nathan, J. R. Dos Passos, and Robert S. Hillyer. Of these men, afterwards celebrated in their own right, after a pruning of middle names or initials along the way, four became lifelong friends of Cummings, and will reappear in this book. He was soon to meet another Harvard man, already an alumnus, with important results for all concerned. Cummings declared in Nonlecture Three:

"Through Harvard, I met Scofield Thayer; and at Harvard, Sibley

Watson—two men who subsequently transformed a dogooding periodical called The Dial into a firstrate magazine of the fine arts; and together fought the eternal fight of selfhood against mobism, the immortal battle of beauty against ugliness."

Of this magazine, of which I shall give an account commensurate with its importance in the career of E. E. Cummings and the cultural life of the country, Stewart Mitchell became the first managing editor. He was, at the time of which I write, editor-in-chief of the *Monthly*. I am indebted to Robert Hillyer for this account of the way in which the *Monthly* board operated:

"It was the custom for the editors to write comments on the material submitted, signing their initials, and the piece was accepted or rejected according to the consensus. Some aspirant handed in a poem that began with the line: 'Thou hast faun eyes.' Cummings's comment took graphic form—a small horned deer with large and soulful eyes. On another poem he wrote, 'Good but poor.' That has always seemed to me an excellent phrase, accurately descriptive of much that is published."

Hillyer told me that when he was elected an editor, "John Dos Passos gave a party for the whole board in his rooms in Thayer Hall. Cummings lived in the same building. Several of us adjourned to his rooms, and after dinner we met there again. It was a Saturday night. We sat up drinking and reading poetry nearly all night, and—I think it was four or five of us—went to sleep where we were on chairs and couches. Early the next morning (or it seemed early) there was a knock at the door. Cummings rightly guessed that it was his father, the Reverend Dr. Cummings, the most famous Unitarian minister in Boston. The room was a shambles. What a to-do there was to whisk bottles and glasses into hiding places and bring some sort of order to the room before admitting the paternal divine! It went off all right; Dr. Cummings was either very unobservant or very wise."

One other meeting deserves mention. In 1913, the Cambridge Dramatic Club on Brattle Street produced Jerome K. Jerome's *Fanny and the Servant Problem*—in which Cummings was cast as Ernest, the second footman. Of this production—he also played Micah in *The Little Minister*—he recalls two things: that he was kissed "by the very beautiful leading lady," and that the hero, "Lord Somebody or other," was brilliantly played by a "cold and aloof" person. This person was T. S. Eliot. They met, formally, for the first time several decades later.

2

I have already referred to what Harvard "officially" presented Cummings. "Unofficially," he related in the same lecture, "she gave me my first taste of independence: and the truest friends any man will ever enjoy." In his senior year Cummings, who had been living at home, moved to a room in the Yard (Thayer Hall, south entry, second floor). He adorned his mantelpiece with four or five china elephants and his walls with "Krazy Kat" comic strips. It is just possible that the typographical arrangements in this famous funny-paper sequence suggested certain things to Krazy Kat's admirer. In this room he painted as well as wrote.

Independence meant, first of all, the freedom to come and go as he pleased. He went. "Now I could roam that surrounding world sans peur, if not sans reproche: and I lost no time in doing so. A town called Boston, thus observed, impressed my unsophisticated spirit as the mecca of all human endeavors—and be it added that, in this remote era, Boston had her points." Some think it still has them: good speech, good manners and, as Slater Brown phrased it to me, "Boston is just the right size for a city," meaning "New York is too big," for which reason he says he left it. But Cummings was to fall overwhelmingly in love with New York; and while he gives a few rowdy details—and omits some others—of his nocturnal wanderings with equally high-spirited Harvards of his acquaintance, and names the tunes that haunted them—the "Turkey Trot" and the "Bunny Hug," "Everybody's Doing It" and "Alexander's Rag-Time Band"— Boston, after all, was only preparation for higher things, although I do not believe that he scanted that preparation. Malcolm Cowley has related (first, in Sanders Theatre introducing Cummings who was to read and then in the pages of the *Advocate*) how this "son of a famous minister was in revolt against ministerial standards, so that his father's car, with its clergyman's license plates, was found parked outside a famous joint near Scollay Square, to the embarrassment of the Boston police."

Cummings had several times been asked to explain the presence of hairpins inside the car; but this was different—the "joint" happened to be a house of ill-fame, and father and son "almost came to blows," I was told, when he defended the girls, saying "They were just as nice as his mother"!

There were the delights of eating and drinking in German, Chinese, and Greek restaurants. S. Foster Damon recalled for me Jacob Wirth's, near Chinatown, where he and Cummings drank seidels of dark Kulmbacher beer; a bona fide Chinese restaurant whose specialty was a chop suey of lobster and pineapple, with no casualties listed; and the Parthenon and Athens, which live on in Cummings's poems. There were also Italian restaurants. And there was, of course, the Howard Athenaeum, affectionately called the "Old Howard," the throne and home of burlesque—whenever the Watch and Ward Society was not snooping around. Writes Cummings, with a regret that has lingered: "When Miss Gertrude Hoffman brought her lissome self and her willowy girls to Boston, they and she were violently immersed in wrist-and-ankle-length underwear."

Damon, who accompanied Cummings on these Athenian rambles, met him first in a morning class in German literature in Cummings's senior year. "I was the first of the D's, he was the last of the C's," Damon said, and thus they became acquainted. He told me that Cummings was terribly shy, that he held a newspaper up to his face when riding in a street car, and that he would not be photographed with the *Monthly* staff. Cummings, he recalled, liked to talk about Shelley and gave him a copy of Shelley's poems; about the Rossetti sonnet, and about Swinburne. At the time they met "Cummings was writing double ballades and all the trick forms."

Cummings was not only experimenting with French forms but others as well. The January, 1916, number of the Harvard *Monthly* has this imitation of

SAPPHICS

When my life his pillar has raised to heaven,
When my soul has bleeded and builded wonders,
When my love of earth has begot fair poems,
    Let me not linger.

Ere my day be troubled with coming darkness,
While the huge whole sky is elate with glory,
Let me rise, and making my salutation,
    Stride into sunset.

The April, 1916, number has an imitation of a Japanese "Hokku":

> I care not greatly
> Should the world remember me
> In some tomorrow.
>
> There is a journey,
> And who is for the long road
> Loves not to linger.
>
> For him the night calls,
> Out of the dawn and sunset
> Who has made poems.

Damon and Cummings also took Dean Briggs's famous course in poetic composition. Students were graded "inexplicably," Damon related with a slightly quizzical look. He is now a professor himself, at Brown University. One day, Dean Briggs—who read Donne aloud "with great persuasiveness and charm," according to T. S. Eliot— read a poem by Damon, in which occurs this line:

> Thy mouth is a fragrant wound of the twilight.

"Everybody, including the Dean," Damon told me, "shuddered."

Briggs told the class that he had shown the line to Professor Barrett Wendell, who termed it "putrescent." Whereupon Cummings stood up and asked:

"Dean Briggs, but why don't you like it?"

Damon said there was no reply—"just a look." But he was quick to add that "we all owe something to Dean Briggs for his teaching."

John Dos Passos and Robert Hillyer were also members of this class. Hillyer wrote me: "Our group in his courses was divided into the Ancients and the Moderns. I was an Ancient, of course; Cummings, Foster Damon and Dos Passos were Moderns." (Hillyer afterwards held the same chair as Dean Briggs—the Boylston Chair of Rhetoric and Oratory, and gave the same courses.)

Among themselves, the undergraduates were in despair. Damon told me:

"We kept saying to each other that no more poetry could be written, that the best poems had already been written, and all the subjects were used up. There could be no more romantic poetry because there would be no more wars, the nations were so economically interdependent."

Damon, an amateur composer, and author of an article on Erik Satie in the Harvard *Musical Review,* told me that he set a poem by Cummings for voice and piano "about a year after it appeared" in the Harvard *Monthly* for November, 1914. It is entitled "Fancies," with the subtitle "Night":

Night, with sunset hauntings;
A red cloud under the moon.
Here will I meet my love
Beneath hushed trees.

Over the silver meadows
Of flower-folded grass,
Shall come unto me
Her feet like arrows of moonlight.

Under the magic forest
Mute with shadow,
I will utterly greet
The blown star of her face.

By white waters
Sheathed in rippling silence,
Shall I behold her hands
Hurting the dark with lilies.

Hush thee to worship, soul!
Now is thy moment of love.
Night; and a red cloud
Under the moon.

In the lecture from which I have been quoting Cummings pays his respects to Damon "who opened my eyes and ears not merely to Domenico Theotocopuli [i.e., El Greco] and William Blake, but to all ultra (at that moment) modern music and poetry and painting." Damon told me that Cummings, who had also become a member of the Musical Club, offered to teach him Greek in exchange for lessons in harmony. "Cummings," he recalled, "wrote several pieces of music for the piano, picking them out on the keys." Presumably Damon wrote them down, for he told me he still has them.

Dos Passos also remembers Cummings at the piano. He wrote me:
"Let's see what I can remember about my *Monthly* days. Cummings's
extraordinary verbal effervescence, the oldfashioned Cambridge household on Irving Street where his father presided at the head of the
long table . . . I've cherished my recollection of it as a link with the
Jameses and all the generations of old New Englanders back to Emerson and Thoreau . . . Italian restaurants and cheap Italian wine in
Boston . . . Cummings improvising on the piano for the edification of
his admiring family. Dr. Cummings booming from the pulpit—was
it the Arlington Street church? or did I hear him preach there on some
special occasion?"

It was probably Damon who showed Cummings the work of an
almost forgotten poet named Donald Evans, the author of five books
of verse, the first of which, *Discords,* appeared in 1912. Evans was a
type of esthete with better manners than the more familiar ones of
the Twenties, who sometimes thought the sword mightier than the
pen. He moved in uptown society circles as well as downtown literary
ones. He wrote with elegance but was smothered by facility. He was
the enthusiastic publisher of Gertrude Stein's *Tender Buttons,* which
he issued under the imprint of "Claire Marie" at Three East Fourteenth Street in 1914. This, too, found its way to Harvard, where
Cummings read it.

"Practically everything I know about painting and poetry came to
me through Damon," Cummings told me. It was Damon who showed
him a little book which was to have a profound influence on his work
—*Ripostes,* by Ezra Pound, published in 1912. He still recalls the
thrill with which he read "The Return" in this volume:

> See, they return; ah, see the tentative
> Movements, and the slow feet,
> The trouble in the pace and the uncertain
> Wavering!
>
> See, they return, one, and by one,
> With fear, as half-awakened;
> As if the snow should hesitate
> And murmur in the wind,
>   and half turn back;
> These were the "Wing'd-with-Awe,"
>   Inviolable.

> Gods of the wingèd shoe!
> With them the silver hounds,
>   sniffing the trace of air!
>
> Haie! Haie!
>   These were the swift to harry;
> These the keen-scented;
> These were the souls of blood.
>
> Slow on the leash,
>   pallid the leash-men!

The lines are sculptured to enduring form.

Perhaps equally important was the Imagist credo in the March, 1913, issue of *Poetry,* which called for "direct treatment of the 'thing' whether subjective or objective," followed by Pound's "A Few Don'ts," which included: "Use no superfluous word, no adjective which does not reveal something."

Cummings is also grateful to Theodore Miller, who not only introduced him to the poems of Catullus, Horace and Sappho in the original Latin and Greek; "but the token of whose most memorable kindness was a volume combining poems and letters by that glorious human being who confessed:

> I am certain of nothing but of the holiness of the Heart's
> affections, and the truth of Imagination.

Whereupon—deep in those heights of psychic sky which had greeted my boyish escape from moralism—an unknown and unknowable bird began singing" (Nonlecture Three).

The quotation is from Keats's letter to Benjamin Bailey, dated 22 November, 1817. Less than a year later, on July 18, 1818, Keats wrote to Bailey, among other things: "when I see you, the first thing I shall do will be to read that about Milton and Ceres, and Proserpine."

I asked Cummings if he was aware of the resemblance between the passage in *Paradise Lost* to which Keats here refers and his own beautiful "Tumbling-hair," and quoted both. He expressed genuine surprise. This is from Book IV of *Paradise Lost:*

>   Not that fair field
> Of Enna, where Proserpin gathering flowers,
> Herself a fairer flower, by gloomy Dis

Was gathered—which cost Ceres all that pain
To seek her through the world. . . .

And this is Cummings's poem written while at Harvard:

Tumbling-hair
              picker of buttercups
                                violets
dandelions
And the big bullying daisies
                          through the field wonderful
with eyes a little sorry
Another comes
              also picking flowers

One other slight but curious echo in Cummings's poetry is also
from Milton; I refer to the last two lines of "The Hymn" in Milton's
"On the Morning of Christ's Nativity":

And all about the courtly stable
Bright-harnessed angels sit in order serviceable.

Cummings wrote:

(and i imagine
never mind Joe agreeably cheerfully remarked when
surrounded by fat stupid animals
the jewess shrieked
the messiah tumbled successfully into the world
the animals continued eating. And I imagine she, and
heard them slobber and
in the darkness)

stood sharp angels with faces like Jim Europe

(a famous colored band leader before World War I. Gilbert Seldes
wrote in *The Seven Lively Arts:* "Jim Europe seemed to have a constructive intelligence and, had he lived, I am sure he would have been
an even greater conductor than Whiteman." A drummer shot him
dead).

There were also direct influences from the poems of Keats. This passage by Cummings is from "Longing," mentioned earlier:

> The Christlike sun
> Moves to his resurrection in rejoicing heights,
> And priestly hills partake of morning one by one.

"The one use of a man's knowing the classics is to prevent him from imitating the false classics," wrote Ezra Pound to Margaret Anderson.

3

Cummings was graduated from Harvard, June 24, 1915, *magna cum laude* like his father before him, but in English and the classics instead of philosophy. Although he did not "make" Phi Beta Kappa, he was invited to speak at the Commencement Celebration in Sanders Theatre. The exercises began earlier than was usually the case in order to include the ceremony which marked the presentation of the Widener Memorial Library to the University. I extract the following from the official account in the Harvard *Alumni Bulletin* of June 30, 1915, but I shall also give an "unofficial" version so far as the effect of Cummings's talk was concerned:

"The weather was unseasonably cool, and the Yard seemed less filled with graduates than in other years. The presence of women as invited guests at the Library exercises made good the deficiency in numbers.

"At the morning exercises in Sanders Theatre, Paul Perham Cram, '15, delivered the Latin Oration; Henry Parkman, '15, had for the subject of his part, 'Neutralization: its Past and its Future'; Edward Estlin Cummings, '15, spoke on 'The New Art'; and Clarence Belden Randall, A.B., of the Law School, on 'The Undertow in Education.'

"President Lowell conferred 1124 degrees."

I have before me a photostat of the original manuscript of Cummings's talk entitled, "The New Art" (from the Harvard Archives). This Commencement Part afterwards appeared in the *Advocate* with some slight changes. If the reader will bear in mind the age of the speaker and the date of the speech, he will be struck by the extraordinary perception which Cummings displayed (and which could hardly be entirely appreciated). His composition begins:

"The New Art has many branches [in the published version he added "painting, sculpture, architecture, the stage, literature, and music"]. In each of these there is a clearly discernible evolution from models. In none is there any trace of that abnormality or incoherence which the casual critic is fond of making the subject of tirades against the new order. It is my aim to sketch briefly the parallel developments of the New Art in the fields of painting and sculpture, music, and literature.

"Anyone who takes Art seriously, who understands the development of technique in the last half century, accepts Cézanne and Matisse as he accepts Manet and Monet. But this brings us to the point where contemporary criticism becomes, for the most part, rampant abuse, and where prejudice utters its storm of condemnation. I refer to that peculiar phase of the New Art called indiscriminately 'Cubism' and 'Futurism.'

"The term Cubism, properly applied, relates to the work of a small group of ultra-modern painters and sculptors who use design to express their personal reaction to the subject, and who further take this design from geometry. By using an edge in place of a curve a unique tactual value is obtained. . . .

"The painter Matisse has been called the greatest exponent of Cubist sculpture. At the 1913 Exhibition, the crowd around Brancusi's 'Mlle. Pogany' was only rivalled by that which swarmed around the painting called 'Nude Descending a Staircase' [by Marcel Duchamp], which Walter Pach has analyzed as 'phrasing of the elements of motion, mass, and accentuation.' "

Of music, he said:

"While Germany has the honor of producing one of the greatest originators and masters of realism, Richard Strauss, it is a French school, inspired by César Franck, which brought new life to music. One of the most interesting of the modern composers is Erik Satie. Twenty-five years ago [1890] he was writing what is now considered modern music. The most striking aspect of Satie's art is the truly extraordinary sense of humor which prompts one of his subjects, the sea-cucumber, to console himself philosophically for his lack of tobacco."

He also praised Schönberg and Stravinsky.

In introducing the portion of his talk dealing with literature, Cummings declared:

"I shall discuss only the most extreme cases, quoting three contemporary authors to illustrate different phases and different degrees of the literary parallel to sound-painting [in the published version he added, "in a rather faint hope that the first two may prepare the way for an appreciation of the third"]. First Amy Lowell's 'Grotesque' offers a clear illustration of development from the normal to the abnormal:

> Why do the lilies goggle their tongues at me
> When I pluck them;
> And writhe and twist,
> And strangle themselves against my fingers,
> So that I can hardly weave the garland
> For your hair?
> Why do they shriek your name
> And spit at me
> When I would cluster them?
> Must I kill them
> To make them lie still,
> And send you a wreath of lolling corpses
> To turn putrid and soft
> On your forehead
> When you dance?

"In this interesting poem we seem to discern something beyond the conventional. The lilies are made to express hatred by means of grotesque images. But there is nothing new in the pathetic fallacy."

It is doubtful if anyone was listening; the audience had not yet recovered from the shock of the first quoted line coming, as it did, on the heels of Cummings's remark that the poem offered "a clear illustration of development from the normal to the abnormal." Professor Damon, the biographer of Miss Lowell, wrote: "Sanders Theatre shuddered in sibilant horror as he recited: 'Why do the lilies goggle their tongues at me,' " and adds:

"One aged lady (peace be to her bones!) was heard to remark aloud: 'Is that our president's sister's poetry he is quoting? Well, *I* think it is an *insult* to our president!' Meanwhile the president's face, on which all eyes were fixed, was absolutely unperturbed. But one of the Boston newspapers, which did not truckle to the Brahmins, came out with the headlines recalled as 'Harvard Orator Calls President Lowell's Sister Abnormal.' "

Unperturbed, Cummings quoted another poem by Amy Lowell—"The Letter":

> Little cramped words scrawling all over the paper
> Like draggled fly's legs,
> What can you tell of the flaring moon
> Through the oak leaves?
> Or of my uncurtained window, and the bare floor
> Spattered with moonlight?
> Your silly quirks and twists have nothing in them
> Of blossoming hawthorns,
> And this paper is chill, crisp, smooth, virgin of loveliness
> Beneath my hand.
> I am tired, Beloved, of chafing my heart against
> The want of you;
> Of squeezing it into little ink drops,
> And posting it.
> And I scald alone, here under the fire
> Of the great moon.

"This poem," Cummings commented, "is superb of its kind. There is probably in the whole field of realistic literature not one image that exceeds the vividness of the first few lines. The metaphor of the chafed heart is worthy of any poet, but its fanciful development would have been impossible in any literature except this ultra-modern."

Leaving Amy Lowell, probably to the relief of her august brother and Damon's "aged lady," Cummings quoted eight lines from a sonnet by Donald Evans, and I give them chiefly for the comment with which he followed them:

> Her voice was fleet-limbed and immaculate,
> And like peach blossoms blown across the wind;
> Her white words made the hour seem cool and kind,
> Hung with soft dawns that danced a shadow fête.
> A silken silence crept up from the South,
> The flutes were hushed that mimed the orange moon,
> And down the willow stream my sighs were strewn,
> As I knelt to the corners of her mouth.

Cummings said: "With the figure 'her voice was fleet-limbed,' and the phrase 'white words,' it is interesting to compare Dante's expressions, occurring in the first and fifth cantos of the Inferno: 'dove il Sol tace,' and 'in loco d'ogni luce muto.' But even Dante would not have dared 'the corners of her mouth' [the last sentence is omitted from the printed text].

"From Donald Evans to Gertrude Stein is a natural step, up or down, and one which I had hoped we might take in security. Gertrude Stein is a Futurist who subordinates the meaning of words to the beauty of the words themselves. Her art is the logic of literary sound-painting carried to its extreme. While we must admit that it is logic, must we admit that it is Art?

"Having prepared the way as best I can for a just appreciation, I now do my best to quote from her book, 'Tender Buttons,' as follows:

(1) A Sound.

> Elephant beaten with candy and little pops and chews all bolts and reckless, reckless rats, this is this.

(2) Salad Dressing and Artichoke.

> Please pale hot, please cover rose, please acre in the red stranger, please butter all the beefsteak with regular feel faces.

(3) Suppose an Eyes.

> . . . .
> Go red, go red, laugh white.
> Suppose a collapse is rubbed purr, is rubbed purget.
> Little sales ladies little sales ladies little saddles of mutton.
> Little sales of leather and such beautiful beautiful, beautiful, beautiful.

Here we see traces of realism similar to those which made the 'Nude Descending the Staircase' so baffling. The book from which these selections are taken is undoubtedly a proof of great imagination on the part of the author, as any one who tries to imitate her style will discover for himself. But as far as these 'Tender Buttons' are concerned, the sum and substance of criticism is zero, for the reason that criticism is impossible. The unparalleled familiarity of the medium precludes its use for the purposes of esthetic effect. And here, in their logical conclusion, impressionist principles are reduced to absurdity.

"The question now arises: How much of all this is really Art?

"The answer is: We do not know. The great men of the future will undoubtedly profit by the experimentation of the present period [in the published version he added here: "An insight into the unbroken chain of artistic development during the last half century disproves the theory that modern is without foundation"], for this very experimentation is the logical unfolding of sound tendencies. That the conclusion is in a particular case absurdity does not in any way vitiate the value of the experiment provided we are dealing with sincere effort. The New Art, discredited though it be by fakirs and fanatics, will appear in its essential spirit to the unprejudiced critic as a courageous and genuine exploration of untrodden ways."

It is a remarkable picture—the straight youthful figure with the erect blond head telling the Cambridge ladies—and gentlemen—who had gotten as far as John Singer Sargent, perhaps, but who undoubtedly knew Longfellow, what the new art was. Cummings's reading and discussions, his attendance at concerts and exhibitions, had borne strange and exhilarating fruit.

4

Cummings stayed on at the Harvard Graduate School of Arts and Sciences for another year, and emerged an M.A. During his final year he helped to organize the Harvard Poetry Society, which met on the top floor of the Union. I am indebted to Malcolm Cowley for this freshman's-eye glimpse of Cummings and his circle at this time:

"I didn't know him when he was in college. By the fall of 1915, Cummings was already a graduate student, outside the horizon of a freshman, but I must have seen him at two or three meetings of the Poetry Society, held in the sanctum of the Harvard *Monthly*. I can't remember whether he read his poems, though I clearly remember readings by others—for example, Foster Damon, whose voice became flat and matter-of-fact when he recited an especially outrageous line; and Robert Hillyer, looking like a wicked cherub; and John Dos Passos, speaking in very low tones as he peered at a manuscript from behind very thick lenses."

The formation of the Poetry Society apparently engendered a certain amount of spiteful or malicious gossip on the campus. Among those who gossiped most were undergraduate poets who were not members. Although its founders were chiefly contributors to the *Monthly,* it was the rival *Advocate* which struck back with an indignant editorial (which incidentally reveals some of the things that were being said) :

"There has been gossip abroad concerning just what sort of an organization the Harvard Poetry Society is. There have been hints of effeminacy, of desires on the part of its members to grasp the flickering halo of aestheticism that hovers about the long locks of pseudo-geniuses. The falsehood of such gossip is something that is not to be discussed. But the seeming malice of what has been the current libel is something to be deplored and to be stopped at once. The Harvard Poetry Society is doing its small best to gain more intellectual and artistic benefit, by their meetings and the privilege of listening to well-known poets than is required to enter 'the brotherhood of educated men' by reason of English A and sixteen other courses. If those who disapprove of such endeavor do not care to join the society, or who, by lack of ability, are unable to secure admission, let them by all means remain absent. And let the howling, that is seemingly so much in vogue, cease. It ill-befits students with any claim to seriousness. Let those who scoff ape gentlemen, or let them at least swallow their sour grape scorn in silence."

A feeling admonition.

On the evening of February 28, 1916, Amy Lowell came to address the new society. In her honor a festive board, consisting of beer and pretzels, adorned the big table at which she was to sit in massive superiority. Also, in order to provide a respectable audience, as regards numbers, the meeting was officially denominated "a candidates' meeting," so that undergraduates who were not members of the *Monthly* staff or of the Poetry Society might hear her. The room was consequently full.

Miss Lowell talked about her favorite subject and practice—*vers libre.*

"I suppose you think that Whitman wrote it; well, he didn't."

That was that.

At the end of her talk she read "Patterns" and "The Cross-Roads" from the manuscript of her forthcoming book, *Men, Women and Ghosts.* This was followed by a discussion.

John Brooks Wheelwright, one of the Society poets who was later to refer to Miss Lowell as "Biggest Traveling One-Man Show since

Buffalo Bill caught the Midnight Flyer to contact Mark Twain," and who had a flair for showmanship himself, rose to ask a question. It had probably been much considered for its "shock" value.

"Miss Lowell, what do you do when you want to write a poem and haven't anything to write about?"

All eyes were on the questioner, who looked—as Horace Gregory has described him—like "a pre-Revolutionary Bostonian," slender, with "a fine head with a nearly 'hawklike' nose, thin lips, and slightly slanted, narrowed eyes"—while the two New England bluebloods peered at each other over an immense silence.

Miss Lowell never answered.

It was now Cummings's turn. He, too, had framed a question. But whether from shyness, or Miss Lowell's abrupt departure, he almost missed his chance. Damon says in his book: "As she was leaving, with a regretful glance at the centerpiece of beer and pretzels, which nobody offered to disturb, E. E. Cummings asked her what she thought of Gertrude Stein.

" 'Do *you* like her work?' Miss Lowell replied, Yankee-wise.

" 'Why—yes—.'

" '*I* don't!' "

And she swept massively out into the night, where her carriage waited.

(Twenty-two years after his Harvard talk and this exchange with Amy Lowell, I innocently asked Cummings what *he* thought of Gertrude Stein. This was his reply: "I tried to read her. I can feel some things, but she doesn't give me as many things as some people get. [Here, I noted at the time, his eyes brightened.] She's a symbol —she's an excellent symbol, like a pillar of Portland cement. You can't budge her. Philistines bump into her and get bruised.")

Gertrude Stein's view of Cummings will be given later.

In the Harvard *Monthly* for March, 1916, appeared:

> All in green went my love riding
> on a great horse of gold
> into the silver dawn.
>
> four lean hounds crouched low and smiling
> the merry deer ran before.
>
> Fleeter be they than dappled dreams
> the swift sweet deer
> the red rare deer.

Four red roebuck at a white water
the cruel bugle sang before.

Horn at hip went my love riding
riding the echo down
into the silver dawn.

four lean hounds crouched low and smiling
the level meadows ran before.

Softer be they than slippered sleep
the lean lithe deer
the fleet flown deer.

Four fleet does at a gold valley
the famished arrow sang before.

Bow at belt went my love riding
riding the mountain down
into the silver dawn.

four lean hounds crouched low and smiling
the sheer peaks ran before.

Paler be they than daunting death
the sleek slim deer
the tall tense deer.

Four tall stags at a green mountain
the lucky hunter sang before.

All in green went my love riding
on a great horse of gold
into the silver dawn.

four lean hounds crouched low and smiling
my heart fell dead before.

It must have been apparent at once, to all his associates, that Cummings was not only the chief poet of the Society he had helped to found, but one to challenge all his contemporaries.

Chapter 4

THE MAKING OF A BOOK

1

It was Stewart Mitchell who conceived the idea of putting into permanent form the work of some of the men with whom he had been associated during this memorable period. Thus was born *Eight Harvard Poets,* a collection which appeared in 1917 and whose contributors were blazoned on the title-page in the following order:

E. Estlin Cummings
S. Foster Damon
J. R. Dos Passos
Robert Hillyer
R. S. Mitchell
William A. Norris
Dudley Poore
Cuthbert Wright

But while the moving spirit behind this project was Mitchell, it was John Dos Passos, ably seconded by his father, who kept the project from foundering.

For a little book—118 pages, in gray boards with a cloth back stamped with crimson lettering—*Eight Harvard Poets* appears to have been as involved a production as any in the history of publishing. In part it was due to the number of contributors, but mostly it was due to the peculiar nature of the undertaking.

Laurence J. Gomme, under whose imprint the book appeared, had been an associate of Mitchell Kennerley whom he succeeded as proprietor of "The Little Book Shop Around the Corner," at 2 East 29th Street, across the street from the church with the similar name. Kennerley had published, in beautiful editions, a number of new writers, notably Edna St. Vincent Millay who had been brought to his shop at the age of seventeen by Louis Untermeyer. Gomme likewise published at the shop a succession of writers that included John Jay Chapman, Joyce Kilmer, Hilaire Belloc, as well as several issues of William Stanley Braithwaite's annual *Anthology of Magazine Verse,* about which a wag once remarked that he "wished he could like *any* poem as much as Braithwaite liked *every* poem."

Some time in 1916 (Gomme told me) Stewart Mitchell brought him the manuscript of *Eight Harvard Poets.* (Gomme was a friend of Mitchell's aunt, Mrs. G. H. Thomas, a concert pianist.) Gomme said that his poetry readers were Joyce Kilmer and Clement Wood, and it was to the latter that the manuscript was sent.

Mr. Wood, whose first volume of verse had just been published by Gomme, was to become, in the Twenties, a more or less prominent literary figure dispensing poetry and criticism with a generous hand, they being his own. He was not, however, much of a poet and not much of a critic (as his volume, *Poets of America,* testifies); as regards the latter role, he depended chiefly on the methods related in *Hudibras.* He was overbearing and a bully, and I suspect, from observing him there, that he was happiest when he had terrified the ladies of the Poetry Society, where his voice was often heard booming in declamation or debate. To him the most felicitous measure in the world, and the one in which he excelled, was "te-dum, te-dum, te-dum." I once happened to see his copy of *The Waste Land* where, in the margin next to the opening lines, he had written: "No rhythm." A man who could believe that could believe, I believe, anything. It was to this man that the work of Cummings and his Harvard associates went.

On October 19, 1916, from his residence at 510 Audubon Avenue, New York City, Mr. Wood wrote Gomme as follows:

"Your 'Eight Harvard Poets' manuscript I am returning herewith;

and I have enjoyed immensely reading it. I do not think it will be a poor book; taking into consideration the fact that the authors are presumably still college men, it is a remarkably good book. It contains, I venture to say, enough good poetry to warrant its publication if it were not the work of collegians; tho there are crudities, of course, that wider experience would eradicate, in a poet or poets whose work had been before the public to a larger degree. That sentence seems unintelligible to me; perhaps you gather what I am trying to say.

"The first poet, Cummings, I might use as an example of this. Even his grammar is sometimes bad (as in line 2 of the opening poem, which should be 'soundest', shouldn't it) [O Mr. Wood! hadst thou never read the curse out of Isaiah, "make the heart of this people fat, and make their ears heavy, and shut their eyes"?]; the line before he has used 'history her heroes,' which is a silly archaism, to me; and, in his third sonnet, the 7th line is a dreadful inversion. To the contrary, the second sonnet's last line is quite effective; and his vers libre, while affected, is pleasing. I feel that more maturity would rub these artificial excrescences from his work, and let him say in a thoroly understandable manner what he is getting at. Take him all in all, he is only fair."

Mr. Wood began his next paragraph with the words: "To the better ones." He found Mitchell "a delight," and liked Norris "almost as much." Poore "belies his name in the 2nd poem," "one or two" of Wright's pieces passed muster; "Hillyer's 'Sea Gull,' his Scarlatti thing, his excellent 'My Peace I Leave With You' sonnet—these are indeed good. Damon I find more like Cummings, inclined to be too much only a fair distiller of overused poetic material; and Dos Passos is good, particularly in his second and third poems, and in certain lines of 'Memory' and 'Nightpiece.' I could pick out the bad things and comment on them, but I don't think this would be valuable to you."

"As a whole, the collection is good; and I hope you make it sell," was Wood's conclusion.

An undated letter to Gomme from Robert Hillyer, then residing at 36 Mt. Auburn Street, Cambridge, states:

> I enclose a sonnet which I should like to be substituted
> for one of the sonnets in my contribution to the "Eight
> Harvard Poets" anthology. The sonnet whose place I

should like this one to fill is the third in my four sonnets from a sonnet-sequence,—the one beginning "Fly joyous wind." Of course, if the change is not convenient, or if the anthology has already been set up, do not trouble to make the substitution. Unless this new sonnet can be substituted for the "Fly joyous wind," I do not care to have it printed, for I have already overstepped my quota of ten pages. I hope this will not cause you trouble.

The substitute sonnet caused no trouble whatever, for it was placed in Gomme's files, where it remains to this day. Between Wood's report and the publication of the book one of the most involved correspondences on record took place.

2

Mr. Gomme wrote for Mr. Mitchell on the occasion of the latter's presentation of the book to Harvard in 1941:

In May 1917, "The Little Book Shop Around the Corner" closed its doors and with it came the end to my publishing business.

As I was already under contract for the "Eight Harvard Poets" which was at this time in the process of printing, I took temporary quarters in the old Washington Irving House, corner of 17th Street and Irving Place, occupying the front room on the ground floor of this historic mansion. "Eight Harvard Poets" was produced from there. It was the last book I published before going into war work.

Early in June of 1917, Mr. Dos Passos sailed for Europe for the American Red Cross Ambulances, he therefore did not see the book until his return. Under the contract thirty copies were sent to each of the authors for their own use.

I have been informed that one of the authors who up to this moment I have been unable to identify, has not thought so well of his appearance in the volume and has destroyed all copies that came within his grasp. Perhaps this accounts for the rarity of this small but interesting contribution to American poetry.

The unidentified author referred to by Gomme was William A. Norris, who became a business man, and is reputed to have bought up all copies of *Eight Harvard Poets* he could lay hands on in order to destroy them. It explains why, in the copy of the book deposited at Harvard by Stewart Mitchell, there are only seven autographs. It also explains Mitchell's letter which accompanied the book:

> This volume was planned at first as *Seven Harvard Poets*. Owing to the insistence of one of the seven, however, an eighth contributor was added—William Allis Norris, of Milwaukee, Wisconsin, of the Class of 1917.
>
> Having secured the autograph of Cuthbert Wright late in September, 1940, I wrote to Norris, asking him if he would be willing to put his name in the volume, which I was going to present to the Harvard College Library. I did not receive the courtesy of a reply.
>
> Obviously the feeling that the appearance of Norris in this book was a mistake is now mutual.

Although Gomme does not mention it, the copies sent to each author were paid for by the author; but anyone who understands the financial transaction or transactions that took place previous to the dispersal of the volumes must have a harder head than mine. To begin with, Gomme, finding himself with one unfulfilled contract remaining on his hands after closing down his establishment, made an effort to withdraw from it. But he had not reckoned with the natural desire of poets to be published, particularly poets who had come so close to publication as a contract. He was persuaded. He was also assisted.

I have before me a letter from Gomme to John R. Dos Passos, the novelist's father, a well-known lawyer with offices at 120 Broadway:

> For the purpose of my records, I would outline the details discussed in our conversation regarding the book we are publishing under the title "Eight Harvard Poets."
>
> We are to print five hundred copies with plates. It is understood that permission has been granted by the various holders of the rights. Upon publication, I am to supply thirty copies to the eight authors at a price of $1.00 less 1/3%. The first five hundred copies will be published

free of royalty. All copies sold after five hundred have been disposed of, will be on a 10% royalty basis.

The price of the book will be $1.00, unless at the time of manufacturing the price of paper is so advanced as to make this impossible. In that case we will have to make the price $1.25, and the price of the book to the eight authors will have to be advanced in proportion. As this was a point I did not take up with you, I submit it to you for your approval now.

The acknowledgement of this letter will be sufficient contract on both sides.

To this, Mr. Dos Passos replied, November 9, as follows:

Your letter dated November the 3rd was directed to me, whereas it was intended for my son, John R. Dos Passos Jr. He is now in Madrid, having gone there to enter the University to perfect himself in Spanish and other courses. He told me all about the terms of the publication of the book, the "Eight Harvard Poets." Your version of the understanding is correct and you can assume this to be a confirmation of the same on behalf of my son. If you will kindly write me about any matter relating to the book I shall be glad to act for my son as to its publication. I am forwarding your letter to him with a copy of this letter also.

The letters were duly forwarded; on December 22, 1916, John Dos Passos wrote to Gomme from Madrid:

Your letter—to which my father replied—has just reached me. If anything should come up in regard to the Anthology—Dudley S. Poore or R. S. Hillyer—Cambridge would be the best people to get in touch with. Still, I hardly think anything will—except the small "i's," which you may be as high handed about as you like as far as I am concerned.

By the way, the terms are completely satisfactory, that is:—each of the eight are to take thirty copies—at the retail price minus a third, and if another edition is thought advisable we are to get 10% royalty.

Lastly, please don't let them forget the "Junior" at the
end of my name on the title page. It would be too bad to
saddle my father with my poems!

>   Yours very truly
>   John R. Dos Passos Jr.

Thus ended the old year. The new began with trepidations on the
part of Gomme, which he seems to have communicated to several
of the contributors.

Mr. Gomme's correspondence, which he kindly placed at my disposal, includes a letter from Cuthbert Wright which was in reply to
one of his, unfortunately missing. But its subject can be guessed—
Cummings's typography, to which Dos Passos briefly referred. Wright,
who seems to have been the only member of the Eight not on the
move or march, wrote on Harvard Union stationery, January 13:

Dear Mr. Gomme:

In regard to *Eight Harvard Poets,* I find that Cummings
has gone to N.Y. and can be addressed in care of Collier's
Weekly. If he makes any difficulty about the poem I should
suggest that it be dropped out. If you will address me as
above I shall be glad to read the proof and be personally
responsible for getting it back expeditiously. I am sorry
not to report on the man to write the preface but will do
so as soon as possible. Mr. Wendell has retired and may
not do it, but either Bliss Perry or W. A. Neilson would
consent I am sure.

I hope I may serve you in the matter if you need any
help at this end.

>   Very truly yours
>   Cuthbert Wright

3

It is not easy at this late date to determine which poem Dos
Passos and Wright had reference to. Cummings led off in the book,
as he did the roster of contributors, with eight poems which occupy
pages 3 to 10. There were four sonnets which—Clement Wood's
comments notwithstanding—are among Cummings's best. They are:
"Thou in whose swordgreat story shine the deeds," "when thou

hast taken thy last applause, and when," "this is the garden: colours come and go," and:

> it may not always be so; and i say
> that if your lips, which i have loved, should touch
> another's, and your dear strong fingers clutch
> his heart, as mine in time not far away;
> if on another's face your sweet hair lay
> in such a silence as i know, or such
> great writing words as, uttering over much,
> stand helplessly before the spirit at bay;
>
> if this should be, i say if this should be—
> you of my heart, send me a little word;
> that i may go unto him, and take his hands,
> saying, Accept all happiness from me.
> Then shall i turn my face, and hear one bird
> sing terribly afar in the lost lands.

The first and third appeared afterwards in *XLI Poems,* the second and fourth in *Tulips and Chimneys.* I give the sonnet as it appeared under Cummings's own supervision; in *Eight Harvard Poets* the lowercase "i" and the opening letters were capitalized without his knowledge.

The four remaining poems were: "i will wade out," "Over silent waters," "your little voice" and "Tumbling-hair" (quoted in the preceding chapter). The first appeared in *XLI Poems,* the third and fourth in *Tulips and Chimneys.* The second, entitled "Finis" in *Eight Harvard Poets,* has never been collected:

> Over silent waters
>   day descending
>   night ascending
> floods the gentle glory of the sunset
> In a golden greeting
>   splendidly to westward
> as pale twilight
>   trem-
>   bles
>   into
>   Darkness

comes the last light's gracious exhortation
                              Lifting up to peace
so when life shall falter
                    standing on the shores of the
eternal
god
        May I behold my sunset
Flooding
            over silent waters

There was one final flurry. Cummings told me that Dos Passos came to see him just before going abroad on war service. "As I remember it, Dos was greatly agitated," he said. "He asked me what I proposed to do about the lowercase 'i's' in the poems, and I replied —I heard myself with surprise—that the poems must stand as they were."

"It was," he added, "the beginning of my style."

But while the typographical arrangements were allowed to stand, someone—Gomme thinks the printer—capitalized all the "i's" when the book went to press. When I asked Gomme what had become of the manuscript, he said it had been broken up and the material returned to the contributing poets.

4

The flurry among the poets was followed by a bombshell from Gomme, who wrote to the senior Dos Passos on February 8 as follows:

Dear Sir:

On November 3rd I wrote to you in regard to the publication of "Eight Harvard Poets." Since that time I find that it has become more and more difficult to publish books, owing to the very high cost of material; and conditions make possibilities of sales extremely uncertain.

It is with this feeling I am writing to ask you to release me from the obligation to bring this book out. Conditions have changed to such an extent recently that I doubt very much whether there will be sufficient demand for books of this character to justify the expense of production. It

is with great regret that I am writing to you in this vein
as I looked forward with a good deal of pleasure to producing what I feel would be a very worthy collection of
poems.

Trusting to hear from you in the near future, I am

Sincerely,

Laurence J. Gomme

On March 29, Gomme addressed a similar letter to 120 Broadway.
The tone of both suggests he, like the poets concerned, was not altogether desirous of having the project dropped. The communica-
tions might be termed "feelers," without offense to anyone. They
proved successful. John Dos Passos wrote me (September 29, 1957):

"My recollection is that I induced my father John R. Dos Passos,
the lawyer, to put up $750 to guarantee the printing costs."

Dos Passos had returned to this country from Spain and, following the death of his father, had enlisted in the Norton Harjes Ambulance Corps. He was not the only one. "A Bord de 'Chicago' " of
the French Line on June 20, 1917, he scribbled a hasty note to
Gomme:

My dear Mr. Gomme—

I didn't get a chance to get to see you this morning—my
wild rush for the boat.

Enclosed is the letter about the upwards $200.

Will you please send your letter to my aunt, Mrs. J. R.
Gordon at the address I gave you.

Also, when that millenial day arrives and the Eight
finally see the light, will you please write Mr. Mitchell to
find out how many copies he wants. If you send me five
copies—or perhaps six—it will be sufficient. Then I shall
send Mr. Poore two & Mr. Hillyer two, as I shall know
where in France they will be.

Best wishes,

J. R. Dos Passos

Address

—c/o American Red Cross Ambulance

7 Rue François Premier

Paris

It would appear that Gomme wrote to Mrs. Gordon without delay. On June 21, from 214 Riverside Drive, Mrs. Gordon wrote:

> Your note of June 20 was rec'd this morning. Mr. Dos Passos asked me to pay you the balance on the printing bill of the volume on its completion—which I shall be glad to attend to for him. He said that he thought the volume would be ready next week.

But it was not until July 12 that the first copy was ready. Gomme wrote Mrs. Gordon on that date:

> Dear Madam,
>
> I have pleasure in sending by this mail the first copy of Eight Harvard Poets off the press. The book is now ready for distribution.
>
> I would esteem it a favour if you would send me a check for the balance on the printing bill as indicated on the enclosed invoice.
>
> I hope you will like the appearance of the book. It has been a very great pleasure to me to see the book through the press and I feel sure it will receive the attention good verse deserves.
>
> Yours very sincerely,
Laurence J. Gomme

Meanwhile, Gomme had notified some of the contributors that the book was "about to be published in a few days." This was on June 26. On June 29, S. Foster Damon replied from Gore Hall, Cambridge:

> Dear Mr. Gomme:
>
> I am very glad to hear that the "Eight Harvard Poets" is to appear so soon. Please send my 30 copies to
>
> S. Foster Damon
54 Dunster St.
Cambridge, Mass.
>
> and mark it *"Please do not forward."*
>
> About two months ago I sent Mr. Dos Passos my check for $20.00 in advance.
>
> Very sincerely yours,
S. Foster Damon

Stewart Mitchell wrote from South Norwood, Ohio, July 2:

> Will you please send me, for the present, ten copies of
> the volume, "Eight Harvard Poets." I will be able to take
> more of them—I know I shall want more—within a few
> months. Please mail one of my ten copies to Mrs. G. H.
> Thomas, 8 Eastern Point Road, East Gloucester, Massa-
> chusetts. The remaining nine mail to me here in Norwood.
> So soon as I become more certain as to my future where-
> abouts, I shall want you to send on a dozen or so more.

Cuthbert Wright wrote from Cambridge on stationery embossed
with the seal of Harvard:

> Thanks for your letter about the Anthology. I enclose
> a cheque for $20.00 and you may send copies to the ad-
> dress below.
> If I were you I should send a consignment to the Har-
> vard Cooperative Store, Harvard Square with the request
> that they make a window display of the book etc. They are
> rather dense about these things and have to be instructed.
> Would you mind telling me what press bureau you
> employ for reviews so that I may apply to them.

It may be that Norris was already feeling some uneasiness about
his role as a published poet. I do not know how many letters Gomme
sent him in all; I know that he wrote him on June 26 and July 9
and 12, after appealing to Wright, who replied:

> Norris is still in the Harvard Regiment and can be ad-
> dressed at his old rooms or care of *Harvard Reserved Of-
> ficers Training Comp., Harvard University.*
> Dr. Cummings' address is *Irving Street, Cambridge,
> Mass.*
> If you have time, drop me a line and let us know what
> Press Clipping Agency to employ.

Mr. Gomme replied the next day:

> Dear Mr. Wright,
> Many thanks for your letter and the addresses necessary
> to complete my records.

I have always subscribed to The Romeike Press Clipping Bureau, 106 Seventh Avenue, N.Y. Mine is an annual subscription but I think they charge 10 dollars a hundred.

I have just received an advance copy of the book and I think it looks very well. I hope you will feel the same way. Your copies will leave New York tomorrow.

> Yours very sincerely,
> Laurence J. Gomme

On July 12, which seems to have been a busy day in the life of Gomme, another letter went to Norris at his new address:

Eight Harvard Poets is to be out next week and I am to send you thirty copies. Would you be good enough to let me know by return mail how and where you want them sent.

When you send this information will you also let me have your check for $20 in payment, in accordance with the arrangement with Mr. Dos Passos.

On the same day he addressed Dr. Edward Cummings:

Dear Sir,

I have pleasure in informing you that the volume EIGHT HARVARD POETS is now ready for distribution. Before leaving for France Mr. Dos Passos requested me to write to you for instructions as to the shipment of the thirty copies due Mr. E. Estlin Cummings.

When you send this information will you also let me have your check for $20 in accordance with the arrangement made with Mr. Dos Passos.

I trust you will like [the] book both in its appearance and content.

> Yours very truly,
> Laurence J. Gomme

Dr. Cummings replied, July 23, on stationery of the World Peace Foundation, 40 Mt. Vernon Street, Boston, of which he was General Secretary:

Dear Sir:

It gives me pleasure to enclose check for twenty dollars, in accordance with the arrangement made by Mr. Dos

Passos, with the understanding that you will forward me thirty copies of the volume entitled "Eight Harvard Poets."

Sincerely yours,

Edward Cummings

On the same day, Damon wrote Gomme on the letterhead of the Reserve Officers' Training Corps, Harvard Barracks, requesting that one copy of the book be sent to "Company K, Barre, Mass., and the rest to the address I sent you before."

A long delay now ensued, vexing to all concerned. Dr. Cummings went to New Hampshire, and returned from New Hampshire, and there was still no sign of the book. On September 19, from his home in Irving Street, he addressed Gomme once more, this time in stern vein. After quoting the whole of Gomme's letter to him of July 12, Dr. Cummings wrote:

> On July 23, I sent you a check for $20, with directions for forwarding the books by parcel post or by express.
>
> More recently, I wrote stating that the check had come back to me with your endorsement, showing that it had been cashed; but that I had received no word with regard to the books which you assured me were ready for distribution on July 12. I heard nothing from this letter.
>
> Do you wish me to begin legal proceedings, or may I have the favor of a prompt reply?
>
> Sincerely yours,
Edward Cummings

However these matters were finally straightened out, the mystery surrounding the publication of *Eight Harvard Poets* persisted as late as 1949, when a Chicago bookseller specializing in British and American 19th and 20th century first editions wrote to Gomme for information.

"I can find no record, in fact, that the book was ever formally published," wrote Jack Potter, the bookseller referred to. "There is no listing of it in the copyright annals, nor was a copy sent to *Publisher's Weekly.* Further, it was apparently never reviewed, as it is not mentioned in *Book Review Digest.*

"I do know that the Library of Congress acquired a copy in 1923, but this was evidently a copy they bought rather than the copyright deposit copy.

"The size of the printing is not so vital a matter as knowing the approximate date of publication. I have always assumed that this latter was Spring, 1917, but the fact that I am unable thus far to trace it at all has made me wonder if it was delayed indefinitely."

To this, Gomme replied, October 27, 1949:

> Regarding the *Eight Harvard Poets,* it was published in August 1917—I had made arrangements to publish it earlier in the year when war duties forced me to close The Little Book Shop Around the Corner. In order to publish this last contracted book of my publishing business, I opened an office in Washington Irving's house, at Seventeenth Street and Irving Place where I read proofs and published the book. *Two thousand copies were printed, one hundred copies of which were sent to each of the contributors* [author's italics].
>
> There is one thing in your letter I cannot quite understand, that the Library of Congress' copy sent to them for Copyright is not in their files—I entered the Copyright in accordance with the Law.

5

Neither Professor Neilson, an eminent Shakespeare scholar and teacher, nor Professor Perry wrote a preface for *Eight Harvard Poets;* the book appeared without one. But one day in Cambridge Neilson asked Cummings if he would like a job in New York. Cummings jumped at the chance. It was not, however, with *Collier's Weekly,* as Wright supposed, but with the parent firm of P. F. Collier & Son, Inc., which ran a mail order business in books, usually in sets. Its offices were at 416 West 13th Street, and there Cummings went to work for $50 a week, an enormous sum in those days particularly for a young man. His job was to answer letters elicited by advertisements in *Collier's Weekly.* Cummings recalled for me the substance and spelling of some of these untutored epistles; in one of them, a woman complained that her "husban" could not stand the "noyz" of her sewing machine. This stumped him, and he turned to his boss, who told him to look at the ads—there was sure to be one of a silent machine. His boss, Cummings told me, used to strike out most of his sentences, with the result, he said, "I learned how to write a business letter." Whenever someone came into the office, he said, his boss stood up, and he did likewise because "I was brought up that way," but this was deprecated by his boss who, he added, was a Yale man. Most of the time, Cummings said, he had nothing to do.

"I read both Eddas in the three months I worked there," he told me.

During this period he lived at 21 East 15th Street, just off Fifth Avenue, with Arthur ("Texas") Wilson, a friend of his college days who had shocked Harvard by a short story called "The Girl Who Advertised." Wilson was also a poet, and later appeared as such in *The Dial;* he is now a painter specializing in seascapes. Of his first home in New York Cummings recalled that there was a photographer's studio upstairs where young women posed in the nude. The women soon discovered that there were no plates in the camera, and that they were being paid merely to display themselves while the photographer, covered with a large hood, made a pretense of pressing the bulb. As they were models, it made no difference to them so long as they were paid. Cummings explained that this was in the days before sex magazines, and the "photographer" liked to look at nudes.

Thus it happened that, in his twenty-second year, Cummings plunged exuberantly—if briefly this first time—into the city that was henceforth to be his home.

"After Harvard," he declared in Nonlecture Three, "I thank (for self discovery) a phenomenon and a miracle. The phenomenon was a telemicroscopic chimera, born of the satanic rape of matter by mind: a phallic female phantasm, clothed in thunderous anonymity and adorned with colossally floating spiderwebs of traffic; a stark irresistibly stupendous newness, mercifully harboring among its pitilessly premeditated spontaneities immemorial races and nations."

The miracle was to come: Paris.

Cummings had arrived in New York not only with Professor Neilson's introduction which resulted in a job, but bearing three other letters to magazine editors from Amy Lowell, who also wrote to the editors themselves. In his biography of her, Professor Damon gives the form she used in addressing the editors of the *Century, Scribner's Magazine* and *Craftsman*:

"I am taking the liberty of giving a letter of introduction to you to a young Harvard graduate, named Erstline [sic] Cummings. He has been specializing in English I believe, and had one of the Commencement parts last year, in which I hear he was very brilliant. He is extremely interested in all forms of the New Poetry, but I do not think confines himself to that branch of literature. He is very anxious to get something to do on a magazine, and although I have very little hope that you will have anything to give him, perhaps you would be so kind as to see him for a few minutes and give him some excellent advice. At any rate, I hope that I am not trespassing upon a very slight acquaintance; if I am, pray ignore both this note and the letter he will bring you."

It is not likely that her notes were ignored, or that the letters Cummings bore would have been. He simply did not present them.

After three months at Collier's, Cummings "fired" himself—"the most intelligent thing I could possibly have done." He had learned, he told me, once and for all, what "having a job" means, how it feels to "earn your living" in a country "where nothing outranks the almighty dollar," and what price a human being pays for "security." Meanwhile "America was becoming less and less secure."

On Thursday, March 29, 1917, the New York *Times* carried the following story on page three:

GOELET GIVES $250,000
TO HARJES AMBULANCE

Fund Will Equip Two Sections
For American Corps, Which
Serves French Army

Robert W. Goelet donated $250,000 yesterday for the establishment and equipment of two additional ambulance sections of the Harjes-Norton American Ambulance Corps, which at present consists of three sections with a total of approximately 75 cars and 120 men, operating with the French Army. Mr. Goelet also announced his intention to furnish funds necessary for the maintenance of the two new sections until the end of the war.

The Harjes-Norton ambulance corps is distinct from the larger organization known as the American Ambulance Field Service. The first and second sections were organized at the beginning of the war by Richard Norton, formerly of Boston, and Henry H. Harjes of Morgan, Harjes & Co., Paris. In September the two sections were combined. At the request of the French Government a third section was added on the first of the year. As a mark of appreciation of their work, the Government bestowed the French War Cross on Norton, Harjes, and several of their assistants, and they were mentioned in the war orders of Feb. 8.

Eliot Norton of 2 Rector Street, brother of the head of the corps, to whom Mr. Goelet announced his gift, said the two new sections would also consist exclusively of Americans. Each car will require two chauffeurs, and will operate from field dressing stations or base hospitals. The men serve for a minimum period of six months and several have been wounded in their work. Eliot Norton will recruit those needed for the new sections, each of which will have twenty to twenty-five autos and forty to fifty men.

On the same page were stories suggestive of the imminent belligerency of the United States. One of them related that Dr. Alexis Carrel was coming here to teach his methods of treating infected wounds "to army surgeons, public health experts, and Red Cross nurses." There was also a cabled dispatch from Berne. "The Germans," it read, "appear to be considerably irritated by the American reply to their proposal that the treaties of 1799 and 1828 should be respected. The Frankfurter Zeitung avers that the United States has no proof whatever to support the statement it makes, for 'the German Empire is most anxious to uphold the old humane agreements.'"

Franklin Simon advertised "Men's *Aquascutum* Showerproof Topcoats $24 up But Mostly $24."

Arthur Wilson, one day, joined the American army as an aviator. It was now, of course, a question of time before Cummings would be called up for service with the American army. He journeyed to 2 Rector Street and signed up as a volunteer ambulance driver.

Among the other volunteers at this time was a good-looking devil-may-care product of Webster, Massachusetts, and Columbia University. His name was William Slater Brown. (When I asked Brown how a New Englander got to Columbia University, he replied: "I couldn't get out of New England fast enough, and the first chance came with college.") He was then twenty years old. Cummings was twenty-two.

Young Americans slipped into Canada to enlist in the Royal Canadian Air Force, among them William Faulkner; they enlisted in the French army, like Alan Seeger, or in the French military transport, like Malcolm Cowley. Many of them, being in Cummings's phrase "neither warrior nor conscientious objector," enlisted in the American Field Service or the Norton Harjes Ambulance Corps.

Cowley wrote in *Exile's Return*: "We were eager to get into action, as a character in one of Dos Passos's novels expressed it, 'before the whole thing goes belly up.'"

Dos Passos wrote me: "Although I was an enthusiastic pacifist I wanted to get into the ambulance service to see what the war was like. There hadn't been any great wars for some time. The attraction was enormous. My eyes were so myopic that it was the only way I could get anywhere near action. Another motive was that I had a horror of serving in the army . . . a good many other young men of my generation felt the same way. Everybody's idea was to get into the war without getting into the army. Later, after I'd seen the front lines a little, I felt quite differently. In fact I went to a great deal of trouble to get into the army after the volunteer services were disbanded and I've always been glad that I did. It was the most valuable part of my education during these years."

Cummings felt the same way. He has great sympathy for conscientious objectors, but never could understand those who were not and yet avoided service, or were resentful over having to serve.

"World War I," he told me, "was the experience of my generation."

He went on to explain that those who had consciously shut themselves off from it were ever afterwards "outsiders." He admitted that he volunteered with Norton Harjes to avoid the U. S. Army. "It was an opportunity to do something useful and to see France at the same time. Of course," he added, smiling, "the army got me afterwards; but I didn't mind."

Chapter 5

THE POET AT WAR

1

Cummings and William Slater Brown sailed, the last week in April, 1917, on *La Touraine* of the French Line. They had not yet met. Brown told me that he was talking to another volunteer ambulance driver who asked Cummings, about to pass them on a stroll around the deck, for a light. Perhaps Cummings was wearing that fur coat which was to figure so comically in *The Enormous Room.* Introductions followed. After this chance encounter—although in the course of the voyage they would have met in any case—Brown and Cummings became inseparable, with the ship's bar a frequent background for their talks. They were still talking when they landed at Boulogne. But eagerly as they looked forward to Paris, little did they suspect that by a missed signal, to which all organized effort is peculiarly susceptible, they would have a fairly lengthy stay there. It happened as follows.

On the boat-train, the leader of their group became more and more excited as they neared Paris. Just before the capital he rushed through the cars shouting for all to be ready to detrain and all—incredible as it may sound—detrained at the next stop, which was not

Paris at all, but a suburb. Brown and Cummings, busy with their own affairs, paid no attention, and consequently arrived where they were supposed to. But when they reported at 7, rue François Premier, they were told to await orders, as they could not be sent to the front as individuals. This was—in Brown's recollection—May 7 or 8. The rest of their group reported as a body after they left, and were quickly assigned and shipped out. Still awaiting assignment, Brown and Cummings spent a blissful month in Paris.

"I participated in an actual marriage of material and immaterial things," Cummings afterwards wrote; "I celebrated an immediate reconciling of spirit and flesh, forever and now, heaven and earth. Paris was for me precisely and complexly this homogeneous duality: this accepting transcendence; this living and dying more than death or life. Whereas—by the very act of becoming its improbably gigantic self—New York had reduced mankind to a tribe of pygmies, Paris (in each shape and gesture and avenue and cranny of her being) was continuously expressing the humanness of humanity. Everywhere I sensed a miraculous presence, not of mere children and women and men, but of living human beings" (Nonlecture Three).

He was to return to Paris again and again; but it was to New York that he returned to live.

In that incredible month he and Brown took in all that Paris has to offer. Among their more memorable experiences was Stravinsky's "Petrouchka." Brown puchased a number of Cézanne prints and placed them in a suitcase which he left at the Red Cross. He never saw them again. In uniform at last, they were assigned together to Section Sanitaire Vingt-et-Un, Ambulance Norton Harjes, Croix Rouge Américaine. They left Paris for the Noyon sector of the front in an ambulance convoy. After an overnight stop in Compiègne they proceeded to a village outside Noyon called Ham, which was to be the scene of their débâcle. To this, two things contributed: their *chef de section,* and Brown's indiscretion as a letter-writer in wartime.

First, the *chef de section.* He was soon looking with a furious eye on two happy nonconformists who thought nothing of letting grease spots stay where they had splattered; and of these there must have been a great many, for they were constantly attending to vehicles. Also, to his furious eye, it appeared from time to time as though

Brown and Cummings had set out to grow beards, a feat quite within their powers as their appearance frequently showed. Brown and Cummings were "a disgrace to the section."

"In this, I am bound to say," Cummings wrote in *The Enormous Room*, "Mr. A. was but sustaining the tradition conceived originally by his predecessor, a Mr. P., a Harvard man, who until his departure from *Vingt-et-Un* succeeded in making life absolutely miserable for both B. and myself. Before leaving this painful subject I beg to state that, at least as far as I was concerned, the tradition had a firm foundation in my own predisposition for uncouthness plus what *Le Matin* (if we remember correctly) cleverly nicknamed *La Boue Héroïque*."

Mr. A.'s advice was, "you boys want to keep away from those dirty Frenchmen" and "we're here to show those bastards how they do things in America." His name was Anderson.

These pungent remarks bring us to the second cause of the débâcle. Brown and Cummings, perhaps not so much disliking their compatriots as preferring the French, easily and quickly made friends with the eight Frenchmen attached to their section, particularly the cook and provisioner (when arrested, Cummings was actually domiciled with the Frenchmen who had made room for him "on their own initiative"). And since the section itself was attached to the French army, they had quickly and easily made friends among the *poilus*. From the latter they heard some disquieting rumors. Brown, who had attended the Columbia School of Journalism, flashed them in letters home. ("Flashed," however, is hardly the word, for the letters were never delivered.) There was also a letter written jointly by the two friends and a third American to the Under-Secretary of State in French Aviation offering to enlist in l'Escadrille Lafayette, in order to continue their fraternization with the French now that the United States was in the war (and had taken over the Red Cross). All letters from section members, of course, were dropped unsealed so they could be inspected for security reasons.

The war was very near. Cummings wrote:

> the bigness of cannon
> is skilful,
>
> but i have seen
> death's clever enormous voice

which hides in a fragility
of poppies . . . .

i say that sometimes
on these long talkative animals
are laid fists of huger silence.

I have seen all the silence
filled with vivid noiseless boys

at Roupy
i have seen
between barrages,

the night utter ripe unspeaking girls.

Three months after their arrival in Ham the blow fell. Brown and
Cummings had just finished cleaning and greasing the *chef de section's* car, a form of punishment, when a Renault drove up. In it were
a police officer and two helmeted soldiers. The two friends were taken
to Noyon in separate cars, which also carried their belongings. And
they were interrogated separately. Cummings met Brown coming out
looking, he afterwards wrote, "peculiarly cheerful." Brown, he added,
cheerfully announced, "I think we're going to prison all right."

Cummings found himself looking into three pairs of eyes, not
all of them unfriendly. One pair belonged to "Monsieur le Ministre
de Sûreté de Noyon." He was asked his name.

" 'You are Irish?'—'No,' I said, 'American.'—'You are Irish by
family?'—'No, Scotch.'—'You are sure that there was never an Irishman in your parents?'—'So far as I know,' I said, 'there never was
an Irishman there.'—'Perhaps a hundred years back?' he insisted.—
'Not a chance,' I said decisively. But Monsieur was not to be denied:
'Your name it is Irish?'—'Cummings is a very old Scotch name,' I
told him fluently; 'it used to be Comyn. A Scotchman named The
Red Comyn was killed by Robert Bruce in a church. He was my
ancestor and a very well-known man.'—'But your second name, where
have you got that?'—'From an Englishman, a friend of my father.'
This statement seemed to produce a very favourable impression in
the case of the rosette, who murmured: *'Un ami de son père, un
anglais, bon!'* several times."

The case against him, if case there was, did not go very well; if he had dissociated himself from Brown he could have walked out of the interrogation almost at any point. But this he refused to do— he even insisted, after hearing the interrogator's view of Brown, that his own be put into the record: "Write this down in the testimony— that I, here present, refuse utterly to believe that my friend is not as sincere a lover of France and the French people as any man living! Tell him to write it."

He was told instead that "We have the very best reason for supposing your friend to be no friend of France."

To this Cummings replied: "That is not my affair. I want my opinion of my friend written in; do you see?"

It was written in.

Finally he was asked: "Est-ce-que vous détestez les boches?"

In *The Enormous Room* he wrote: "I had won my case. The question was purely perfunctory. To walk out of the room a free man I had merely to say yes. My examiners were sure of my answer. The rosette was leaning forward and smiling encouragingly. The moustache was making little *oui's* in the air with his pen. And Noyon had given up all hope of making me out a criminal. I might be rash, but I was innocent; the dupe of a superior and malign intelligence. I would probably be admonished to choose my friends more carefully next time, and that would be all. . . .

"Deliberately, I framed the answer:

" 'Non. J'aime beaucoup les français.' "

An effort was made to extricate him. If only he would admit that the Germans were hateful. "But you are doubtless aware of the atrocities committed by the boches?" "I have read about them." "You do not believe?" "Ça se peut." "And if they are so, which of course they are, you do not detest the Germans?" "Oh, in that case, of course anyone must detest them."

It was all over. "I breathed freely once more. All my nervousness was gone. The attempt of the three gentlemen sitting before me to endow my friend and myself with different fates had irrevocably failed.

"At the conclusion of a short conference I was told by Monsieur:

" 'I am sorry for you, but due to your friend you will be detained a little while.'

"I asked: 'Several weeks?'

" 'Possibly,' said Monsieur."

With this, Cummings as well as Brown disappeared. The Red
Cross was, seemingly, indifferent to their fate. It took the combined
forces of their families, friends in the government, the American
Embassy in Paris, the State Department in Washington, and a letter
to the President, to find them. By a species of poetic justice, a man
named Anderson was to be instrumental in bringing them aid and
succour. Meanwhile, from the Enormous Room, Cummings sent an
account of what had befallen him and Brown to his mother.

Dearest of Mothers!

At 11 A.M. Monsieur le ministre de Sureté plus 2 or 3
gendarmes convoyed my friend and me in separate voitures
to his abode in N. Here we dined,each with his gendarme,
still apart,and later were examined. Then removed to separate cells where we spent the night. My friend must have
left the following day:I spent another night in my cell
(sans sortir) having enjoyed a piece of bread,a piece of
chocolate(thanks to friend)a small pail(or marmite)of
grease-meat soup,more bread,ditto of beans,ditto soup &
bread. This sound[s] like a lot. At 10 A.M. I left in the
company of 2 gendarmes for the station of N. A distance of
about ½ mile. Had some trouble with a gendarme,who
told me if I didn't want to carry my baggage I could leave
it(I had a duffle-bag,chockfull,a long ambulance coat,a fur
coat,a bed-roll,&blankets,total + 150 lbs.)by the wayside
—which I naturally refused to do. We finally compromised
by my hiring a sweet kid to lug the bed-roll(which he did
with greatest difficulty). Chemin-de-fer till 5 o'clock when
landed at G. where supped on grease-meat-soup in a better
cell,and slept on planks in blankets(other baggage forbidden)till 4 A.M.,when another pair of gendarmes took
me to the station of G.(I with baggage)where we boarded
c.def. for Paris,arriving at 6 A.M. Wait till 12 noon. In
interval coffee & newspapers. At 1 train left for B.,where
we arrived at 9:30 PM,I having dined on bread. All this
time my friend was 1 day ahead of me. Arrived at B.,we
checked big duffle-bag & roll in gare,and set off on foot for
la Ferté Macé, I carrying this time merely a small bag of

letters,n.books,& souvenirs,which a gendarme had always carried hitherto. Douze kilometres. Arrived midnight. Given a straw pallet & slept on floor sans blankets. In morning found self in hugely long room with my long-lost friend and about 30 others as I guess—very cosmopolite group.

The following program is ours now till 15th October, when a commission comes to examine us for pacifism or something of the sort:6—up. Coffee. 7—down to yard. 9:30 up. 10 down to salle a manger. 10:30-3:45 yard. 3:45 up.4 down to salle a manger. 4:30-7 yard. 7 up. 9—lights out. I am having the time of my life. Never so healthy. Our meals are both soup,but we are allowed a spoon,which is better than eating with fingers,as we did in prison. By the way,a gendarme assured me this is not prison.

By the time this reaches you I shall have been out for some time. It's a great experience. Monsieur le Surveillant is a fine man. We(my friend & I) have instituted "3 old cat",which we all play in the yard when it's fair. I couldn't possibly want anything better in the way of keep,tho' you have to get used to the snores,and they don't allow you a knife,so you can't cut the air at night which is pretty thick, all windows being shut.

Elos's [Elizabeth Cummings] letter I got before leaving the "front" and please thank her & give her my much love,as to all.

You can't imagine,Mother mine,how interesting a time I'm having. Not for anything in the world would I change it! It's like working—you must experience it to comprendre—but how infinitely superior to Colliers! If I thought you would excite yourself I wouldn't write from this place,but I know you will believe me when I reiterate I am having *the time of my life!*

Always—
Estlin

P.S. my bagg[ag]e has been given back. I have
    my bed and am finely off! No more floor-sleeping.
P.P.S. arrested a week ago today.

2

I have before me the personal and official correspondence dealing with the arrest and detention of Cummings and Brown, including
Brown's intercepted letters. With the exception of Dr. Cummings's
letter to President Wilson, and another by him to an officer on the
staff of the Judge Advocate General, A. E. F., in Paris (parts of
which appear in the Foreword to *The Enormous Room*), none of
this material has ever been published before. Although at the time,
which was of course a period of great anxiety for the families of the
two young men, nothing appeared to be happening in their behalf,
the documents reveal an extraordinary amount of activity, and this
in very high quarters.

The first word of the plight of his son reached Dr. Cummings in
the form of a cablegram from Paris. It was dated October 17, 1917,
and read:

> EDWARD E. CUMMINGS HAS BEEN PUT IN A CONCENTRA-
> TION CAMP AS RESULT OF LETTERS HE HAD WRITTEN
> STOP AM TAKING UP THE MATTER THROUGH EMBASSY TO
> SEE WHAT CAN BE DONE

It was signed "Norton." This was Richard Norton, head of the Norton Harjes Ambulance Corps, the son of Charles Eliot Norton and
a friend of Dr. Cummings.

Following the cablegram from Norton are two pencil drafts of
replies by Dr. and Mrs. Cummings. The first one reads:

> Thanks—Do everything—Draw on me Advise me what to
> do—Will come if needed Cable progress.

The second one is addressed to "E. E. Cummings care Richard
Norton" and reads:

> Please act on Norton's advice Take greatest care for my
> sake Cable immediately.

It is signed "R. H. Cummings," the poet's mother.

On October 20 Norton dispatched another cablegram to Dr.
Cummings:

> NOTHING TO BE DONE FOR PRESENT UNDERSTAND COM-
> MISSION WILL PASS ON SONS CASE NO NEED TO COME

WILL MYSELF DO ANYTHING THAT IS POSSIBLE TO BE
DONE

Again there is a draft of the reply, the date—"Oct. 21"—in
pencil, the text in ink:

Norton Ameredcross Paris
Unless Ambassador is assured of prompt release provide
best legal counsel for defence. Am prepared to take up
Case at Washington [here "and appeal to country" is
crossed out] if necessary France cannot afford to alienate
American sympathy by disregarding rights of Citizens
or dealing harshly with youths who volunteered to help
her [here "Notify French Govt" has also been crossed
out].

The note is signed "C," which greatly resembles the famous single-
letter signature of his son. The word "youths" indicates that Dr.
Cummings had learned, possibly from Brown's family, that Brown
was also involved.

To this Norton replied by cable on October 25:

REVEREND DOCTOR CUMMINGS
104 IRVING ST CAMBRIDGE (MASS)
SO FAR AS I AM INFORMED EVERYTHING GOING SLOWLY
BUT WELL STOP YOU MUST NOT FORGET ALL PERSONS
IN THE SEASON [? SERVICE] OF THE ARMIES WHETHER
VOLUNTEERS OR CIVILIANS ARE SUBJECT TO MILITARY
LAW STOP CAN SEE NO HARM IN EMBASSY BEING ASKED
TO AND [? AID] YOU.

This cablegram indicates that Norton had not yet turned for assist-
ance to the United States Embassy in Paris, which seems strange for
an official used to "chains of command" and "channels." (As it turned
out, the Embassy had requested information on the matter from the
American Expeditionary Force, Liaison Group, on October 24.) A
note, in ink, in Dr. Cummings's handwriting, dated "27 Oct.," and
presumably the draft of a cable in reply, reads:

Taking no action—Relying entirely on you—Grateful
for good report—.

Two days later, on the 29th, Norton wrote to Arthur Hugh Frazier, First Secretary, American Embassy, 5, rue Chaillot, as follows:

> Dear Mr. Fraser [sic],
>
> I enclose a letter for young Cummings who as you know is locked up by the French.
>
> I have a cable from his father to-day, and he is awaiting my report as to what can be done. I have told him that for the present, he has to be patient and that there is nothing to do but await the action of the French. If you have any later information you can give me, I shall be very grateful for it.
>
> Very truly yours,
Richard Norton
Director Red Cross Ambulance Service

Mr. Frazier replied the next day:

> My dear Norton,
>
> Your letter of October 29th 1917 with enclosure, relating to the father of Cummings has been received.
>
> The Embassy has made repeated representations both through the 2^e Bureau and the American General Headquarters, to ascertain the status of the case against Cummings and another young ambulance driver under detention. At the present time the Embassy has received nothing definite beyond the fact that letters which these two young men wrote to their parents were intercepted by the French authorities and that their detention was the direct result of statements made in such letters. I will, however, not fail to communicate with you on receipt of definite news.
>
> Very sincerely yours,
Arthur Hugh Frazier

On the same day that Norton wrote to Mr. Frazier, he also wrote a long letter to Dr. Cummings. (The envelope bears this note in Dr. Cummings's handwriting: "NB complains of 'amazing lack of action on part of Red Cross.' ") Norton's letter follows:

7, rue François 1er
Paris, le Octobre 29th, 1917.

My dear Dr. Cummings,

I entirely sympathize with the shock you must have had when you received my cable about your son. I am sorry not to have been able to write to you before. The fact was I could not get sufficient information to be able to write intelligently. This was partly due to the fact that I was tied here and could not myself go to the Front and talk with the Leader of the Section in which your boy and a fellow named Brown who was also taken in charge by the authorities were, but it was still more due to what seemed to me an amazing lack of perception on the part of the Red Cross authorities. I could not induce them to do anything in any efficient and vigorous manner for a long time. I have at last got the matter cleared up.

It turned out that your boy and Brown attracted attention to themselves by always being together, by never going with the Americans, but always with the French, and by a great deal of what seems to have been extremely foolish talk. The letters that the men in our sections write are always censored. It is in the power of the American Leader of the Section to do this, himself, or turn the duty over, as is generally done, to one of the French officers attached to the section. It was a Frenchman who was censoring the letters of Section 21 to which your boy and Brown belonged. His attention was attracted one day by a letter addressed to the Minister of War. It is contrary to all military law for an individual in the position of a soldier, as these two boys were, to write directly to the Minister of War. He opened this letter and found that it was a request to the Minister from your boy and Brown to be accepted in the Aviation Corps. Why they should have thought this was the way to go about things I do not know [note in margin, by Dr. Cummings: "They did so on the advice of the French lieutenant attached to the Section. E. C."]. It seems to me to show that they are both of them lacking in common sense, to a marked degree. This led to talk. It appeared that they were both desirous of getting into Aviation, but said that they would not want to drop bombs or do any damage to the Germans [marginal note: "Nonsense!"]. This might be for a professional pacifist, a possible point of view, but naturally the Frenchmen in the Section now became suspicious and this apparently led to the letters of these two boys being regularly censored.

It turned out that Brown certainly, (and I am not sure about your son) was writing frequently to a German Professor in Columbia College and according to accounts that have come to me, expressing generally most traitorous sentiments. At any rate, the letters were considered so bad that one day two gendarmes appeared at the camp and took the boys away for an examination. As a result of this examination, they have both been put in a concentration camp where they are, as I understand it, merely under surveillance until their papers can be properly gone into, and the whole matter settled. The Embassy are looking after their interests and my impression is that the authorities will merely recommend that the two boys be shipped out of the country, dishonourably discharged from the Service, and probably with a warning to the American authorities that owing either to lack of common sense or to crooked education, they are at present, dangerous people.

I will do the best I can to keep you informed of anything that turns up but I believe it is a matter where you will simply have to be patient.

Believe me,
Very truly yours,
Richard Norton

Before this letter arrived, another cablegram from Norton reached Dr. Cummings. Dated November 6, it read:

HAVE BEEN RELIEVED OF ALL WORK WITH REDCROSS STOP IMPOSSIBLE FOR ME TO DO MORE FOR YOU STOP ADVISE USING ALL INFLUENCE TO STIR AUTHORITIES TO MORE VIGOROUS ACTION

A note in ink on a small sheet of pad paper gives Dr. Cummings's reply:

> Asking help from Washington Please inform boys and visit them if you can. Am still sending mail your care.

To get help from Washington, Dr. Cummings turned to another friend, the Hon. George W. Anderson, head of the Interstate Commerce Commission, who proved a friend indeed. There is no written record of the first communication between the two men, which was probably by telephone. But on November 8 the following telegram was received at 104 Irving Street:

> STATE DAPARTMENT CABLES PARIS TODAY FOR FULL REPORT WILL SEE YOU TOMORROW IN BOSTON
>
> G W ANDERSON

Their meeting probably took place in the office of the World Peace Foundation, 40 Mt. Vernon Street, Boston, of which Mr. Anderson was a trustee.

3

No mere routine communication from the State Department followed. The cable to Paris was signed by Robert J. Lansing, Secretary of State. This is the official paraphrase, made in the American Embassy:

> 2789 November 8, 4 P.M. Edward Estlin Cummings, member of Norton Harjes Ambulance Corps, is reported under arrest by French authorities since Octoberthird, as a result of letters he had written. Ascertain what charges are made against him. Kindly cable full report.
>
> Lansing

With this interposition by the Secretary of State, the United States Ambassador took charge. On the same day, presumably at the request of Ambassador Sharp, the American Military Mission in France, by direction of General J. G. Harbord, Chief of Staff, sent the Embassy its dossier on Cummings and Brown. The dossier read as follows:

From: The Chief Liaison Group, G.Q.G.
To: The American Embassy in Paris
           (Thro' the Chief of Staff, A.E.F.).
Subject: Two American volunteers sent to distribution
           center.

October 26, 1917.

1. Reference telegram from U. S. Embassy in Paris, signed Lt. R. Simmons and dated 24 October.

The following is the report on the two Americans BROWN and CUMMINGS mentioned therein.

BROWN, William Slater, born November 13, 1896, at Webster, Massachusetts, U. S. A., resident at Webster. College man. Bachelor. Volunteer attached to Automobile Sanitary Section N° 21.

CUMMINGS, Edward Estlin, born October 14, 1894, at Cambridge, Massachusetts, U. S. A., resident at Cambridge. College man. Bachelor. Volunteer attached to Automobile Sanitary Section N° 21.

They arrived at S.S.U. N° 21 on June 15, 1917.

They generally lived quite by themselves, not mixing with their American comrades.

2. On September 7, 1917, the French Postal Control stopped the accompanying letters written by W. S. BROWN to:

1.—Charles Francis Phillips, New-York.

2.—Lewis G. Levenson, New-York, Journalist School, 2940 Broadway.

3.—Dr. Gerhardt Lower, New-York [read "Lomer," emendation by Brown].

3. M. ANDERSON, Chief of the S.S.U. N° 21, to whom BROWN was signaled as Germanophile by another American volunteer, thinks that Brown is an undesirable in the Zone of the Armies, that he should not be permitted to go freely in France and that his immediate return to America would be dangerous. Declaration was made officially by Mr. Anderson to this effect.

4. BROWN's letters are forwarded herewith without comment.

5. CUMMINGS is the friend of BROWN. Although his correspondence was not censored, his intimacy with Brown, under whose influence he seems to be and whose ideas he seems to approve, has made him similarly suspected. His Chief, Mr. ANDERSON, thinks that he is as undesirable as Brown in the Zone of the Armies and that his immediate return to America would be dangerous.

On the other hand, it has been proved that on several occasions he expressed pro-German feelings and endeavoured to come into contact with French soldiers with suspicious intentions.

6. By order of the Commander in Chief, both BROWN and CUMMINGS were evacuated separately to the distributing center for such cases, La Ferté Macé (Orne), the first on the 22nd September 1917, the second on the 23rd September 1917.

Moreover, request was made by the French General Headquarters that both should be sent to a concentration camp under surveillance.

The Interministry Committee which examines suspects, at its meeting of 17 October 1917 has concluded as follows:

With regard to BROWN, that he be sent to a concentration camp;

With regard to CUMMINGS, that he be set free.

The French Home Ministry, in agreement with the French War Ministry, will take final decision.

Frank Parker
Colonel U.S. Army

Letter addressed to Mr. Lewis G. LEVENSON, 10, Pineburne Avenue, New-York.

August 29, 1917.

Dear Levenson,

I am writing this letter with a quill pen which I made last night from the feather of a goose. It writes very well don't you think?

At present the French Division to which we are attached is on repos and we are quartered in a small village in the

North of France doing nothing. There is a Church here, a
pump, seven or eight houses, a chateau and a café. At the
café one can buy beer that tastes as if it had been brewed in
the stomach of a horse. It is rather a nice place and we are
within four kilometers of a city—a very ugly one where
one drinks white wine au Grove [read "or Grave," emendation by Brown].

For a month I have not heard the screaming and whis-
tling of a shell and I am gradually dropping into a state of
ennui. Everybody in France is terribly tired of the war and
if it does not end very soon there will be all kinds of trouble. The war will [not] end with victory for either side.
That is impossible—and every one despairs of a revolution
in Germany.

I may stay over here in Europe for the remainder of the
war. It cannot last for ever, and as soon as France finds that
she can fight no longer it will end then.

By the way I wish you would send me, if you have time,
my copy of Blake. The red Oxford edition which I think I
left with you. I miss Blake very much, for some reason or
other.

How is Bishop and the rest of my friends getting along?
Have any of them been conscripted? If they have already
been and are among the first troops to get over here, they
might as well do away with themselves now, for the first
large contingent of American troops is going to have hell
handed to them by the Germans.

What is the news. I wish you would write, but perhaps
I may come home soon to drink Neady Beer [read "Near
beer," emendation by Brown] or the rest of those foul
drinks which the prohibitionists have vomited into
civilization.

Love to every one.

As ever.

(Signed) W. Slater Brown.

Convois auto, S.S.U. XXI.

Letter addressed to Charles Francis PHILLIPS, 838, West
End Avenue, New-York.

September 4, 1917.

Dear Charlie,

I find myself writing you again. Whether you have received the five letters which I have mailed you during the
last month and a half, I do not know. In this letter I will
try to say nothing which may be censored, so that at least
you will receive one letter from me.

As soon as the Americans arrived in France, people at
once began telling stories about them which of course have
not the slightest ground of truth to them. One of them is
that syphilis in the American training camp is spreading
like an epidemic, and of course this is laid to the work of
spies. It is said that the syphilis is of the virulent variety
and is contracted through cuts and open places in the skin.
There is another story of less truth than this one however,
and you know Americans too well to consider the story of
the slightest truth. It is said that the Americans are already
considering shooting of the officers whom they do not like.
From what I hear, the French who are in their camp have
taught them this. It is a well known fact that this has happened to a large extent in the English Army, due to the
fact that the superior officers used to charge "over the hill"
[read "over the top," emendation by Brown] with their
men, which gave their men a good chance to shoot them if
they felt like it. It is rather easy to shoot the officers, or at
least so I am told. It would be the simplest thing to follow
out Bernard Shaw's advice on this matter it would cure all.

A propos of this story a French soldier told me the other
day that in his company there were two officers whom the
soldier did not like and one night they were both found
dead. When the doctors examined them they found French
bullets in their backs. I guess the man was a liar. The
French soldiers adore their officers, as any one with a little
observation would see.

This French soldier also told me that once the French
made a gas attack on the Germans. After this gas attack, as
is customary for humanitarian purposes, they send either
black men or French soldiers over into the German trenches
with knives to clean up the rest of the Germans who have

not been killed by the gas. One night a French priest went over with these "cleaners" and came back some time later. "I finished 18 of them" he said. "I don't believe that" said the Lieutenant. The priest then pulled out 18 ears which he had in his pocket and proved it.

This incident only proves to what a state of bravery and self-sacrifice war leads men. If it is not true, it matters little, the man who told it to me admired the act by the priest, and admiration of brave and fine deeds of course leads other men to an emulation of them.

I have heard many other thrilling stories of valor here in France, and it all leads me to an intense admiration of those men who have the power and the brains to lead men to the ways of valor and bravery.

If I come back to the States soon, and it is quite possible that I may, I will tell you many other things which you may use to prove that war is a great purgative—the great purgative. It robs men of selfishness and makes them do great deeds for the common good. I do not think that the American people realize this enough. Perhaps if they did they would be more enthusiastic for the war.

At times it seems that the war will never end, such [?but] at other times it seems that it will end in a few weeks. It is all so terribly complex that one simply decides it with the emotion and little else. Germany is far from being defeated but as I read in a French paper the other day, a German General admitted that the allies were more eager for the war than were the Germans. A rather important statement or at least it seems to me. Tell Ed Meyer to write to me, that is if you see him, I should like to hear what he is doing.

Give my love to all my and your friends. I miss you and my good friends in a way far more than I miss my family.

I suppose Estelle Albert thinks I left for Europe because I loved her too much. I have not heard from her or have not written either. I had forgotten all about her until the other night when I talked to a drunken French soldier who had eyes exactly like hers. So much like hers that it gave me a terrific start and I could not remember for some time whose eyes they resembled.

Regards to Eleanore, I know she thinks that I am an embuscade, to use that dreadful word, but I am learning a great deal over here, much more than I have written you.

Tolstoi is absolutely right.

Love to all again,

As ever,

(Signed) W. Slater Brown

P.S.—I have written this letter with a quill pen which I made, a very fine pen too.

Thought of a fine poem last night which for its simplicity of diction, its freedom from classical rhyme, its feeling for social equality is unrivaled in literature, it is:

The moon is very democratic

It sits in pools so people can look at it.

Letter addressed to Dr. Lower, Columbia School of Journalism, 2940, Broadway, New-York.

August 29, 1917.

Dear Dr. Lower.

I am writing this letter in a little village in Northern France a long way from the front. We are supposed to be taking a rest, but I have been drinking so much white wine at a little café in town that I feel as if I had been through many campaigns. The beer here is terrible and tastes as if it had been brewed in the stomach of a horse, I drink very little of it.

This letter is being written with a quill pen which I made myself and considering the circumstances I think it is a very good one.

I have not met your brother yet but we are near the British lines and some day I may come across him. At any rate I shall speak to any doctor whose name is Lower.

Every one is sick of the war here and I look forward to a revolution in France soon. The French soldiers are all despondent and none of them believe that Germany will ever be defeated. They maintain the war just as they hold on to the Church, or marriage, or any senescent institution. I remember seeing senescent in a poem by Poe. Have I used it correctly?

I hope that none of my friends will ever have to come

over to this damn place and fight. It makes me feel very ill
when I think how many fellows are going to be killed for
no reason whatsoever. How any one can hate the Germans
is more than I can imagine. While I have been here I have
not heard a French soldier say anything against the Germans, in fact they admire the Germans very much. I think
the French dislike the English a great deal more than they
do the Germans.

My love to all my friends whom you may happen to see.
Love to Mr. Hall too.

> (Signed) W. Slater Brown
> Convois auto, S.S.U. XXI.

Slater Brown wrote me, October 7, 1971:
"Dr. Lower. The name was Lomer, not Lower, and he was not German but Canadian-English. His brother served as an officer in the
Canadian Army in World War I in France. Dr. Lomer was not a member of the German Department at Columbia but taught English Lit.
(I feel sure that this was all an effort of the French authorities to tar me
with pro-German proclivities.)"

He also told me: "Unless I can see the originals of my letters in my
own handwriting I won't be persuaded that some of the letters—
particularly the one beginning at the bottom of page 92 [in the original
edition of *The Magic-Maker,* letter to Charles Francis Phillips], were
written by me. They seem to contain all sorts of interpolations expressing pro-German and anti-French opinions which neither Cummings
nor I held."

The dossier reached the Embassy on November 12. On the 13th,
Brown's twenty-first birthday was "celebrated" with cups of cocoa
which he and Cummings made on top of the stove mentioned in
Chapter IX of *The Enormous Room.* On the 16th, Ambassador Sharp
cabled Lansing as follows:

SECSTATE

WASHINGTON

2755 Nov. 16, 10 P.M. Your cable No. 2789 in reference
to Edward Estlin Cummings and William Slater Brown,
who were evacuated from Section 21 Norton Harjes Ambulance Corps, on September 22nd and 23rd, to Ferté
Macé, because of letters Brown had written to persons in
the United States, who authorities considered pro-German.

Cummings was suspected because of his intimacy with
Brown, but wrote no letters of this kind. On Oct. 17th
Examining Board decided that Cummings be released and
that Brown be interned. Final decision will be made by
Ministry of Interior. Have endeavored, through this Ministry, to learn present whereabouts of Cummings and will
cable you reply. Copies of letters written by Brown and
preliminary report will be sent by next pouch.

Sharp

4

On the same day—November 16—Norton cabled Dr. Cummings, who sent the new information to Commissioner Anderson in
the form of a telegram, of which the following is the draft (in pencil
and ink):

Just received Cable as follows Letters for son arrived
and put in hands of Embassy stop Believe everything going
smoothly and boy will shortly return signed Norton So
your efforts seem to be bearing fruit. Many thanks—

Mr. Anderson did not reply until November 19. It would appear
that he checked with the State Department and was promised additional information; hence his delay. On November 19 he wrote as
follows:

Interstate Commerce Commission
Washington

offices of
>   George W. Anderson
>   commissioner

November 19, 1917.

Rev. Edward Cummings,
>   40 Mt. Vernon Street,
>   Boston, Mass.

Dear Mr. Cummings:

This afternoon I received from Mr. William Phillips,
Assistant Secretary of State, the following:

"PARAPHRASE OF TELEGRAM FROM PARIS, RECEIVED
NOVEMBER 18TH.

William Slater Brown and Edward Cummings were removed from Norton-Harjes Ambulance Section 21, on
September 22nd and 23rd to Fersingere Mace, because of
Brown's letters to persons in the United States which were
considered by the authorities to express pro-German sentiments. Because of his intimacy with Brown, Cummings
who had written no such letters was also suspected. On
October 17th the Examining Board decided that Cummings
be released and Brown be interned. The final decision will
be made by the Ministry of the Interior and will be cabled
as soon as received. Copies of Brown's letters with preliminary report will be forwarded by the next pouch."
Sincerely yours,
G. W. Anderson

From Paris, on the 21st, came more welcome news in the form of
a cablegram from Norton, apparently filed on the 20th:

HAVE FINALLY SEEN ALL PAPERS IN CASE ABSOLUTELY
NOTHING AGAINST YOUR BOY WHO I UNDERSTAND AFTER
CERTAIN FORMALITIES WILL BE IN FEW DAYS HIS OWN
MASTER

Norton appears to have had an interview with the Ambassador, and
afterwards with an Embassy secretary, who showed him the files in
the case. For he now wrote Dr. Cummings as follows:

November 20th, 1917

My dear Dr. Cummings,

After endless trouble, I have just seen all the papers
regarding your son and his friend Brown, at the American
Embassy. There is nothing whatever of the slightest description against your boy except that he was an intimate
friend of Brown whom I judge to be a bumptious ass. I
am told by the Embassy that your boy has been recommended to be sent home, and as soon as certain formalities
are gone through, that he will be, as I have cabled you
today, his own master. I hope to see him and have a talk,
possibly ram a few ideas into his head.

As for Brown, unless I can persuade the powers that be
to take strong measures, he will, I am afraid, be kept in a

Concentration Camp. Knowing my own compatriots as I do, this seems to me ridiculous. There is nothing of any criminal intent, of any possible sort in his letters; he obviously has, however, little breeding or education and 'gasses' in his letters about stories he has heard in regard to officers being shot, everybody being sick of the war, and propounds very unbaked philosophical doctrines, and quotes idiotic poetry. It looks to me as if most of the trouble had come from people reading his letters who did not know English, and certainly did not know the American nature, possibly also, because he had made himself unpopular with his section as I am told your son did too, from a general lack of neatness—in fact, I will put it stronger and say that they have been reported to me, both of them, as being dirty and unkempt. I do not know whether you have passed much life under canvas; if you have (as I have many years) you will realize that this is a real sin and may well get on people's nerves, so that they cannot bear the sight of a person who shows these faults, and are apt to think worse of such a person than he deserves. I do not vouch for the absolute truth of what I say, but merely give it to you as a suggestion to explain the conditions, believing that you would rather know anything I can possibly tell, or suggest, than that I should keep anything hidden from you.

With best regards,
Yours sincerely,
Richard Norton

On the envelope are the following notations in Dr. Cummings's handwriting:

Quote 'After endless trouble . . . & there is nothing whatever of the slightest description against your boy except that he was an intimate friend of B.
NB One month before release!
Quote Cable Nov. 12
    ''   ''   ''   16
    ''   ''   ''   6

These notations were made several weeks later, and they were made because of certain developments which impelled Dr. Cummings

to seek help from the President himself. The first of these developments was a telegram to Mr. Anderson, who was again in Boston,
from the Assistant Secretary of State in Washington:

FOLLOWING TELEGRAM JUST RECEIVED FROM PARIS
QUOTE HAVE LEARNED FROM AMERICAN NAVAL AUTHOR-
ITIES THAT EDWARD ESTLIN CUMMINGS EMBARKED FOR
UNITED STATES ON THE ANTILLES AND THAT HE IS RE-
PORTED AMONG THOSE LOST END QUOTE
                                        WILLIAM PHILLIPS

It was received by Mr. Anderson practically simultaneously with
the receipt of Norton's cablegram at 104 Irving Street on November
21. It was now Mr. Anderson's painful duty to communicate the
dreadful news to his friend. They must have met at once to confer,
as indicated by the following telegram from Mr. Anderson to Mr.
Phillips:

TELEGRAM RECEIVED NEWS INCONSISTENT WITH CABLE
FROM NORTON SENT CUMMINGS FATHER TODAY SAYING
CUMMINGS INNOCENT AND SHORTLY RELEASED KINDLY
CABLE FOR CORRECTION OR VERIFICATION

Dr. Cummings also set out to get information, as his notations
show:

Anderson cabled Phillips to verify & find out what Cummings sailed on Antilles Oct. 15.

On the same sheet of paper there is a draft of a cable:

Camb. Nov. 21, 1917 to Norton
          Ameredcross Paris—
Informed son sailed on Antilles and reported lost Cable
truth immediately
                                        Cummings

Following receipt of this cable, Norton wrote to Ambassador
Sharp:

                          Paris, le 22. Nov. 1917.
          To H. E.
                The American Ambassador:
          Sir:
                Confirming our conversation of two days ago may I ask
          you to look into the matter of Messrs. Cummings (E. E.)

& Brown (W. S.) formerly in Section 21 of the American Red Cross Ambulance Service. These two men were arrested by the French authorities because of the character of letters they wrote to friends in America. Your secretary, Mr. Wiley, tells me that he has been informed that Cummings was to be liberated but that Brown was to be interned, the reason for the difference in treatment being that Cummings' only fault was his friendship for Brown. Mr. Wiley has shown me copies of the letters which form the basis of the charge against Brown & while they are unquestionably extremely foolish I cannot but feel that a serious error would be committed were Brown to be interned.

Respectfully yours,

Richard Norton

Norton, apparently, was of the opinion that Cummings was still in France, and does not appear unduly alarmed.

Three days were to pass before additional word came to Dr. Cummings from Washington, four before additional word came from Norton in Paris. (Cummings told me that during this period of anguished suspense his mother never faltered in her belief that he was still alive.) At 4:15 on the 24th, Mr. Phillips dispatched the following telegram to Dr. Cummings:

TELEGRAM JUST REC'D FROM PARIS STATES H H CUMMINGS AND NOT E E CUMMINGS LOST ON ANTILLES AMBASSADOR IS RENEWING ENDEAVORS TO LOCATE YOUR SON AND WILL REPORT LATER

The next day Norton cabled:

SAME REPORT REACHED ME SIX WEEKS AGO STOP CHECKED IT UP AND FOUND ERROR STOP EMBASSY DENY IT TODAY STOP AM PRESSING FOR DECISION

5

On December 8, Dr. Cummings addressed a letter to President Woodrow Wilson, using the various notations he had made as a guide to his principal points. This letter appears in the Foreword he

wrote to *The Enormous Room* in somewhat abbreviated form, and
I give the full text from the original in the State Department files:

104 Irving Street,
Cambridge, December 8, 1917.

President Woodrow Wilson,
White House,
Washington, D. C.
Mr. President;

It seems criminal to ask for a single moment of your
time. But I am strongly advised that it would be more criminal to delay any longer calling to your attention a crime
against American citizenship in which the French government has persisted for many weeks,—in spite of constant
appeals made to the American Minister at Paris; and in
spite of subsequent action taken by the State Department
at Washington, on the initiative of my friend Hon. George
W. Anderson, of the Interstate Commerce Commission.

The victims are two American ambulance drivers,—
Edward Estlin Cummings of Cambridge, Mass., and Wil-
liam Slater Brown, of Webster, Mass., son of a Contract
Surgeon in the United States Army, and nephew of Spaul-
ding Bartlett, probably known to you as a member of the
Textile Commission.

More than two months ago these young men were arrested, subjected to many indignities, dragged across
France like criminals, and closely confined in a Concentration Camp at La Ferté Macé; where according to latest
advices they still remain,—awaiting the final action of the
Minister of the Interior upon the findings of a Commission
which passed upon their cases as long ago as October 17.

Against Cummings both private and official advices from
Paris state there is no charge whatever. He has been subjected to this outrageous treatment solely because of his
intimate friendship with young Brown, whose sole crime
is,—so far as can be learned,—that certain letters to friends
in America were misinterpreted by an over-zealous French
censor.

It only adds to the indignity and irony of the situation,

to say that young Cummings is an enthusiastic lover of France, and so loyal to the friends he has made among the French soldiers, that even while suffering in health from his unjust confinement, he excuses the ingratitude of the country he has risked his life to serve, by calling attention to the atmosphere of intense suspicion and distrust that has naturally resulted from the painful experience which France has had with foreign emissaries.

Be assured, Mr. President, that I have waited long—it seems like ages—and have exhausted all other available help before venturing to trouble you:—

1. After many weeks of vain effort to secure effective action by the American Ambassador at Paris, Richard Norton of the Norton-Harjes Ambulance Corps to which the boys belonged, was completely discouraged, and advised me to seek help here.

2. The efforts of the State Department at Washington resulted as follows:

i. A cable from Paris saying there was no charge against Cummings and intimating that he would speedily be released.

ii. A little later a second cable advising that Edward Estlin Cummings had sailed on the Antilles and was reported lost.

iii. A week later a third cable correcting this cruel error, and saying the Embassy was renewing efforts to locate Cummings,—apparently still ignorant even of the place of his confinement.

After such painful and baffling experiences, I turn to you,—burdened though I know you to be, in this world crisis with the weightiest task ever laid upon any man.

But I have another reason for asking this favor. I do not speak for my son alone; or for him and his friend alone. My son has a mother,—as brave and patriotic as any mother who ever dedicated an only son to a great cause. The mothers of our boys in France have rights as well as the boys themselves. My boy's mother had a right to be protected from the weeks of horrible anxiety and suspense caused by the inexplicable arrest and imprisonment of her

son. My boy's mother had a right to be spared the supreme
agony caused by a blundering cable from Paris saying that
he had been drowned by a submarine. (An error which
Mr. Norton subsequently cabled that he had discovered six
weeks before). My boy's mother and all American mothers
have a right to be protected against all needless anxiety
and sorrow.

Pardon me, Mr. President, but if I were president and
your son were suffering such prolonged injustice at the
hands of France; and your son's mother had been need-
lessly kept in Hell as many weeks as my boy's mother has,—
I would do something to make American citizenship as
sacred in the eyes of Frenchmen as Roman citizenship was
in the eyes of the ancient world. Then it was enough to ask
the question, "Is it lawful to scourge a man that is a Roman, and uncondemned?" Now, in France, it seems lawful
to treat like a condemned criminal a man that is an American, uncondemned and admittedly innocent!

Very Respectfully,

Edward Cummings

Dr. Cummings's letter to the President is stamped in the upper
left hand corner "RESPECTFULLY REFERRED FOR ACKNOWLEDGMENT
AND CONSIDERATION," and signed "J. P. Tumulty," the President's
secretary. In a copy of this letter in the National Archives there is a
typed notation at the end: "Hon George W. Anderson delivered this
letter by *Messenger* from his office, Washington (Dec. 10?)."

There is no record of a reply by the President. But on December
15, Secretary of State Lansing dispatched the following cablegram
(given here in Embassy paraphrase) to Paris:

2952 Dec 15 5 P.M. Other telegraphic correspondence and
your 2755 regarding Brown and Cummings. The Department has not received the promised preliminary report.
Reasons for failure of Embassy to follow up matter cannot
be understood Cable reply promptly

While the Embassy, presumably, was seeking clarification from the
Foreign Office, Cummings left La Ferté Macé and was proceeding to

Paris with a police pass. He was released on December 19, and arrived at the Embassy on the 20th, apparently at the very moment when Ambassador Sharp was dictating a reply to Secretary Lansing's cable:

SECSTATE

WASHINGTON

2926 Dec. 20, 7 P.M. Referring to your 2952 information has been received from the Foreign Office that definite orders have now been given for the internment of Brown at Ferte Mace and that Cummings' release has been ordered stop This case has been followed with close attention by me in order to try and get in touch with Cummings but in spite of repeated and energetic representations to Foreign Office and Ministry of the Interior I have been unable to obtain any information from these two departments of the French Government until today when I learned that in accordance with my request he was being sent to Paris stop Cummings reported at Embassy just now and on Saturday will leave on the Espagne for the United States stop Departure will be facilitated by me stop By next pouch copies of letters which Brown has written will be forwarded.

SHARP

The next day the Ambassador set out to explain by letter:

The Honorable
    The Secretary of State,
        Washington.
Sir:
    Referring to my telegram No. 2926 of the 20th instant, relative to the release by the French authorities of Mr. Edward Estlin Cummings who has been interned at Ferté Macé and recently at the College de Presigny (Sarthe) and reporting his approaching departure for the United States on board the "Espagne," sailing tomorrow the 22nd, I have the honor to transmit herewith a copy of a report on the arrest drawn up by Colonel Parker as well as copies of letters addressed by Mr. William Slater Brown to persons in the United States. These letters had been intercepted by

the French censors and were believed by them to express progerman sentiments and they served as evidence in the proceedings against both Cummings and Brown.

As will be noted in the enclosed report, suspicion was only directed against Mr. Cummings because of his intimacy with Mr. Brown and these suspicions have been ascertained to be unfounded.

The internment of Mr. Brown has been definitely ordered and he is now confined at Presigny.

I am now investigating his case and shall report thereon in a separate communication.

I have the honor to be, Sir,
            Your obedient servant,
                        Wm. G. Sharp

The separate communication in the case of Brown was filed from Paris, January 23, 1918, and reads (in paraphrase):

3084 Jan. 23 4 P.M. With reference to my despatch 5889 dated December 21'st, I decided after a talk with Cummings to make informal representations to the French Government having in view the release of Brown. I have just received a communication from the Foreign Office in which it is stated that instructions which have in view the assurance of his departure to the United States have been given.

As in the case of Cummings, powerful influences had been brought to bear to bring about Brown's release, including that of Senator Henry Cabot Lodge of Massachusetts. Brown had been taken to the prison at Précigné about the middle of December. There were approximately 400 prisoners there, including several who had been with him and Cummings at La Ferté Macé. The food there consisted only of bread, beans and potatoes, Brown told me, and he came down with scurvy. He said:

"I was at Précigné until the middle of February [1918], when I was taken to Bordeaux, held in prison for a week and then placed aboard the 'Niagara' of the French Line, which brought me to New

York. I stayed with my family in Webster for a couple of months recovering from scurvy, and then joined Cummings who was living on Christopher Street."

Meanwhile, on Christmas Eve, Dr. Cummings had received a letter from the Assistant Secretary of State, the address on the envelope— "104 Irving Street, Boston"—having been corrected in pencil by the Boston post office:

> Washington
> December 21, 1917

Dear Sir:

> At the request of Commissioner Anderson, to whom I have read the telegram, I beg to send you enclosed a para- phrase of the cable just received from the American Em- bassy at Paris with regard to your son. You will note that he has now been released and is about to sail for the United States.

> Very truly yours,
> William Phillips

The enclosure repeated the information contained in Ambassador Sharp's cable to Secretary Lansing.

The last item in the documents from which I have drawn the fore- going correspondence is the draft of a telegram from Dr. Cummings to Mr. Phillips:

> Cambridge, Dec. 24, 1917

> Your letter just received enclosing Cable brings the most welcome of Christmas gifts. Profoundly grateful for good offices. Please accept holiday greetings and best wishes from Mr. and Mrs. Edward Cummings. Correct address 104 Irving St. Cambridge—not Boston.

Cummings arrived in New York on New Year's Day, 1918. Here is his second glimpse of his future home (from the last paragraph of *The Enormous Room*):

"The tall, impossibly tall, incomparably tall, city shoulderingly up- ward into hard sunlight leaned a little through the octaves of its parallel edges, leaningly strode upward into firm, hard, snowy sunlight; the noises of America nearingly throbbed with smokes and hurrying dots which are men and which are women and which are things new and curious and hard and strange and vibrant and immense, lifting with a great ondulous stride firmly into immortal sunlight. . . ."

He was met at the pier by his mother and James Sibley Watson.

Chapter 6

THE ENORMOUS ROOM

1

"No classic resembles another," said Ernest Hemingway. No; but all classics have this in common—each one, being unique, contributes to a community of uniqueness. There is something else: they all have a life of their own, regardless of current tastes, and this life they share. *The Enormous Room* is indubitably a classic, and does not resemble any other. It has survived many vicissitudes, and shows the right kind of durability. It is very much alive today, and my readers as well as I may be hard put to it to name a book published in 1922 which has lasted at all or lasted as well. Like all true classics, *The Enormous Room* easily passes the supreme test: it can be reread, and it is reread with all the attendant excitement of its first appearance.

It has often been pointed out that the best preparation for a writer of prose is the writing of verse, and it is true that a great many prose writers, particularly in Europe, have begun their careers with the proverbial slim volume. Cummings, after leaving Harvard, not only continued to write poems—he wrote them steadily, voluminously; the critics who afterwards thought they saw new developments or new departures in his work were as mistaken as only critics can be. For

what Cummings did in making up his first three volumes of verse was
to select what he himself fancied from the "millions of poems," as he
confessed to James Sibley Watson, that he had written over a six-year
period (loosely, from 1917 to 1923; but some of the poems are even
earlier).

Having established this much, I wish to go a step further: *The
Enormous Room* is not only the work of a poet, but it is a poet's work;
no mere writer of prose could have written it. For the beauty and
surprises of many of its pages are of the same sort, the same quality,
that afterwards made Cummings's books of verse so memorable.
Indeed, were certain of his poems and certain paragraphs from this
book placed side by side, it would be seen at once that their authorship
is the same. Here, it may be useful to point out that Cummings—
whether in conversation or letters, in poetry or prose, including the
drama—has only one style, and that style, an instrument of great
range and flexibility, is his own. It does not exist before him, and falls
flat when imitated. The reason is simple—Cummings's style springs
from what he is. He expressed it in *The Enormous Room* as follows:

"There are certain things in which one is unable to believe for the
simple reason that he never ceases to feel them. Things of this sort—
things which are always inside of us and in fact are us and which
consequently will not be pushed off or away where we can begin
thinking about them—are no longer things; they, and the us which
they are, equals A Verb: an IS."

2

The book was written at the insistence of Dr. Cummings,
whose indignation did not abate with the passing months or years.
He has related, in the Foreword, what shape his son was in when released—"very much under weight [and] suffering from a bad skin
infection." However, he added, "a month of competent medical treatment here seems to have got rid of this painful reminder of official
hospitality."

There was one other reminder. Philip Hillyer Smith, a Cambridge
neighbor who was a senior at Harvard in 1918, told me he used to
see Cummings take a live coal from the grate with his fingertips, light
his cigarette with it, and set the coal down without burning his fingers
—a trick picked up at La Ferté Macé, where matches were scarce.

In the fall of 1920, at his New Hampshire farm, Dr. Cummings finally persuaded his son to set down the record of his imprisonment. William Slater Brown was there to jog his memory when Cummings started to write. Cummings also drew from notes he had made at La Ferté Macé, for he apparently goes nowhere without a notebook, not even to prison. In Chapter Five of *The Enormous Room* there is an example of a note made on the spot, together with its "interpretation" —i.e., expansion. Although Cummings refers to this note as a "specimen of telegraphic technique," and Robert Graves terms it "telegraphese" in his Introduction to the English edition of the book, it is really, in language and construction, a portrait like the portraits to be found among Cummings's early poems under the heading of "Realities." When Dr. and Mrs. Cummings went back to Cambridge, Cummings and Brown stayed on in New Hampshire; and in a cottage on Silver Lake, on a spur of land called Hurricane Point, the book was written in two months.

A letter to Stewart Mitchell describes Cummings's procedure:

> Here I've been working (as worked the sons of Egypt to build the pyramids, you understand—in other words like H.) upon a little historical treatise of vast import to my Family and Nobody in General—comprising my experiences in France, or more accurately *en prison*. Honestly to say, I haven't done nawthing else. Strenuous is no name therefor—3 pages a day, since my family left, on an average of 2 hours to a page. ID EST, a six hour day, splendid for the good of humanity, and if so, and so forth.

The letter is dated October 6, 1920. Mitchell, at this time, was managing editor of *The Dial,* in which Cummings had made his sensational debut as a poet with the first—January, 1920—number.

Some time in 1921 the manuscript of *The Enormous Room* was taken to Boni & Liveright by Dr. Cummings. When I asked Cummings why this particular firm had been chosen, he replied: "It was a good firm at that time." I have been told by several authors published by this firm that when Horace Liveright finally met Cummings at a party, he rushed toward him exclaiming: "Your father turned my hair white!"

It is an inclusive remark. Cummings, having finished his book, gave it to his grateful and enthusiastic father—instructing him to allow no publisher to make any change whatever in the manuscript—and left for Paris. A letter from him, from Autun, France, authorized Dr. Cummings to sign the contract for him. This, Dr. Cummings did. In sending the contract back to Liveright, he wrote, November 4, 1921: "There are a few sentences to be added to the end of one chapter. My son seems to attach considerable importance to having this addition made. I will see that it is forwarded at once." He also sent the letter from Cummings, saying: "The sketches to which my son refers in this letter are, as I recollect them, rough pencil portraits of some of the characters he describes, made on small slips of paper which happened to be available. Do you want to consider using them?"

To this, Liveright replied: "I think it would help the book very much if we use the sketches your son did. I hope that there are a number of them. Please send them all." He also suggested a title for the book—*Hospitality*. One sketch was reproduced on the jacket. There is no further mention of the suggested title in the surviving correspondence. On April 8, 1922, Liveright wrote that he expected copies of the book from the binders on the 18th and that he was "endeavoring to have the New York *Times* give Dos Passos the book for review."

Thus far, and until after the book appeared, the correspondence between Liveright and Dr. Cummings appears cordial. On June 5, Liveright had some disquieting news to impart:

> I have just learned through a friend of your son, Estlin Cummings, who had word from him from Paris, that he cannot understand why we have omitted two or three chapters from The Enormous Room. This is the first I have heard of any omissions other than a few phrases or words which we felt it was necessary to delete in order to make the publication of the book possible in this country.
>
> I would appreciate it very much if you would let me hear from you at once regarding the mysterious missing chapters. It may be that you in your great good judgment edited the book before it came here and I have no reason to believe that there is any complaint to be found with your editing; but, naturally, I want to be in position to intelligently answer your son's inquiry.

Dr. Cummings's reply, dispatched the next day, is sufficient to account for Liveright's rueful remark a few years later. Dr. Cummings wrote:

My son, E. E. Cummings, wrote me in regard to the omissions of certain parts of THE ENORMOUS ROOM, about which you make inquiry in your letter of June 5. He wanted to know who was responsible for these omissions, —as well as for certain pretty obvious and rather stupid mistakes in spelling, punctuation, etc.

I wrote him that I accepted entire responsibility, because the proofs submitted to me did not contain these passages, and because the passages in question had been deleted from the manuscript returned to me with proofs, and because under the circumstances I did not think it worth while delaying the publication of the book and trying to persuade you to reinstate the omitted passages. If any passages had to be omitted, those which you had deleted seemed to me less of a sacrifice than any others which could have been chosen.

All you have to do to verify my statement with regard to the deletion of the passages in question, is to consult the manuscript, which you asked me to return with the corrected proof. Incidentally, I would suggest that if there is no serious objection to so doing, you return the original manuscript to me.

So you will perceive that "your great and good judgment edited the book" before it came to me,—not the reverse, as your letter suggests. So, also, you will pardon me for expressing some surprise at the statement that the information recently received from Paris was "the first you had heard of any omissions other than a few phrases or words which we felt it was necessary to delete in order to make the publication of the book possible in this country." I suppose you also may have been ignorant of the pressure that was brought to bear upon me to return the proofs immediately, on the ground that I was delaying your publication schedule, etc., etc. All of which had considerable to do with my decision as above stated.

Please observe that in writing to my son I have accepted entire responsibility. I further reminded him that if anyone was to blame beside me, it was himself; because I cabled him to come back at my expense and see the book through the press. He said he was too happy where he was. I daresay he would be happier now if he had come. I hope you have seen the review of THE ENORMOUS ROOM in the *Nation* of June 7. It is superb.

Isidor Schneider, a poet employed by Boni & Liveright, told me that, at the last moment, just before the book went out to reviewers, a report came that John S. Sumner, Secretary of the Society for the Suppression of Vice, planned a raid because of a four-letter word on page 219. The passage read:

"You don't say! Look, the king of England is sick. Some news! . . . What? The queen, too? Good God! What's this?—My father is dead! Shit. Oh, well. The war is over. Good." —It was Jean le Nègre, playing a little game with himself to beguile the time.

Schneider told me the offending word was inked out to avoid entanglement with Sumner.

"A little girl in the office had to go through the copies—the whole edition—inking out the word," he said.

The passage is now in French, as Jean le Nègre spoke it (Modern Library edition, page 271).

3

The New York *Times Book Review and Magazine* reviewed *The Enormous Room* on May 28, 1922. The reviewer was Thomas L. Masson. He wrote:

"Mr. Cummings has taken John Bunyan's 'Pilgrim's Progress' as a kind of model, and gives us his own Apollyon, and certain Delectable Mountains who inhabited the Enormous Room. But in his book he misses the great lesson taught by Bunyan, the lesson that the apparent injustices so universal in the material world of senses are as nothing compared with the true vision of the saints. 'Naked I came into the world,' exclaimed Job, 'and naked I shall depart.' What happens in between is of small individual consequence."

To be sure.

"Mr. Cummings undoubtedly belongs to the Harvard school of writers, headed by that joyous and chivalric and mistaken spirit, John Reed, whose sad death in Russia excited the sympathies of all those who love youth and who are tolerant of its blindness for the sake of its glorious promise. Then, there is Dos Passos, whose 'Three Soldiers' evoked such controversy, and now Mr. Cummings, with his bitterness toward government, his flings at patriotism, his great doubt about poor old America, his implication that there is a revolution coming soon. 'Ah, well,' he exclaims, 'the revolution—I refer, of course, to the intelligent revolution—is on the way.'

"And of the American public he says, just before this, that it is 'the most aesthetically incapable organization ever created for the purpose of perpetuating defunct ideals and ideas.' "

Mr. Masson, having finally got around to the book, is aghast at a split infinitive and finds, "to be brutally frank," that "this book is old stuff"; and worse—"this book is a Bolshevist book." But now his superior nature, achieved by contemplation of the saints, comes to the fore: "Apart from its crudities, its mistaken, disgruntled attitude and its bad writing, the book is quite worth while. Any one who has the superb energy to sustain enough interest in his own past sufferings to write such a long book cannot be dismissed as being utterly useless."

The next day, Monday, May 29, the *Times* took cognizance of the book in "Topics of the Times," which appeared regularly on its editorial page. The column was headed "Turning From a Book to Its Author," and here *The Enormous Room* was examined "from the point of view taken by one to whom a book is not entirely a product of good or bad art—an end in itself—but something with a relational content and an influence on its readers.

"That is, of course, to judge the writer of a book as revealed by his achievement, and it is not literary criticism, yet it is fair enough, and, anyway, it is inevitable, though the consequences do not often get into print.

"The ordinary reader of 'The Enormous Room' sees, as the reviewers did, that Mr. Cummings, in spite of the strainings and the obscurities of his style, does make a picture, and the one he intended to make. That is success, in its way, but the book does more than that. It discloses, for instance, that its author, if he had the faintest notion of what the war was about—of its rights and wrongs—carefully concealed his knowledge all through these many pages."

To this, I venture to reply that Cummings's "aunt" knew enough for both the author and the commentator (and certain other reviewers) :

> my sweet old etcetera
> aunt lucy during the recent
>
> war could and what
> is more did tell you just
> what everybody was fighting
>
> for,
> my sister
>
> isabel created hundreds
> (and
> hundreds) of socks not to
> mention shirts fleaproof earwarmers
>
> etcetera wristers etcetera, my
> mother hoped that
>
> i would die etcetera
> bravely of course my father used
> to become hoarse talking about how it was
> a privilege and if only he
> could meanwhile my
>
> self etcetera lay quietly
> in the deep mud et
>
> cetera
> (dreaming,
> et
>   cetera, of
> Your smile
> eyes knees and of your Etcetera)

4

I should like now to contrast two important reviews. In the May 10, 1922, issue of the *New Republic,* Robert Littell wrote, under the heading of "Garbage and Gold":

"I feel as if I had been rooting long, desperate hours in a junk heap, irritably but thoroughly pawing over all sorts of queer, nameless garbage, rotting tin cans, owls' skeletons, the poisonous fragments of human apparatus rusting into morbid greens, yellows, oranges, and yet as if prodding about among these and other objects best touched only with a stick, I had come away at last with some lumps of curious, discolored but none the less precious metal."

A curious and discolored framework of reference; yet he wished—strenuously—to praise the book:

"Could any sensitive person be locked up in a small, filthy French prison with a riff-raff of suspected spies and write an honest book which did not give something of this effect? I doubt it. Mr. Cummings is honest. He is also sensitive, so sensitive that the lightest tremors of life make his tongue, like some cubistic seismograph, record them in a cryptic, half insane dance of words.

"This sensitiveness has a tinge of self-pity, which the indignant letters of the introduction do nothing to diminish." Here he explains the arrest of the author "on charges none too clear, but apparently not more serious than that a friend of his had written home in a revolutionary vein disliked by the censor. He does not take this fate easily, of course, but too often his bitterness is venomous. It also leads him into a rather unpersuasive account of his own ease and dignity." Mr. Littell lists a number of words and phrases to which he takes exception, including "a sharp, black, mechanical cry in the spongy organism of gloom," and asks:

"Do such expressions mean that reality has tortured their author's nerves into a snarl? Can the other parent of such obvious children of disorder be any kind of light?" The answer is going to be yes; but Mr. Littell, at the time he wrote his review of *The Enormous Room,* was in the literary phase of his career, and first he quotes part of a long sentence from the book, which he does not particularly care for, following it with this, which he apparently liked:

"If one gives one's imagination (in this case out of Nerves by Dictionary) a free rein, this sort of thing is not hard to do. Such a horse shies easily at reality, bolts into oxymoron and by way of self-expression bucks with hallucinating turgidity. It reminds one of sonal pools of insanity, bulging neatly but enormously with bat-wingèd words.

"It is strange that Mr. Cummings does go oftener into these tailspins, since he has mastered their technique so thoroughly, and so much seems to enjoy them. He is also a master of conveying to you the essence of disagreeable smells, putrescences and vilenesses. I have nothing to say against anyone's describing a stinking French prison just as it is. But Mr. Cummings has a real flair and gusto for filth. Read his eager description of Ça Pue, beginning on p. 27."

I have said that Mr. Littell wished to praise the book, and he does so: "I should however rather dig with him for his tarnished treasure than enjoy all the sane and competent enamelware which is the bulk of literature today." He concludes: "A queer, strong, defeated book, all smeared and spattered with genius." Mr. Littell went on to higher things. He became a drama critic.

The second of the two reviews I have referred to appeared in the *Nation,* June 7, under the heading "Man and Animal." The author of it was Ben Ray Redman, a scholarly critic, translator, essayist and poet, in later years the best of the contributors to the *Saturday Review* when it was the *Saturday Review of Literature.* His opening paragraph is fused by the excitement of his discovery:

"Two experiences I expect to remember always. One of them is a visit, at meal time, to the dining-hall of a state institution for the feebleminded and insane; the other is reading E. E. Cummings's 'The Enormous Room.' Contacts with two equally memorable infernos; contacts, in each case, with sights, sounds, and smells that are unobliterable; contacts with humanity degraded. But between these two experiences there lies a vast difference: the one was all horror and disgust; the other is horrible, disgusting, and glorious. I would choose to forget the first: I would pray to remember the second. Mr. Cummings has written a terrible book, but it is a profoundly beautiful book; it is among the most beautiful that I have ever read. In 'The Enormous Room' we view the tragedy Man, with man in the victor's role.

"Briefly, this is the story of the author's imprisonment—or, with him, we should say 'confinement'—by the French Government in the Camp de Triage de la Ferté Macé, Orne, France. No charge was preferred against Cummings. He was a voluntary driver in Sanitary Section 21, Ambulance Norton Harjes, American Red Cross. His crime was that he had a friend, a closest friend, who wrote home to America in somewhat unguarded terms. We lack information regarding the exact nature of B's epistolary indiscretions: perhaps he was so ill-advised as to question some of the major premises of the war for civilization, or perhaps he unidealistically squirmed at certain of its individual aspects. However, 'the excellent French Government' found B. a suspicious and potentially dangerous character. Mr. Cummings was his friend. It requires only a superficial knowledge of governmental spy-phobia in war time to follow the impeccable logic which necessitated the 'confinement'—pending trial—of Cummings and B. in La Ferté, more specifically in the Enormous Room which housed an average of some sixty other criminals at least as dangerous as themselves. In this room the author existed for a little more than three months—a period terminated by release and polite official regrets. This book is the story of those months. It is not a chronological story, for it is the tale of a timeless world. As the author explains, 'the diary or time method is a technique which cannot possibly do justice to timelessness,' and, abjuring it, he writes: 'I shall (on the contrary) lift from their gray box at random certain (to me) more or less astonishing toys; which may or may not please the reader, but whose colors and shapes and textures are a part of that actual Present—without future and past—whereof they alone are cognizant who—so to speak—have submitted to an amputation of the world.'

"Mr. Cummings's technique is well chosen, and from his gray box he has lifted inspiredly. The individual portraits in this book are superb: portraits of his fellow-prisoners and of his captors; of the Wanderer, Pompon and Haree, *les plantons,* Bill the Hollander, Surplice, the Surveillant, *les femmes,* Mexique, the Zulu and the rest. And the portrait and tale of Jean le Nègre is Homeric. The farewell to Jean—beginning 'Boy, Kid, Nigger'—is sheer, and amazing, poetry. These superlatives are hackneyed; they have been too often used when they meant precisely nothing. To me their use here is accurate."

Mr. Redman concludes: "This book is not an indictment of war, or of prisons, or of the French Government, as has been variously suggested. It is at once an indictment and glorification of the incredible animal Man."

5

In *The Shock of Recognition,* Edmund Wilson wrote: "One of the most important elements in the literary activity that followed the War was the return from military service of a number of first-rate young writers: John Dos Passos, William Faulkner, Ernest Hemingway, E. E. Cummings. These men had had a deeper experience than Stephen Crane and Sherwood Anderson had had in the Spanish War; they had been involved in a world crisis, and they had seen what it meant at first hand. They had come back with a vivid memory of what human society looks like when the laws and the conventions are suspended, and with a conviction that they knew the reality which the civilians at home could not imagine."

These remarks serve as the preface to John Dos Passos's review of *The Enormous Room* which appeared originally in the July, 1922, *Dial*. Dos Passos wrote with the reviews he had read in mind:

"Why is it that when anyone commits anything novel in the arts he should be always greeted by this same peevish howl of pain and surprise? One is led to suspect that the interest people show in these much-talked-of commodities, painting, music, and writing, cannot be very deep or very genuine when they wince so under any unexpected impact.

"The man who invented Eskimo Pie made a million dollars, so one is told, but E. E. Cummings, whose verse has been appearing off and on for three years now, and whose experiments should not be more appalling to those interested in poetry than the experiment of surrounding ice-cream with a layer of chocolate was to those interested in soda fountains, has hardly made a dent in the doughy minds of our so-called poetry lovers. Yet one might have thought that the cadences of

> Or with thy mind against my mind, to hear
> nearing our hearts' irrevocable play—
> through the mysterious high futile day
>
> an enormous stride
>   (and drawing thy mouth toward
>
> my mouth, steer our lost bodies carefully downward)

would have melted with as brittle freshness on the senses of the readers of the *Dial* as melted the brown-encrusted oblongs of ice-cream in the mouths of tired stenographers and their beaux. Can it be that people like ice-cream and only pretend to like poetry?

"Therefore it is very fortunate that this book of E. E. Cummings has come out under the disguise of prose. The average reader is less self-conscious and more open to direct impressions when reading prose than verse; the idea that prose is ART will have closed the minds of only a few overeducated people. Here at last is an opportunity to taste without overmuch prejudice a form, an individual's focus on existence, a gesture unforeseen in American writing. The attempt to obscure the issue, on the paper-cover blurb and in the preface, will fool no one who reads beyond the first page. It's not as an account of a war atrocity or as an attack on France or the holy Allies timely to the Genoa Conference that *The Enormous Room* is important, but as a distinct conscious creation separate from anything else under heaven.

"Here's a book that has been conceived unashamedly and directly without a thought either of the columnists or the book trade or Mr. Sumner, or of fitting into any one of the neatly labeled pigeon-holes of novel, play, essay, history, travel book, a book that exists because the author was so moved, excited, amused by a certain slice of his existence that things happened freely and cantankerously on paper. And he had the nerve to let things happen. In this pattern-cut generation, most writers are too afraid of losing their private reputations as red-blooded, clear-eyed, hundred-percenters, well-dressed, well-mannered, and thoroughly disinfected fashion plates, to make any attempt to feel and express directly the life about them and in them."

Another perceptive review appeared in *Current Affairs*, September 4, 1922. It was signed "E.H.P." He wrote:

" 'The Enormous Room' came to my hands in an odd way which I commend to sophisticated book buyers in Boston (all fourteen of them). I was in a bookstore and heard the most correct clerk tell the most respectable looking customer that 'The Enormous Room' was no good. My eaves-dropping cost me two dollars. . . ."

After quoting numerous sentences and paragraphs, "E.H.P." says he called his doctor to share his find (and confirm his sanity):

"We read through 'The Enormous Room' before daylight and I felt some surprise that the sun did not come up green and playing on a corn fiddle. There will undoubtedly be columns of solemn nonsense as to what Mr. Cummings was trying to achieve and what rules he violated successfully and unsuccessfully. Unless I am very far wrong, Mr. Cummings made this tremendously significant contribution because, for the first time in the history of the world, a writer wrote just exactly as he felt and did not afterwards reduce it to a common and respectable denominator by the use of a grammatical lawn mower. . . .

"The style, I reiterate, is the most natural and unaffected I have ever come in contact with. Mr. Cummings' prose has an unmistakable flow, even when it is cut up in the most extraordinary manner by italics, capitals, parentheses, dashes and shifts from French to English. He has a genius for rhythmic arrangement of syllables unlike anything else in America. His unfailing humor, and his utter freedom from resentment or sentimentality, recall a remark of Dostoievsky that men can laugh where the Gods go mad.

"The only part out of tune is the introduction by Cummings, Sr. It requires no affidavits to convince anyone of the authenticity of the incidents. Even a publisher should have sensed that. For such things to happen is quite a stretch upon the credulity, but for any human to imagine such absurdities is obviously impossible. The author gets his delicious sense of humor, it seems, from his maternal forbears."

6

Although it is clear that the Liveright edition of *The Enormous Room* received, on the whole, a very good press, its sale was meagre. It would appear that the book was remaindered some time after publication, although the plates were stored. For there was a second printing in March, 1927, and a third in August, 1929. The sudden revival of interest in *The Enormous Room* in 1927, after a lull of five years, was due to the fact that word had reached the Liveright offices that Lawrence of Arabia had not only praised the book but recommended its publication to an English firm. The story is told by Robert Graves in his Introduction to the English edition of *The Enormous Room* (Jonathan Cape, London, 1928). Lawrence's note of recommendation read, in part:

"To produce it in England will be an honourable adventure for a decent publisher (it's a strong book). It would be bought by writers in the first place, because it's an exceedingly good book; and by those interested in life and its materials, served up raw . . . and people who are particular will savour its occasional stylistic strangeness. He uses some new alloys of words, and has rare passages as iridescent as decay in meat. The book is modern in feeling and new-world in pedigree, and all the more exciting on this side in consequence. It seems to me so much the best American war-period book."

Mr. Graves concluded his Introduction with these words:

"It is important to add that this edition of *The Enormous Room* is reprinted from Cummings' original manuscript, contains a good deal of material that does not appear in the American edition, including five or six Portraits in Chapter V, and corrects a very large number of misprints that do."

The Modern Library edition, 1934, with an Introduction by the author, is—though still marred by a number of misprints—the most important, the result of the collation by Cummings of all the various manuscripts of his book.

A year before *The Enormous Room* was included in the Modern Library, Isidor Schneider wrote (in *Contempo,* April 5, 1933):

"It is significant that this piece of attested autobiography is generally listed and referred to as a novel. Most reports of experiences serve their brief purpose and have no real existence apart from that purpose. But *The Enormous Room* does more than report an experience. Out of the past experience it creates a present one. It is a novel in the sense that it *is* a creation and will have a life of its own long after the imprisonment that it memorializes has become irrelevant. For that reason its classification as fiction is a tribute to it.

"A book of such outstanding quality obviously belongs among the few established modern classics. Why then does *The Enormous Room* require periodic rescue from neglect?

"I was working at Liveright's when they decided to put out a new edition of *The Enormous Room.* Here was an instance where a publisher had faith in a good book and was willing to bet good money on it. The occasion for the new edition was the praise given it by Lawrence of Arabia. This praise was printed either as a preface or a jacket blurb, I don't remember which, but even the praise of the British sheik didn't turn the trick and *The Enormous Room* settled back into its brilliant obscurity. I say brilliant obscurity purposely because the book, while it went into retirement, so to speak, was lit on its way by critical pyrotechnics and by a publisher's advertising campaign that turned on the headlights.

"I don't mean to suggest that *The Enormous Room* was then or at any time after its publication without readers. The critics' send-offs, and the reminders of it in general literary articles and surveys, and the efforts of its several publishers have pushed it, I should judge, into the hands of five thousand book buyers. Relatively, however, this is obscurity, and I have often tried to think out the reason for it.

"*The Enormous Room* wasn't published in a bad year, and if it had been, it was reissued enough times to have known a good year.

"Its rhetoric, so alive and so integral in the narrative, could not have distressed readers, for *The Bridge of San Luis Rey* and more recently, *The Fountain,* with their colder rhetoric, nevertheless accomplished their hundred thousand.

"There is a broader and yet subtler reason.

"*The Enormous Room* is opposed in spirit to our time.

"Contemporary humanity, apparently, wants to revile, to arraign, to mock, to deny itself.

"It has no will for affirmation.

"And *The Enormous Room* is an affirmative book. Written as a protest against the stupidity and brutality of officialdom, it affirms the dignity and beauty of the mankind whom the state opposes. . . .

"Our generation, in self-punishment, has wanted instead to see the common American satirized by Sinclair Lewis, bulldozed by Mencken, pitied by Dreiser, reduced to a behavioristic automaton by Hemingway, corn-cobbed by Faulkner."

7

The question of Cummings's style in *The Enormous Room* and possible influences on it has interested writers and critics ever since the book appeared. Earlier in this chapter I have tried to show that Cummings's prose style grew naturally out of his poetic one, plus a factor to which I have also called attention—namely, his extraordinary reportorial skill. If other influences were at work I have not been able to find them; nor has anyone else. In this connection, I quote Gertrude Stein:

"In those early days Hemingway liked all his contemporaries except Cummings. He accused Cummings of having copied everything, not from anybody but from somebody. Gertrude Stein who had been much impressed by The Enormous Room said that Cummings did not copy, he was the natural heir of the New England tradition with its aridity and its sterility, but also with its individuality. They disagreed about this."

But on another visit to 27, rue Fleurus, Hemingway "brought a manuscript he intended sending to America. He handed it to Gertrude Stein. He had added to his stories a little story of meditations and in these he said that *The Enormous Room* was the greatest book he had ever read. It was then that Gertrude Stein said, Hemingway, remarks are not literature" (*The Autobiography of Alice B. Toklas*).

In *No Thanks* Cummings memorializes his fellow writer as follows:

> what does little Ernest croon
> in his death at afternoon?
> (kow dow r 2 bul retoinis
> wus de woids uf lil Oinis

Cummings himself has confirmed that his book "just growed." The confirmation occurs in an exchange of letters with Malcolm Cowley in the spring of 1951. Cowley wrote him:

> I'm putting together a book of which the real subject is the contributions to prose fiction of the new writers who appeared in the 1920s. They were big and varied contributions, if you add them all together or even if you take them separately. You never wrote any prose fiction that I know of, but The Enormous Room comes into the story because it had a very great influence on other writers. It was something absolutely new when it appeared, as your poems in the first issue of the monthly Dial were absolutely new. There had been a big change since 1915, when you were a kid writing for the Advocate, and the question I wanted to ask was how the change came about. It isn't the old question of literary influence, as if I wanted to end by saying that Cummings 'was influenced by' or 'derives from' and so on. You found something that was new and your own —the real question is what started you to looking for it? Was it mostly your reading (and of whom?) or was it partly because you started painting and wanted to get some of the same immediate effects in words? And also when did you write The Enormous Room?—I know it was some time before the book was published, but was it in 1919?

To this, Cummings replied, April 30, 1951, on the eve of sailing to Paris with his wife:

> TheER wrote itself as a(n however microscopic)
> gesture of thankfulness toward my father;who,
> despite every effort of Norton Harjes & l'armée
> francaise, boosted not only me but B out of hell.
> B & I were together at the writing, which sans
> his memory of events would have proved impossible.
> And he can probably tell you when this happened
>
> as for the "big change":(1)our unhero wrote for a
> literary mag called The Harvard Monthly, not for
> a special sheet called The ditto Advocate—what-
> ever the Advocate "Anthology" 's editor may say or
> not(2)perhaps,& here's hoping,I Just Growed
>
> Marion joins me in wishing you & yours good luck

In *Contexts of Criticism,* Professor Harry Levin of Harvard, who sees an affinity between Cummings and Hemingway because of certain poems (example, "i sing of Olaf glad and big"), quotes an interesting observation by the English critic, Cyril Connolly:

"There are three writers I envy America—Hemingway as a novelist, Edmund Wilson as a critic, and E. E. Cummings as a poet. America possesses many more good writers, but those three have something which we are inclined to lack (perhaps because they are father's boys and our literature is apt to be made by those more influenced by their mothers): that is to say, they are illusion-free and unite a courageous heartwhole emotional drive to an adult and lively intellectual toughness."

The experience at La Ferté Macé was decisive. Pound said to Cummings in St. Elizabeth's Hospital: "How fortunate for you to have served your term of imprisonment when you were young!" Cummings would have rebelled, in any case, against the coming society of anonymous mass-men with rubber-stamp inanities and cruelties; as it happened, he became, on the very threshold of his career, a champion of the individual man and a spokesman for the universal underdog. Bunyan did not glimpse the Delectable Mountains until his release from prison; Cummings found them inside, the individual and the underdog in combination.

It may come as a surprise to new readers of *The Enormous Room* that concentration camps were not the peculiar property of the latter-day Germans, and that guilt by association was not invented in the United States:

"For who was eligible to La Ferté? Anyone whom the police could find in the lovely country of France (*a*) who was not guilty of treason, (*b*) who could not prove that he was not guilty of treason. By treason I refer to any little annoying habits of independent thought or action which *en temps de guerre* are put in a hole and covered over, with the somewhat naive idea that from their cadavers violets will grow whereof the perfume will delight all good men and true and make such worthy citizens forget their sorrows. Fort Leavenworth, for instance, emanates even now a perfume which is utterly delightful to certain Americans."

This, presumably, is a reference to political prisoners and conscientious objectors immured in World War I, a procedure repeated in World War II, when there was somewhat better treatment. It appears, then, that Cummings was liberal without labelling himself. Those who have criticized him as politically ignorant or naive can only have meant that he did not share their views. In the light of events he has been, at least, consistent, while those intellectuals who became most vociferous politically were at last struck dumb or sick, or turned into informers, their own choice having been an unmitigated catastrophe.

Part Two

Chapter 7

THE TWENTIES: NEW YORK

1

In the spring of 1918, Brown joined Cummings in New York, in a tumbledown wooden building of three stories at 11 Christopher Street. There was an outhouse in the back. The building has long since disappeared and the space it occupied is now a parking lot. In the summer Cummings was drafted and reported to Camp Devens, Massachusetts, where he underwent training as an infantry soldier until the Armistice. It was at Camp Devens that he became acquainted with Olaf, the "conscientious object-or" of his poem. Brown was also drafted, but "scurvy had left my health, particularly my teeth, in such bad shape that I was discharged when I reached camp," he told me. In the fall he resumed his studies at Columbia, and when Cummings was mustered out they took a studio together at 15 West Fourteenth Street, opposite Hearn's department store. The building was a rundown loft building with studios; theirs was the top floor rear. They were there about a year. Brown told me that Cummings painted "all the time."

Brown says he and Cummings "walked for hours" all over New York and "sat for hours" in New York restaurants. It was not the

city's "stark irresistibly stupendous newness" (as Cummings phrased
it at Harvard) that fascinated them, but the quarters which had more
of the Old World in them than the New, the enclaves of "immemorial races and nations." Of these, the Jewish section on the lower
East Side, whose Fifth Avenue was Second, drew them daily to its
streets. And gradually a pattern evolved.

At the southwest corner of Second Avenue and Twelfth Street was
the Café Royale, the rendezvous of Yiddish writers and actors; this
might be said to have marked the northernmost bounds of the quarter,
as Fourteenth marks that of the Village. At the Café Royale, now
defunct, Cummings and Brown soon made friends, despite language
barriers. Brown told me that, in 1919 at least, he and Cummings saw
more of Yiddish writers than American ones. He was particularly
impressed, he said, that when he and Cummings walked down Second
Avenue with a Yiddish writer, everybody on the street—"even the
pushcart peddlers"—said "hello."

"It was very pleasant to walk with them," Brown said.

Two of these writers were Milton Raisin, a poet, then about
seventy years old, and Nachum Yud, "a sweet, gentle man," who
wrote fairy tales. Both lived in the faraway reaches of The Bronx, but
both came to the Café Royale every night. One night, Nachum Yud
created a sensation by driving up to the café in a taxi. Out he leaped,
and hastily borrowed four dollars for his fare.

"But if you're so broke, why a taxi?" he was asked.

"Because I didn't have a nickel," he explained.

(The subway fare was then a nickel.)

At the southern, or lower, end of Second Avenue, at the corner of
Houston, was the National Winter Garden Burlesque theatre, and
past the theatre, also on Houston Street, was Moscowitz's Rumanian
restaurant. The restaurant, which had a cosmopolitan clientele and a
Middle European atmosphere, served the "little meats" or "mititei"
of Rumania (a little like hot dogs, of finest meat spiced with garlic)
and filet mignon broiled over charcoal. I have been told that the
broiling of steaks in the Rumanian fashion was so fine an art that
even in that remote period the chef was handsomely paid. This
restaurant drew European visitors as well as celebrities from the
American literary, theatre and film world, among them Charles Chaplin. Moscowitz himself, tall, mustachioed and distinguished-looking—
"with the very look of a great gallant and ladies' man," as a Rumanian

habitué described him to me—was not only host but entertainer; he played, for his own delight and his clients' pleasure, skilfully and triumphantly, upon an instrument known as a cymbalon. His most sensational number was the "Poet and Peasant" overture, which always brought down the house. Mr. Moscowitz was no amateur, for he gave solo concerts uptown.

In the warmth of their welcome among people so different from themselves, and who spontaneously took the two attractive gentiles to their hearts, Cummings and Brown basked in continual pleasure and surprise. In a prose poem which belongs to this period—"my eyes are fond of the east side"—Cummings has catalogued the sights, smells, colors—and tastes—of the quarter which he observed with the eyes of a painter and the mind of a poet. He remembers a scarlet pepper which he ate. Result: "my eyes were buttoned with pain." In another poem: "I have not eaten peppers for a week."

The two friends also spent many afternoons and evenings drinking ale in McSorley's Saloon, now "McSorley's Old Ale House," fronting Hall Place east of the Bowery on Seventh Street. McSorley's was already in business when Abraham Lincoln spoke at Cooper Union, a bottle's toss away, in 1860. It has two rooms, each with its individual admonitory sign, "Be Good or Be Gone." The walls are crowded with photographs and lithographs in which a vanished city dwells, and dead, buxom ladies and derbied men. The room in front has the bar, but the room in back boasts a famous lady of a smooth and beautiful nudeness. She does not receive too much competition from the other decorations on the wall—Gilbert Stuart's Washington, the American flag and a Dublin Horse Show poster. She is propped on visible and invisible bolsters, recliningly, and is looking at a parrot. The parrot is looking at her. She is a durable symbol, although I am not sure of what, for women were not permitted to enter McSorley's. A Village nymph who essayed it once, in fedora and trousers, was quickly ejected; more recently, a bevy from Women's Lib invaded it.

Here writers, artists and laborers still meet on equal terms, without other distractions, to sluice down amber pints in the abiding gloom. Said the man at the table next to mine to the chef, or sandwich-maker, who emerged briefly from his cubicle: "Hear about the girl who was raped on Rivington Street? She thought it was Grand." The chef didn't get it. There is still sawdust on the floor, but something new has been added: a TV. The bare table-tops are crisscrossed with

names and initials; what must have been a jolly party is suggested by
this vertical muster chiselled in wood:

> Lippi
> Joe
> Pot
> Tony
> Curti
> Chappy

Cummings also, but elsewhere, has memorialized time spent in those
pleasant environs:

> i was sitting in mcsorley's.   outside it was New
> York and beautifully snowing. . . .

2

Greenwich Village, of course, offered attractions of its own,
restaurants not least. There was Romany Marie's, on the southeast
corner of Washington Square and Thompson Street, a candle-lighted
rendezvous in a pre-Revolutionary brick building whose walls bulged.
It was said that Washington and Lafayette had reviewed troops there
when the Square was a parade ground, but whether from a window or
the roof was never made clear. The roof sloped steeply. The presiding
genius of the place was Romany Marie herself, a handsome Rumanian
woman who read cards, hands, tea-leaves, and was the mother con-
fessor of Villagers in trouble; she was seldom idle or alone. I remember her "poets' table" where none durst sit except writers, whether
established or not. She also had a special dinner, with a special price,
for her Bohemian clientele: tasty coarse black bread, thick soups,
Turkish coffee—rather sustaining fare, 50¢, not always paid for. The
uptowners who dined there, and made it possible for impecunious
Bohemians to eat, were rewarded by Bohemian sneers. The building
was torn down in 1928.

A block south, on Thompson Street, was the Grand Ticino, still a
flourishing and pleasant place though long minus the huge pool table
downstairs where old paysans played and two enormous mastiffs,
somnolent with ossi bucci bones and scallopini scraps, dozed in its
shade.

There was also Polly's restaurant on West Fourth Street, rendezvous of prominent Bohemians, and the Lafayette on University Place, where dining may have been out of the question, but whose café with marble-topped tables was a pleasant and inexpensive place for coffee and rolls in the morning and coffee and liqueurs at night. In those days, the Brevoort on Fifth Avenue still had a noble staircase; staircase, Brevoort, Lafayette, have all been swept away in the inexorable march of progress, preceded by the depression that followed Prohibition.

And there were book shops—Albert and Charles Boni's book shop on Macdougal Street, where the Washington Square Players was born, and from which sprang the Provincetown and the Theatre Guild; and the Washington Square Book Shop on Eighth Street, which later moved to Tenth, next door to Patchin Place. Across the street from the Provincetown Playhouse was "The Black Knight," where liquor was always plentiful during Prohibition and the French cooking was first-rate and inexpensive.

Prohibition! There was Luke O'Conner's famous Columbian saloon —also known affectionately as the "Working Girls' Home"—on the corner of Christopher Street and Sixth Avenue, where beer flowed as copiously as when John Masefield worked there as a youth, and not only beer but stout and the best whiskey the mobs were purveying. There was also the "Golden Swan," at the corner of West Fourth Street and Sixth, but better known as the "Hell Hole," probably with reason. Mobsters mingled there with actors from the Provincetown and drifters from the Bowery, but it was probably as safe as the Waldorf if you behaved yourself. The "Hell Hole" was the favorite resort of Eugene O'Neill. Gaunt, appearing underfed, he listened to everyone, saying little himself, sustained by whiskey and the plots leaping to life in his tortured brain. Here also were to be found the painters Charles Demuth, who has recorded the "Hell Hole's" sinister interior, and Marcel Duchamp.

In the Village Cummings and Brown were soon joined by Edward Pierce Nagle, a sensitive, highly strung young man who was a painter, and M. R. Werner, afterwards well known for his biography of Barnum and a history of Tammany Hall. Werner, a native New Yorker, had been a classmate of Brown's at the Columbia School of Journalism.

Through Nagle, the son of Mrs. Lachaise by her first husband, Cummings met Gaston Lachaise, the French-born sculptor whose studio was on Fourteenth Street. Lachaise was twelve years older than

Cummings. With his dark, unruly hair falling over his brow, his alive and brooding eyes, his scowl and sullen mouth, and his powerful build, he resembled Thomas Wolfe. His favorite word was "simple," as pronounced in French. He was romantic—he had seen Mrs. Nagle in Paris and followed her to America—and he was imbued with a feeling about art which can only be described as tender. Cummings has recalled an incident which took place at the Society of Independent Artists during one of those catch-all, hang-all exhibitions which provoked derision and occasionally riots in the early Twenties.

"I was wrestling some peculiarly jovial mob of sightseers at possibly the least orthodox of all Independent 'openings', when out of nowhere the sculptor Lachaise gently materialized," Cummings wrote in the foreword to the catalogue of one of his own shows at the University of Rochester in May, 1957.

" 'Hello Cumming' his serene voice (addressing me, as always, in the singular) sang above chaos 'have you seen one litel cat?' I shook my head. He beckoned—and shoulder-to-shoulder we gradually corkscrewed through several huge rooms; crammed with eccentricities of inspiration and teeming with miscalled humanity. Eventually we paused. He pointed. And I found myself face to face with a small canvas depicting a kitten.

" 'Dis ting' Lachaise reverently affirmed(in the course of what remotely resembled a lull) 'is paint with love.' "

Lachaise's sculpture made a profound impression on Cummings, who was shortly to give it incomparable praise in *The Dial*.

The chief focus of the pattern earlier alluded to was the National Winter Garden Burlesque on Houston Street. This was literally as well as figuratively heaven to an old habitué of The Howard Athenaeum in Boston—literally because it was reached by elevators, it being on the roof of an old theatre, once the home of Boris Thomashefsky's Yiddish troupe. Werner told me that over the proscenium arch were the startling words: "The Show's the Thing—W. Shakespeare." A runway, lighted from beneath, projected into the audience and on it the girls paraded to whistles and calls. Strip-tease, of course, was the main feature, and to this American art the impassive Chinese in the audience responded with applause. They did not respond to the comedians.

"Every week," Werner said, "there was the same joke: 'Would you hit a woman with a child?' No, I'd hit her with a brick."

As for the American portion of the audience, Cummings was to write: "It was not only peculiarly demanding, it was extraordinarily well mannered. I have not sat, and I never hope to sit, with tougher or more courteous people."

The chief comedian at the National Winter Garden was Jack Shargel, of whom Cummings made a pen drawing which appeared in *The Dial*. He also wrote an article in praise of him, from which the above was taken, for *Vanity Fair*. Shargel had two roles which brought the roof down. One was downright earthy—as Anthony in a skit entitled "Anthony and Cleopatra." In a tin helmet and cigar as big as a guided missile he is seen on a divan with Cleopatra, a strip-tease queen. Enter Caesar, who wallops him in the right place with the flat of a gigantic sword. Anthony jumps up and does a loping stagger around the stage.

ANTHONY: "I'm dying! I'm dying!"
CHORUS: "He's dying! He's dying!"
ANTHONY: "I hear de voices of angels!"
CAESAR: "What do they say?"
ANTHONY: "I don't know—I don't speak Polish!"

In the other role, Shargel is handed a rose by a siren, who promptly disappears. He looks longingly after her, enraptured; sniffs the rose, kisses it, sniffs it some more; then, as though his ecstasy is too great to bear, with an exquisite gesture of renunciation, he tosses the rose to the stage, where it falls with the noise of shattered glass.

"To sum up," Cummings wrote in *Vanity Fair,* "the creations of the National Winter Garden possess, in common with the sculpture of Gaston Lachaise, the painting of John Marin and the music of Igor Stravinsky, the virtue of being intensely alive; whereas the productions of the conventional theatre, like academic sculpture and painting and music, are thoroughly dead—and since 'art,' if it means anything, means TO BE INTENSELY ALIVE, the former constitute art and the latter are balderdash. Furthermore, the fact that this highly stylized, inherently 'abstract,' positively 'futuristic' art known to its devotees as burlesk is indubitably *for the masses,* knocks into a cocked chapeau the complaint of many so-called 'critics' that 'modern art' is 'neurotic,' 'unhealthy,' 'insane,' 'arbitrary,' 'unessential,' 'superficial' and 'not for the masses.' "

Lachaise, with whom Cummings built a durable friendship, and for whom he sat, also became a devotee of burlesque, and was soon sketching and casting Minsky belly dancers.

North and south stretched the limitless city. The Aquarium drew them—almost every day, Brown told me, he and Cummings walked to the Battery, stopping at Khouri's on Washington and Rector to eat delectable Syrian dishes. The Aquarium was one of the most delightful places, in a delightful setting, in New York; but the park commissioner had it torn down.[1] The Bronx Zoo drew them—and Cummings has left a record of a visit there. It was in the spring of 1919 that he, Brown and Nagle squired Elizabeth Cummings and a Radcliffe classmate, a Miss Gay, to the Zoo.

Cummings purchased "two bags of lukewarm peanuts" and gallantly offered one to Miss Gay, who declined in what must have been so polite a Cambridge fashion, saying "No, thank you, I have one"— meaning a single peanut—that almost two score years later Brown could hardly tell the story for laughing. The incident is enshrined in a poem, which also states, "unhappily, the denizens of the zoo were that day inclined to be uncouthly erotic," with the result that "Miss Gay had nothing to say to the animals and the animals had nothing to say to Miss Gay."

A climax to the excursion came when they entered the alligator house. As they pressed eagerly forward to peer at the saurian, an unfortunate butterfly, innocently skimming the surface of the muddy tank, was instantaneously snapped up by ponderous jaws, which so upset Nagle that he had to make an abrupt exit.

Cummings has recorded his explorations of New York in an early sonnet:

> by god i want above fourteenth
>
> fifth's deep purring biceps, the mystic screech
> of Broadway, the trivial stink of rich
>
> frail firm asinine life
>   (i pant

---

[1] No one opposes
Commissioner Moses;
Even the fishes
Must do as he wishes.
    —*Francesco Bianco*.

for what's below. the singer. Wall. i want
the perpendicular lips the insane teeth
the vertical grin

               give me the Square in spring,
the little barbarous Greenwich perfumed fake

And most, the futile fooling labyrinth
where noisy colors stroll . . . . and the Baboon

sniggering insipidities while. i sit, sipping
singular anisettes as. One opaque
big girl juggles thickly hips to the canoun

but Hassan chuckles seeing the Greeks breathe)

The poem appeared in *Broom* (May, 1922). Professor Damon
told me that it occasioned the first reference to Cummings in England
—in *Punch*.

One other aspect of Cummings's discoveries during this period
might be mentioned here. He said at Harvard:

"Last but most, I thank for my self-finding certain beautiful givers
of illimitable gladness

       whose any mystery makes every man's
       flesh put space on;and his mind take off time."

3

In 1920, Cummings, Brown, Nagle and Werner were joined
on their tours of the city by Stewart Mitchell, in New York to take
up his post as first managing editor of *The Dial*. Mitchell told me
that two of his chief recollections of this period were of Second
Avenue and the National Winter Garden. John Dos Passos was living
at 3 Washington Square, at work on *Three Soldiers*.

With the establishment of *The Dial*, an account of which will be
found in the next chapter, Cummings became intimately associated
with a number of men and women who were at the center of New
York's literary and artistic life.

To begin with, there were the owners of the new publication,
Scofield Thayer who, with James Sibley Watson, not only encouraged
Cummings as a writer, but had begun to purchase his pictures before
the magazine appeared.

There was Paul Rosenfeld, the music critic of the new publication, a brown-eyed, stocky, round-faced man with red hair and red mustache who, wrote Edmund Wilson, "when I first knew him—in 1922, I think—was one of the most exciting critics of the 'American Renaissance.' " Rosenfeld, a bachelor, liked to give parties which were, says Mr. Wilson, "all the more agreeable for being of rather an old-fashioned kind." There was little liquor served, which was of course unusual during Prohibition. To these parties came writers, musicians, and poets. Mr. Wilson wrote: "One met Ornstein, Milhaud, Varèse; Cummings, Hart Crane, and Marianne Moore; the Stieglitzes and all their group; the Stettheimers, Mumford, Kreymborg. One of the images that remains with me most vividly is the bespectacled figure of Copland, at that period gray-faced and lean, long-nosed and rather unearthly, bending over the piano as he chanted in a high, cold, and passionate voice a poem of Ezra Pound's, for which he had written a setting." Van Wyck Brooks has recalled, in *Days of the Phoenix,* that "one met virtually all the contributors" to *The Dial* there. "There one saw E. E. Cummings, the last of the Yankee come-outers, who came out all the way in his poetry and drawings, and I remember Marianne Moore, on the long sofa by the fire, reading aloud some of her early poems. The mantel and the walls were covered with Marins, Doves, Hartleys and O'Keefes."

Rosenfeld's apartment was on Irving Place, a street afterwards memorable as the site of the Minsky Brothers' reborn burlesque in a rundown theatre in which Gypsy Rose Lee stripped herself to everlasting renown.

In addition to the individual writing and other creative work that members of Cummings's circle were doing, they shared certain aesthetic views and enthusiasms. They looked askance at reputations, both recent and back-dated, and warred continually against "The Great God Bogus," Gilbert Seldes's phrase, afterwards incorporated in *The Seven Lively Arts* where, under that heading, he listed the following beliefs:

> That Al Jolson is more interesting to the intelligent mind than John Barrymore and Fanny Brice than Ethel;

> That Ring Lardner and Mr. Dooley [Finley Peter Dunne's creation] in their best work are more entertaining and more important than James Branch Cabell and Joseph Hergesheimer in their best;

That the daily comic strip of George Herriman (Krazy Kat) is easily the most amusing and fantastic and satisfactory work of art produced in America today;

That Florenz Ziegfeld is a better producer than David Belasco;

That one film by Mack Sennett or Charlie Chaplin is worth the entire *oeuvre* of Cecil de Mille;

That *Alexander's Ragtime Band* and *I Love a Piano* are musically and emotionally sounder pieces of work than *Indian Love Lyrics* and *The Rosary;*

That the circus can be and often is more artistic than the Metropolitan Opera House in New York;

That Irene Castle is worth all the pseudo-classic dancing ever seen on the American stage; and

That the civic masque is not perceptibly superior to the Elks' Parade in Atlantic City.

Admiration for America's comic strips was not limited to natives. Gertrude Stein has told in her autobiography that as long ago as Picasso's Montmartre period—before World War I—she and her brother Leo used to give the painter their Sunday supplements from home so he could follow the Katzenjammer Kids. In *Civilization in the United States,* Harold E. Stearns declared that "Bringing Up Father" "symbolizes better than most of us appreciate the normal relation of American men and women to cultural and intellectual values." He also declared (in *The Freeman*) before rushing off to Paris: "There is something the matter with a culture whose youth is eager to desert it." Hemingway has recorded what they replaced it with.

4

Another member of the Cummings circle, who joined it early and stayed late, was Joseph Ferdinand Gould, afterwards better known as Joe Gould or Little Joe Gould, self-styled "Last of the Bohemians." He, too, was Harvard *magna cum laude,* a contemporary of T. S. Eliot, Walter Lippmann, Conrad Aiken and Gluyas Williams.

Joe was five feet four, bearded, and—with the passage of time—
fringed on top with a frieze of hair like hoarfrost, which gave him the
appearance—in cast-off clothing generally too large for him—of a
gnome or pint-size, grubby Santa Claus. He weighed around 100.

Joe had several legitimate claims to attention. He was a shrewd
observer and a wit, his remarks gaining from the peculiarly slow,
nasal manner in which he uttered them. He gave lectures, in Village
dives, on the work of Cummings and Dos Passos. And he was the
author of a mammoth (and unpublished) work entitled *An Oral
History of Our Time,* which once reached the staggering total of
11,000,000 words. At that point the manuscript towered seven feet
high, which led him to boast that he was the only author in history
who had written a book taller than himself. The *Oral History,* on
which Joe worked for a quarter century, was at first a painstaking
record of conversations overheard anywhere—saloons, streets, subways and flophouses—plus the author's occasionally pithy observations.

"My general idea," he explained, "is that every human being is as
much history as a ruler or a celebrity because he illustrates all the
social forces."

Joe used to be a familiar sight in Greenwich Village streets with
a battered, bespattered portfolio hugged to his bosom; but in recent
years he no longer lugged portions of his work around with him and
was evasive about the fate of his manuscript. (Cummings told me
that he can still remember the start he got the first time he saw Gould
without his portfolio.) Great chunks of the *Oral History* may have
been left behind in abandoned rooms and in the clutches of irate land-
ladies who were optimistic about his coming back to ransom his
dearest possession. Homeless for decades, Joe slept on park benches,
in hallways and subways, and was occasionally picked up for va-
grancy. He had only fond recollections of his sojourns on Ward's and
Riker's islands, however; when other inmates talked of getting out,
he pondered how to stay in to continue eating three times a day and
smoking cigarettes supplied by the city.

Joe also wrote poetry. His verse was terse, viz.—

> In winter I'm a Buddhist,
> And in summer I'm a nudist,

lines as often quoted, perhaps, as a couplet by Dorothy Parker or
Ogden Nash. With this couplet, Joe became a member of the Raven

Poetry Society of Greenwich Village, though not without opposition. He was accused of not being serious enough, whereupon he retorted that neither were most of its members since they wrote only on such "trite themes as life, love and death." Supported enthusiastically by the late Maxwell Bodenheim, Joe was admitted. He immediately translated a poem by his sponsor into "seagull," a language which Joe claimed to know. This offended everyone, especially Bodenheim. "Screek—squawk—screek," went the translation, with Joe making appropriate gestures to personate a gull, and he was ejected.

Newcomers to the dives where Joe hung out in Greenwich Village sometimes reacted to the thrill of meeting him by inviting him to dinner. He always had enough to drink; for like other cadgers he found that bar-flies would buy him liquor to be amused, but turned their backs at the suggestion of food, which carried a hint of troubles. As a result, he too often settled for the liquor, which worked havoc with his system. In part it was his own fault, for he approached strangers with a gambit of his own. "I believe in democracy," he would say with an ingenuous, blue-eyed stare. "I believe everyone has the right to buy Joe Gould a drink." The right was frequently exercised. After a while, he resisted the harder varieties, contenting himself with beer or ale. It sufficed, particularly on an empty stomach. "British beer," he told me, "has only hops; American beer has hops, skips and jumps."

Joe told me in 1952, just a few weeks before he was picked up in the street and taken to a hospital for the mentally ill, that his last square meal was in June, 1936, when he attended a class reunion at Harvard. Classmates, who may have remembered him as a thin, spectacled, serious-eyed fellow student, must have been jolted by the bearded and soiled satyr in their midst stoking himself with gusto. In any event, one sight of Joe Gould eating is forever memorable. New England to the core, he preferred clams to cutlets, and after devouring a platter of them was so bespattered that a paper napkin disintegrated on application, leaving his beard like a hedgerow after a snow flurry. Having got that far with his ablutions, Joe rested; and the rain of sauces and juices, dribbles of ale and coffee, dried where they fell on his tie and suit, to merge imperceptibly with the stains and smears of decades. "Give me a cigarette," he would say to his host. "I feel naked without a cigarette." He smoked with a holder.

Joe took a naive delight in his fame. "I find it natural," he said of

the attention paid him wherever he went—which was chiefly to
saloons. "It's like the home town I grew up in—everybody knows
me." He was born in Norwood, Massachusetts, the son of a doctor
and grandson and namesake of a professor in the Harvard Medical
School, and grew up among people who had known Hawthorne,
Emerson and Thoreau. He once said of his father that he held "the
pessimistic belief that the Americans were the best people God ever
made." Joe ran away from home at the age of twelve, but was recognized a few miles down the road by a neighbor, who hitched up his
horse and buggy and brought him back. A vagabond by nature, Joe,
surprisingly, had never been to Europe. "Why should I go slum-
ming?" he asked in mild surprise. "In the United States I meet a
better type of European. If I went abroad I would only run into
second-rate Americans." He told me he once "spent seven years in
Philadelphia one Sunday afternoon."

In addition to hanging around saloons and cafeterias in the lower
depths of Greenwich Village, Joe was an indefatigable bellringer.
His "route" included many famous residents. A quarter or half dollar
brought him back in a day or two, a dollar kept him away for a week;
and once M. R. Werner, unseasonably flush (after a movie sale), gave
him $25. "Reckon this lets you out for quite a while," Joe said, and
stayed away six months. He never mentioned *money*. The bell rang,
and there he was, the shyest—and wittiest—of panhandlers. When
money was finally passed, it was accepted like a light, without fuss.

Rain had a particular fascination for Joe. Everyone on his "route"
knew when it rained that he was sure to turn up. Residents of the
Village, huddled in doorways during a shower, watched with fascination as he trudged like an automaton through rain-swept streets,
soaked to his socks, his battered hat running water like a spout.

Joe's portrait was painted by Cummings and other artists. Once,
when Lachaise put him up for a night, Mrs. Lachaise suggested that
Joe would make a good subject, but the sculptor demurred. "He is too
formé," Lachaise said of Joe. "He is his own bust." Joe also posed
for hundreds of beginners at the Art Students' League and Cooper
Union, where he went often to pick up a slow buck. Cummings wrote
about him in "little joe gould," as well as in a kind of grace-note to
this famous poem, which is a superb example of Gould's manner of
speaking, bearing in mind his nasal Yankee twang which all but
smothered his Harvard accent:

as joe gould says in
his terrifyingly hum
man man
ner the only reason every wo
man

should

go to college is so
that she never can(kno
wledge is po
wer) say o

if i

'd
OH
n
lygawntueco

llege

Joe is also mentioned in the *Cantos* of Ezra Pound.

Joe complained, with some reason, that he was "the most quoted and least published author" of his acquaintance. Sometimes he quoted himself: "I have slept with Lady Poverty but I am a conservative person and do not consider that an introduction." I asked him once whether he had really said "The Goulds were the Goulds when the Lowells and Cabots were clam-diggers," which had been much quoted. He at first denied it. Then, with a shy, pleased smile, he corrected himself: "What I really said was, 'When Sir Ferdinand Gould was returning from the Crusades, he stopped off at Hanover to buy a loaf of pumpernickel from the ancestors of the present kings of England."

Joe never married. A chapter in the *Oral History* entitled "Why I Never Expect to Marry" follows in its entirety:

"I never expect to marry becaust my horoscope says I will marry outside my own race, and I have never met a human group that I did not think of myself as belonging to."

Joe's interest in racial groups once led him to make a survey in his home town. He thereupon concluded that "the greatest invention in the world may have been the wheelbarrow, because it taught the Irish to stand on their hind legs." While interviewing some English immigrants he found himself talking with two men who had seen the Charge of the Light Brigade. In Boston, he organized a society known as the Friends of Albanian Independence. Asked why he had interested himself in Albania, he replied: "After all, Boswell had his Corsican period." He ascribed his deep sympathy for minority groups to his short stature—he was himself a lifelong underdog. He added, however, "I think of myself as at least six feet tall." This led him to act accordingly when he was rebuffed or otherwise affronted, with the result that he sometimes took a barroom licking. In the *Oral History* he confessed: "I have delusions of grandeur; I believe myself to be Joe Gould."

Chapter 8

THE DIAL AND THE POET

1

Although a good portion of Greenwich Village has begun to look like Park Avenue, some of its streets have managed to retain an almost unaltered appearance before the glacier-like march of massive apartment houses. Such a street is Thirteenth, between Sixth and Seventh avenues, with its three-story houses and sidewalks thickly sown with flourishing plane trees. Its landmark is the Village Presbyterian Church, now shared with the Brotherhood Synagogue, so that the Sabbath as well as Sunday draws worshippers to its white-pillared, Greek Revival portico. Up and down the street are restaurants— Felix's, Mario's, Little Venice, the Mandarin House—long known to Villagers and uptowners. Next door to Felix's, at 152, is the three-story house that was the home of *The Dial* for nine and a half years.

The *Dial* which is the subject of this chapter was not the publication founded in 1840 with Margaret Fuller and Ralph Waldo Emerson as its first editors; that venture lasted only four years, despite notable contributors and a market situated in the "Athens of the West" and the "Hub of the Universe." In 1880, it was reestablished in Chicago, "hog-butcher to the world," and lasted longer; it was still

going in 1917 when it moved to New York where it became a fortnightly with advanced social and liberal views. Some of its editors and
contributing editors were Robert Morss Lovett, Thorstein Veblen,
Randolph Bourne, Van Wyck Brooks, Lewis Mumford and Harold E.
Stearns. But it was soon in financial difficulties, and two men, one of
whom had been at Harvard with Cummings, decided to buy it. They
were Scofield Thayer and James Sibley Watson. Dr. Watson, who
could have practiced medicine but preferred editing, told me:

"Thayer said he would either start a magazine or set up a fund for
artists. If he started a magazine, would I come in with him? The
answer was 'yes.' Then came the question—should we start a new
magazine or get hold of an old one? Because I had written for the
fortnightly *Dial* I suggested we get hold of it. But we did not want
to approach Martyn Johnson, the owner, directly. So Thayer wrote
a check for $10,000, I wrote one for $2,500, and we gave the money
to Harold Stearns, who was to act as go-between. Time passed, and
nothing happened. Harold simply disappeared. He afterwards returned the entire sum."

Poor Stearns (who lives on as Harvey Stone in *The Sun Also Rises*)
had many lovable qualities, but he turned vague and unreliable. In
time the favorite sport and chief preoccupation of the editor of *Civilization in the United States* was the race track.

"About a year later," Dr. Watson continued, "we heard that the
magazine was on the point of suspending. This time we approached
Johnson through our lawyers, and the deal was closed. We got the
Dial in November, 1919, and let it continue as a bi-weekly for a
couple of issues. In January, 1920, it became a monthly. We took
with us Lewis Mumford, who did not stay long. Bruce Rogers, the
Harvard typographer, designed the new format.

"We paid for contributions on acceptance—and had the usual
tendency to stock up in advance. For prose, we paid two cents a word.
Poetry was paid for at the rate of $20 a page or any part of a page.

"The more copies of the magazine we published," he continued,
"the more we lost. When the circulation went up to 22,000—the
highwater mark—we lost too much and let it sink back to 4,000, a
normal run. Towards the end of the Twenties this seemed a natural
number. Our annual deficit was usually around $30,000; but some
years it was $50,000."

Watson's munificence was not confined to *The Dial*. Margaret

Anderson, the editor of the *Little Review*—which serialized Joyce's *Ulysses*—tells in her autobiography of a visit to her office of this tall, spare, diffident American with his marked resemblance to Edwin Arlington Robinson. It was a Christmas day; she does not give the year, but it could not have been long after *The Dial* was purchased, so it was probably Christmas, 1919. She does not give the address, but it must have been in the basement of the "old Van Buren house" at 31 West Fourteenth Street, a four-story brownstone built by Abraham Van Buren in 1846. The brownstone, which was torn down in 1927, was next door to the loft building where Cummings and Brown lived in 1918 and 1919. Miss Anderson wrote:

"At tea time a tall blond man arrived, introduced himself as J. S. Watson of the *Dial,* and said he wanted to buy a copy of Eliot's 'Prufrock.' We had published most of the poems in this collection and kept the book on sale. It cost seventy-five cents. Mr. Watson gave me a dollar bill, took the book and left, saying: 'Oh no, I don't want any change.' As I put the dollar away I chanced to look at it. It was a hundred-dollar bill. I ran after Mr. Watson to tell him he had made a mistake.

" 'Oh no,' he said again, so embarrassed that he began falling down the stairs. 'I brought it for the *Little Review*. It's good, I assure you.'

"I made him come back and talk. We became friends and so remained during all our attacks on the *Dial* as 'a de-alcoholized version of the *Little Review*.' Watson came several times with his salutary hundred-dollar bill which kept the magazine alive when otherwise it would have succumbed" (from *My Thirty Years' War*).

2

The introduction of a new poet must be a memorable event to those who are present at the introduction, who respond to the poetry, and who live to see their original response generally confirmed. Such is probably the case as regards Cummings with some portion of the reading public old enough to have read *The Dial* and young enough to be alive today. His work appeared in it throughout its existence. Pound wrote a decade and a half later: "E. E. was undoubtedly the white-haired boy for that outfit." Dr. Watson told me that "it was always exciting when we had his poems or drawings in the office." He added that, so far as the editors were concerned, "a good thing had intensity; if not, 'it was not profoundly enough imagined,' in Thayer's phrase."

The first number—January, 1920—had for frontispiece a bas-relief of a female nude by Gaston Lachaise. The leading article was "An Autobiographic Chapter" by Randolph Bourne. This was followed by "Seven Poems" and four line drawings—of a comedian, hoofer, and ladies of the National Winter Garden—by E. E. Cummings. A contributors' note states that Cummings "has not previously published in any of the regular periodicals." He was then twenty-six years old. (Other contributors to the first number were Paul Rosenfeld, who wrote on music; Edwin Arlington Robinson, Maxwell Bodenheim, Carl Sandburg, Evelyn Scott and Walter Pach.) The first of the "Seven Poems" was

> little tree
> little silent Christmas tree
> you are so little
> you are more like a flower
>
> who found you in the green forest
> and were you very sorry to come away?
> see   i will comfort you
> because you smell so sweetly
>
> i will kiss your cool bark
> and hug you safe and tight
> just as your mother would,
> only don't be afraid
>
> look   the spangles
> that sleep all the year in a dark box
> dreaming of being taken out and allowed to shine,
> the balls the chains red and gold the fluffy threads,
>
> put up your little arms
> and i'll give them all to you to hold
> every finger shall have its ring
> and there won't be a single place dark or unhappy
>
> then when you're quite dressed
> you'll stand in the window for everyone to see
> and how they'll stare!
> oh but you'll be very proud

and my little sister and i will take hands
and looking up at our beautiful tree
we'll dance and sing
"Noel Noel"

This was followed by "the bigness of cannon" (given in Chapter 5), the poem about Buffalo Bill (in Chapter 1), "when god lets my body be," "why did you go," "when life is quite through with," and "O Distinct" (first lines: *Poems 1923-1954*).

After Buffalo Bill, the poem that made the greatest impact at the time was the fourth:

> when god lets my body be
>
> From each brave eye shall sprout a tree
> fruit that dangles therefrom
>
> the purpled world will dance upon
> Between my lips which did sing
>
> a rose shall beget the spring
> that maidens whom passion wastes
>
> will lay between their little breasts
> My strong fingers beneath the snow
>
> Into strenuous birds shall go
> my love walking in the grass
>
> their wings will touch with her face
> and all the while shall my heart be
>
> With the bulge and nuzzle of the sea

The February number marked the appearance of Cummings as an art critic. His essay was entitled "Gaston Lachaise" and it was illustrated by Lachaise's drawings and sculpture. (Selections from it will be found in my chapter entitled "The Poet as Painter.") He did not appear again until the May number, this time with five poems: "into the strenuous briefness" (given in Chapter 8), "O sweet spontaneous," "but the other," "in Just-spring" (in Chapter 2), and "spring omnipotent goddess," which he afterwards revised for book publication. The two versions present an interesting study in the

methodology of composition, and I give them here. The first is from
The Dial of May, 1920:

> spring omnipotent goddess Thou
> dost stuff parks
> with overgrown pimply
> chevaliers and gumchewing giggly
>
> damosels Thou dost
> persuade to serenade
> his lady the musical tom-cat
> Thou dost inveigle
>
> into crossing sidewalks the
> unwary june-bug and the frivolous
> angleworm
> Thou dost hang canary birds in parlour windows
>
> Spring slattern of seasons
> you have soggy legs
> and a muddy petticoat
> drowsy
>
> is your hair your
> eyes are sticky with
> dream and you have a
> sloppy body from
>
> being brought to bed of crocuses
> when you sing in your whiskey voice
> the grass rises on the head of the earth
> and all the trees are put on edge
>
> spring
> of the excellent jostle of
> thy hips
> and the superior
>
> slobber of your breasts i
> am so very fond that my
> soul inside of me hollers   for thou comest
>
> and your hands are the snow and thy
> fingers are the rain
> and your
> feet O your feet

freakish
feet feet incorrigible

ragging the world

In *Tulips and Chimneys* it became:

spring omnipotent goddess thou dost
inveigle into crossing sidewalks the
unwary june-bug and the frivolous angleworm
thou dost persuade to serenade his
lady the musical tom-cat, thou stuffest
the parks with overgrown pimply
cavaliers and gumchewing giggly
girls and not content
Spring, with this
thou hangest canary-birds in parlor windows

spring slattern of seasons you
have dirty legs and a muddy
petticoat, drowsy is your
mouth your eyes are sticky
with dreams and you have
a sloppy body
from being brought to bed of crocuses
When you sing in your whiskey-voice
                                        the grass

rises on the head of the earth
and all the trees are put on edge

spring,
of the jostle of
thy breasts and the slobber
of your thighs
i am so very
                glad that the soul inside me Hollers
for thou comest and your hands
are the snow
and thy fingers are the rain,
and i hear
the screech of dissonant
flowers, and most of all

          i hear your stepping
                              freakish feet
                              feet incorrigible
          ragging the world,

All of the poems thus far referred to appeared afterwards in *Tulips and Chimneys* (1923) and *XLI Poems* (1925). Stewart Mitchell told me that, beginning in January, 1920, he took the original manuscript of *Tulips and Chimneys* to five publishers, all of whom declined it, including Cummings's present publisher. A glance at the group, particularly the first poem—"little tree"—will reveal an eye familiar with visual forms, for Cummings, being a painter as well as a poet, gives many of his lines a shape as well as movement. A Greek of the *Anthology;* George Herbert in the seventeenth century, and Dylan Thomas in the twentieth, would have completed the typographical image of the Christmas tree.

Those who profess to see a connection between Guillaume Apollinaire's *calligrammes* and Cummings's quite different use of typography misunderstand, I believe, the separate aims and achievements of the two poets. Apollinaire was inspired by certain baroque poems, shaped to visual images, of the seventeenth and early eighteenth centuries. His *calligrammes* present a series of pictures which achieve their ultimate end at first glance. They are, therefore, closer to the graphic arts than to poetry.

This is not strictly true of Cummings's poems, although in a letter to a Harcourt, Brace editor he referred to them as "poem-pictures." It is only rarely that he is concerned with a typographical *image;* an example is the portrait poem, "so little he is," about Jimmy Savo, whose fluttering hands strewed the stage with bits of paper in gestures extremely birdlike—hence its ending:

                              s:
                               A
                               V
                               o(
                                 .

                                 :

                                 ;

                                 ,

Another example: having written very beautifully about stars, it was not unreasonable of Cummings to conjure one right out of—or into—the heavens, the gradual emergence of the star being the whole poem instead of ornament for another kind of occasion:

> brIght
>
> bRight s??? big
> (soft)
>
> soft near calm
> (Bright)
> calm st?? holy
>
> (soft briGht deep)
> yeS near sta? calm star big yEs
> alone
> (wHo
>
> Yes
> near deep whO big alone soft near
> deep calm deep
> ????Ht ?????T)
> Who(holy alone)holy(alone holy)alone

He even spells it out: *????Ht* to *?????T* (bright) and *s???, st??, sta?,* finally *star*—"big alone soft near." It was a stroke of genius for Cummings to choose a question mark from the typographical units available, since it is a physical metaphor, so to speak, shaped like the filament in a lamp, and by gradual combination made to glow. I would not labor the point if others had not belabored the poem.

Cummings is really closer to the Symbolists who, in a laudable desire to strip poetry of verbiage, projected at length pure metaphor without connecting appliances. An example is his early poem:

> of evident invisibles
> exquisite the hovering
>
> at the dark portals
>
> of hurt girl eyes
>
> sincere with wonder

> a poise a wounding
> a beautiful suppression
>
> the accurate boy mouth
>
> now droops the faun head
>
> now the intimate flower dreams
>
> of parted lips
> dim upon the syrinx

Whatever clue may be needed is provided in the last word which, in fact, once served as the title.

But Cummings's use of Symbolist methods quickly went further. His outstanding contribution is metaphor and simultaneity—plus, of course, music. In "cruelly, love," from *XLI Poems,* this combination results in a masterpiece. Here, his invention encompasses divergent aspects of a single situation; all the strands of a mood, perhaps the deepest a poet can feel, are brought together, and single words—an example is "winter"—are made to serve the structure of the poem with all the weight of stanzas, as though the poet stood at a crossroads leading to simultaneous seasons:

> cruelly, love
> walk the autumn long;
> the last flower in whose hair,
> thy lips are cold with songs
>
> for which is
> first to wither, to pass?
> shallowness of sunlight
> falls and, cruelly,
> across the grass
> Comes the
> moon
>
> love, walk the
> autumn
> love, for the last
> flower in the hair withers;

thy hair is acold with
dreams,
love thou art frail

—walk the longness of autumn
smile dustily to the people,
for winter
who crookedly care.

Cummings constructs an edifice of lines which are his steel and
concrete, then walls his building with music. His poems offer few
difficulties when read aloud, either to the reader or to the listener.
This achievement is quite different from pictures formed out of type
or calligraphy. Not only the baroque poets, but Lewis Carroll did it
before Apollinaire, and the Greeks did it before Lewis Carroll and
the baroque poets. But Cummings was the first to introduce and develop those structural elements on the printed page which act as doors
and passageways to ultimate effects. A simple test is to take any of his
poems and note how his lines and divisions of lines help to establish
meaning and accent as well as movement. In this respect, he is an
innovator.

Cummings's view differs from mine. He wrote me after reading
the foregoing: "from my standpoint, not EEC but EP is the authentic
'innovator'; the true trailblazer of an epoch." Pound is assuredly "the
true trailblazer," but this has nothing to do with the effects achieved
by Cummings independently of him. Pound, incidentally, agrees with
me. He wrote me (November 20, 1957): "I do not think Mr. Cummings is indebted to me for any of the brilliance of his style, which is
intensely personal."

3

In the June issue, Cummings reviewed Eliot's *Poems,* published that year. He unerringly chose not only the poems that were to
become so familiar, but revealed Eliot's method. He wrote:

"Between the negative and flabby and ponderous and little bellow-
ings of those multitudinous contemporaries who are obstinately always 'unconventional' or else 'modern' at the expense of being (what
is most difficult) alive, Mr. T. S. Eliot inserts the positive and deep
beauty of his skilful and immediate violins. . . . Some Notes on the

Blank Verse of Christopher Marlowe are, to a student of Mr. T. S., unnecessarily illuminating:

> '. . . this style which secures its emphasis by always hesi-
> tating on the edge of caricature at the right moment . . .
> '. . . this intense and serious and indubitably great poetry,
> which, like some great painting and sculpture, attains its
> effects by something not unlike caricature.'

Even without this somewhat mighty hint, this something which for all its slipperyness is after all a door-knob to be grasped by anyone who wishes to enter the 'some great' Art-Parlours, ourselves might have constructed a possibly logical development from Preludes and Rhapsody on a Windy Night along J. Alfred and Portrait up the two Sweeneys to let us say The Hippopotamus."

He praises Eliot's technique, explaining: "By technique we do not mean a great many things, including: anything static, a school, a noun, a slogan, a formula, These Three For Instant Beauty, Ars Est Celare, Hasn't Scratched Yet, Professor Woodbury, Grape Nuts. By technique we do mean one thing: the alert hatred of normality which, through the lips of a tactile and cohesive adventure, asserts that no-body in general and some one in particular is incorrigibly and actually alive. This some one is, it would seem, the extremely great artist: or, he who prefers above everything and within everything the unique dimension of intensity, which it amuses him to substitute in us for the comforting and comfortable furniture of reality. If we examine the means through which this substitution is allowed by Mr. Eliot to hap-pen in his reader, we find that they include: a vocabulary almost brutally tuned to attain distinctness; an extraordinarily tight orches-tration of the shapes of sound; the delicate and careful murderings—almost invariably interpreted, internally as well as terminally, through near-rhyme and rhyme—of established tempos by oral rhythms."

This was high and exact praise, delivered when it counted, and in a medium in which everyone wanted to appear. But two years later Cummings had other views, according to Malcolm Cowley, who wrote in Exile's Return: "When The Waste Land appeared, complete with notes [it had been published in The Dial without them], E. E. Cum-mings asked me why Eliot couldn't write his own lines instead of borrowing from dead poets. In his remarks I sensed a feeling almost of betrayal."

"Betrayal" seems an odd word and may reflect more accurately the feeling of shock with which Cowley and other young poets interpreted the poem. He wrote:

"The seven-page appendix to *The Waste Land,* in which Eliot paraded his scholarship and explained the Elizabethan or Italian sources of what had seemed to be his most personal phrases, was a painful dose for us to swallow. But the truth was that the poet had not changed so much as his younger readers. We were becoming less preoccupied with technique and were looking for poems that portrayed our own picture of the world. As for the question proposed to us by Eliot, whether the values of past ages were superior or inferior to present values, we could bring no objective evidence to bear on it. Values are created by living men." But Eliot was a living man; and, as Cowley points out, he "was saying that the present was inferior to the past" and "we were excited by the adventure of living in the present."

Not all of the young poets shared this view. In Paris, John Peale Bishop told Cowley that he had begun to study Italian, "so that he could get the full force of the quotations from Dante." On the other hand, Ernest Hemingway threatened to go to London with a sausage grinder "if I knew that by grinding Mr. Eliot into a fine dry powder and sprinkling that powder over Mr. Conrad's grave Mr. Conrad would shortly appear, looking very annoyed at the forced return, and commence writing." This appeared in the *Transatlantic Review,* edited by Ford Madox Ford.

The June number of *The Dial* also carried "The Fourth Canto" of Ezra Pound, "Gavotte in D Minor" by Amy Lowell, and an appreciation of Rimbaud by "W. C. Blum," in reality James Sibley Watson, who also translated "A Season in Hell," which appeared in July. Cummings did not appear again until the January, 1921, issue in which were published four of his drawings and the 290-line "Puella Mea," the most ambitious love poem of modern times, in which sensual thought and sensuous imagery provide a feast with music. Out of its intricate and vivid orchestration spring these lines:

> Her body is most beauteous
> being for all things amorous
> fashioned very curiously
> of roses and of ivory.

The immaculate crisp head
is such as only certain dead
and careful painters love to use
for their youngest angels (whose
praising bodies in a row
between slow glories fleetly go.)

The poem is also a rhythmic catalogue of his reading, for he compares
his beloved with the ladies of the past about whom other poets and
chroniclers had written:

(Whoso rideth in the tale
of Chaucer knoweth many a pair
of companions blithe and fair;
who to walk with Master Gower
in Confessio doth prefer
shall not lack for beauty there,
nor he that will amaying go
with my lord Boccaccio—
whoso knocketh at the door
of Marie and of Maleore
findeth of ladies goodly store
whose beauty did in nothing err.
If to me there shall appear
than a rose more sweetly known,
more silently than a flower,
my lady naked in her hair—
i for those ladies nothing care
nor any lady dead and gone.)

With this affirmation he proceeds to list and describe his lady's
charms, with a little more frankness than Spenser used on a similar
occasion. "Puella Mea" appeared in *Tulips and Chimneys,* was un-
accountably omitted from the *Collected Poems* of 1938, but is now
back in its proper place in *Poems 1923–1954.*

4

I have mentioned a few of the other contributors to *The Dial*
during the period under review. His friends appeared early in its
pages: Slater Brown, S. Foster Damon, Malcolm Cowley, Edmund

Wilson, John Dos Passos. Gilbert Seldes became an associate editor with the February issue, with a department to himself, "The Theatre." Soon another department was added, conducted by Henry McBride. Called "Modern Forms," it was devoted "to exposition and consideration of the less traditional types of art." The names which are at the heart of the literary Twenties began to be familiar to readers of the magazine: Sherwood Anderson, Djuna Barnes, Edna St. Vincent Millay, Conrad Aiken, Alfred Kreymborg, Marianne Moore, James Stephens, and Ernest Boyd. Yeats contributed an essay entitled "A People's Theatre—A Letter to Lady Gregory," and Louis Untermeyer reviewed ten books of verse in one fell gobble and swoop. More names: H. D., William Carlos Williams, D. H. Lawrence, Padraic Colum, George Moore, Ford Madox Ford, Paul Morand, Joseph Conrad, Anatole France. Important and memorable work appeared: Pound's "H. S. Mauberley," Eliot's "The Possibility of a Poetic Drama," and "Ten Poems" by Yeats, including "The Second Coming." There were also reproductions of the work of Picasso, Vlaminck, Redon, Marin, Stuart Davis and Wyndham Lewis.

In the December, 1921, issue appeared, as frontispiece, "Leda," by the sculptor Gleb Derujinsky. Leda is seated, her right thigh raised. Her back is to the beholder, and the swan, seen only by his grasping wingtips, holds her in strong embrace. I have not seen the original; judging by the photograph in *The Dial* it is a lovely thing. But old Henry Holt, head of the publishing house that still bears his name, was aghast when he saw it. Dr. Watson told me that Holt exclaimed, "Why, it's coitus!" and promptly withdrew his advertising.

In the same issue, among other comment by the editors marking *The Dial's* second year, occurs this sentence: "The Dean of the College of Liberal Arts at the University of North Dakota makes the occasion felicitous by the following letter." The Dean had written:

I have been following *The Dial* for some time with considerable curosity. I can remember when *The Dial* was a distinct credit to American letters, but that day has certainly gone by. Indeed, I am at a loss to know its reason for existence. Perhaps it is to be regarded as a humorous publication. If so, its humor is too dull and gross to merit attention. It is equally a failure if one attempts to take it seriously. Its ethics are rotten, its style is often loose and

inartistic, its illustrations are disgusting. It represents nothing but degeneracy. I shall certainly not recommend it to
any of my students. In fact, I have given orders to have it
stopped at the library as soon as our present subscription
expires.

Yours, with scant respect,
Vernon P. Squires

It is because of this letter that I have listed the more important
contributors to *The Dial* up to that point. And now, more names: A.
E. Coppard, May Sinclair, Kenneth Burke; Ivan Bunin with "The
Gentleman From San Francisco"; Louis Aragon, translated by Seldes;
"More Memories" by Yeats; Hugo von Hofmannsthal, Arthur
Schnitzler, Richard Aldington, Thomas Mann, Stefan Zweig, Kath-
erine Mansfield, Betrand Russell, Van Wyck Brooks, Benedetto Croce,
Roger Fry, David Garnett, Knut Hamsun, Manuel Komroff, Luigi
Pirandello, John Cowper Powys, Llewelyn Powys, Glenway Wescott,
Virginia Woolf, Miguel de Unamuno, Mary M. Colum, E. M.
Forster, H. L. Mencken (on Stephen Crane), Edwin Muir, J. Middle-
ton Murry, George Santayana, Carl Van Vechten, Jules Romains,
Clive Bell, Elie Faure, Maxim Gorki, José Ortega y Gasset, Oswald
Spengler, Siegfried Sassoon, Paul Valéry, Liam Flaherty, John Peale
Bishop. The issues containing their contributions were embellished by
reproductions of work by Picasso, Maillol, Jean Cocteau and Matisse,
among others. Meanwhile, of course, Cummings's work continued to
appear.

To this bill-of-fare for its readers the owners of *The Dial* added a
special dessert for a few of its contributors, an award of $2,000 which,
as they were careful to point out, was not a prize, for it was not to
be competed for, but was for proved merit. In 1922 it went to T. S.
Eliot for *The Waste Land,* in 1924 to Marianne Moore for her
Observations, and in 1925 to E. E. Cummings.

The issue containing the announcement of the award was embellished by three busts by Lachaise—of Cummings, Watson and Thayer
—photographed by Charles Sheeler. There was also a review, by
Marianne Moore, of XLI *Poems* and &, both of which appeared in
1925, the latter privately printed. The announcement, written by
Watson, states:

"*The Dial* Award for 1925 was offered to Edward Estlin Cummings and we are happy to announce that he has accepted it. His

distinguished service to American letters will be obvious to all who have read either his story, *The Enormous Room* (1922), or any of his three books of verse, *Tulips and Chimneys* (1923), XLI *Poems* (1925), and *&* (1925).

"The two books of verse published this year are not as some think, made up of poems written more recently than those of his first volume. With the exception of a few poems written in 1915 and earlier, the whole lot is the result of six years of acute activity, 1917-1923, during which, to use his own expression, he wrote literally 'millions of poems.' *&* does indeed contain more stylistic experiments than the other volumes, but this is due not to any recent development of the poet's, but to the fact that he himself selected the contents of the book. These innovations could mean a great deal to some other poet but are not I think the key to any important change in his own quality or mood.

"Some of the younger writers, the writers under thirty, who may or may not yet be famous, but who belong after all to the only class who will or for that matter can read a new book of poems with insight, have preferred to see a new departure for Mr. Cummings in what they call his satirical verse. In spite of the excellence of some of those satirical poems, notably of the four poems published in *Secession* 1924 [read 1922], nightmares of magnificent caricature, it seems to us that they close an epoch rather than begin one.

"And now let people chuckle all they have a mind to over the solemn way in which we speak of epochs and developments. One learns at school that much poetry called great has been written by very young men. As for the public's 'great poets' they are dead poets—or poets who have lived down to two or three generations. Meanwhile Mr. Cummings is one of this generation's great poets.

"The *Dial Award* therefore finds him when he has finished an epoch, and no matter how much difference it may make to *The Dial* to see no more of this poetry at once over-ripe and with the dangerous beauty of glare ice, it makes very little difference to Mr. Cummings. He has become more and more absorbed in painting. If he has begun writing again by millions no doubt his new millions will be different."

The good blond poet had arrived.

Marianne Moore, who was managing editor at the time of the award to Cummings, told me:

"Winners of the *Dial Award* were supposed to contribute to the issue announcing the award. But instead of a poem, Cummings preferred to publish a painting. He invited me to his Patchin Place studio, on the top floor of No. 4, to help him choose one. It was not a very big piece of work. We let him choose it, he was to like that issue. He was very careful about the reproduction, its proportion and size," she recalled.

She described for me Cummings's rare appearances in her office, "in a light tweed suit, an unequivocal person of convictions. He looked exactly like the Lachaise bust of him." She added: "There was nothing ambiguous or cowardly or vague about his views. And he was very witty; but of course one can deduce that from his verse."

Neither *Tulips and Chimneys* nor XLI *Poems* carried a dedication. & was dedicated to "E. O.," the former Elaine Orr, Cummings's first wife by whom he had one child, a daughter. Her first husband was Scofield Thayer. Stewart Mitchell told me that she had violet eyes and was so breathtakingly lovely that women as well as men, passing her on the street, stopped to look back. Dos Passos wrote: "To romantic youth she seemed the poet's dream. Those of us who weren't in love with Cummings were in love with Elaine."

She lived on Washington Square. Her apartment was a meeting place for Cummings's friends. Dos Passos recalled: "Those New York nights none of us wanted to waste time at the theater when there was a chance that Cummings might go off like a stack of Roman candles after dinner." Cummings's mind, he observed, was "essentially extemporaneous."

"After a couple of brandies on top of the wine," he wrote, "Cummings would deliver himself of geysers of talk. I've never heard anything that remotely approached it. It was comical ironical learned brilliantly colored intricatelycadenced damnably poetic and sometimes just naughty. It was as if he were spouting pages of prose and verse from an unwritten volume. Then suddenly he would go off to Patchin Place to put some of it down" (*The Best Times*).

5

Little remains to be said here of the memorable publication launched in 1920 by Thayer and Watson. To the names already listed I wish to add that of MacKnight Black, a forgotten poet who wrote with precision of the machine age. Other late contributors were Archibald MacLeish, Havelock Ellis, L. A. G. Strong, Gertrude Stein,

John Collier and Louis Zukofsky. Among the artists, there was a self-portrait by Marie Laurencin.

Only two more issues need to be mentioned—that of August, 1927, and the last one. The former had for frontispiece a still-life by Derain and began with Yeats's "Among School-children." It also contained six excerpts from Cummings's play *Him,* to which I have devoted a later chapter. A painting by Cummings embellished his text.

The July, 1929, issue—the last—had for frontispiece "Portrait of the Artist" by Picasso (the "property of Hugo von Hofmannsthal"), a forceful composition of individual and daring brush strokes which are broad, brutal and startlingly effective. The issue led off with "Ten Poems" by D. H. Lawrence. Two of the other contributors were Pound and Aiken. The issue ends with the following "Announcement" by Dr. Watson:

"Nine and a half years is a rather long time for one management in the present journalistic mêlée. On the edge of quitting we want to express our immense gratitude to the distinguished men and women who, with us, have edited and helped edit *The Dial* since 1920. These are: Stewart Mitchell, Gilbert Seldes, Alyse Gregory, Kenneth Burke, Marianne Moore. We are also grateful to our readers, always bearing in mind that although a magazine can get along somehow without readers it cannot exist without contributors—who were, however indignantly, *The Dial*."

Thus did he pay tribute to all concerned in the great publishing venture of the Twenties; and by use of a non-editorial "we" memorialized his absent partner, who retired because of illness in 1926. Dr. Watson now lives in Rochester, New York, where he is head of the Radiology Department of the University of Rochester's School of Medicine.

> Who killed *The Dial?*
> "I," said Joe Gould,
> "With my inimitable style,
> I killed *The Dial.*"

Thus Joe, nasally, on his rounds of Greenwich Village after the magazine's end. He, too, had appeared in it, with an excerpt from the *Oral History.*

Miss Moore afterwards wrote in *Predilections:*

"I think of the compacted pleasantness of those days at 152 West

Thirteenth Street; of the three-story brick building with carpeted stairs, fireplace and white-mantelpiece rooms, business office in the first story front parlor, and in goldleaf block letters, THE DIAL, on the windows to the right of the brownstone steps leading to the front door. There was the flower-crier in summer, with his slowly moving wagon of pansies, petunias, ageratum; of a man with straw-*ber*-ies for sale; or a certain fishman with pushcart-scales, and staccato refrain so unvaryingly imperative, summer or winter, that Kenneth Burke's parenthetic remark comes back to me—'I think if he stopped to sell a fish my heart would skip a beat.' "

In her own quiet way she has conveyed the excitement that was part of the "compacted pleasantness," an excitement generated as much by notable personalities as by notable contributions:

"Ezra Pound's precision as translator of Boris de Schloezer—reinforced by an almost horrendous explicitness on returned proofs. . . . Padraic Colum's clemency and afflatus. . . . And John Cowper Powys, inalienable verbalist and student of strangeness, inventor of the term 'fairy cardinal' for Padraic Colum, seemed himself a supernatural being; so good a Samaritan, any other phase of endowment was almost an overplus. As Mrs. Watson said of his conversation, 'He is so intense, you don't know whether he's talking or listening.' And his brother Llewelyn's dislike of 'a naturalist with an umbrella.' "

From her roll-call I select two more characterizations:

"Gaston Lachaise's stubbornness and naturalness were a work of art above even the most important sculpture. Admitting to an undiminishing sense of burden that made frivolities or time-killings a sort of poison to him, he was as deliberate as if under a spell. I remember his saying with almost primitive tribal moroseness, 'But I believe in a large amount of work'; as on another occasion, 'Cats. I could learn a million of things from cats.' And there was, *when* there was, E. E. Cummings, the really successful avoider of compromise, of scarecrow insincerity, of rubber-stamp hundred-per-cent deadness."

No wonder she was able to write:

"I recall a visiting editor's incredulity when I said, 'To me it's a revel,' after being asked if I did not find reading manuscripts tiresome—manuscripts meaning the requested, the volunteered, and the recommended; that third and sometimes uneasy entrant inducing a wish, not infrequently, that the roles of sponsor and author might be interchanged, as when in a letter of introduction a (Persian, I think) typographic neighbor wrote us, 'In the country where I came from, the people say: "Ham Liyarat, ham Tújarat"—Both pilgrimage and business, and so it is. Miss Z would like to have you see some of her poems.' "

"Miss Z" eludes me; could it have been Marya Zaturenska? The Persian was S. A. Jacobs.

Harry Hansen, in his column, "The First Reader," in the Sunday *World,* May 13, 1928, referred to S. A. Jacobs as "typographer for E. E. Cummings, a position that, I take it, has all the importance and weight of being camera man to Douglas Fairbanks." The occasion was a letter from Jacobs:

> Dear Mr. Hansen: As typographer to E. E. Cummings, let me take issue with the last paragraph of Tuesday's "First Reader," in which you suggested that "the new poetry is going to make life much easier for the printer's apprentice." The typography of Cummings is not a matter of shutting the eyes and dipping into caps or lower case. There is to me a definite reason for everything he does with special values on the page, and there is a concomitant result in that remote and underlying field of aesthetic phenomena—the kinaesthetic. In short, there are elements of empathy, of einfuhling, in the typography of Cummings that cannot be arrived at by a haphazard use or misuse of those spacial elements.
>
> S. A. Jacobs

Such a letter from a typographer suggests the immense change that had taken place in the realm of printing since the Elizabethan period, let us say, when Thomas Nashe lumped all its practitioners in an enduring epithet: "Printers are madde whoresonnes." Mr. Jacobs, it is obvious, was no mere printer. He had been "typographer to E. E. Cummings" for five years at the time he wrote the letter to Hansen, and he was to remain in that post for another twenty.

One of my earliest impressions of him—it was in 1925—is, fittingly enough, against the background of a printing press. It was in a building on Eighth Street. In the room with him and the press were a famous editor, Guy Holt, and a famous bibliographer (and poet), Francesco Bianco. Also present was a young poet with a sheaf of

galleys in his hand. The young poet was rather upset. He had discovered—almost too late—at the end of a stanza, a comma where a
period should have been. The forms were locked, the book ready for
printing. Mr. Jacobs smiled. He produced from somewhere a short-
bladed knife with a round tip. He climbed into the press and almost
disappeared from view. He was gone several minutes and emerged,
unstained and triumphant. In the ink-black jaws of the press he had
found the offending page, he had cut off the tail from the comma, and
had rounded what remained into a period like the others in the book.
Everyone congratulated him.

Mr. Jacobs was

> Deferential, glad to be of use,
> Politic, cautious, and meticulous;
> Full of high sentence—

almost as in Eliot's description of someone else. His name in Persian
was about a yard long—or so I judge from a reference to it in *Time,*
viz.: "Jacobs is loth to give his full name in Persian, admits that part
of it is Samuel Yakob Aivaz Sheraaobode Azerbajode Muradkhan."
He was dark-complexioned, and his skin seemed to glow. He was
of average height, but full-fleshed, with an air of Eastern well-being.
Not a man to lose his temper; gentle, understanding, and imbued
with a passionate loyalty. He was not only Cummings's typographer
—he was Cummings's friend, explainer and defender. It was to him
that interviewers went in the Twenties to learn something about
Cummings.

It seems almost a thing of fate that Jacobs and Cummings should
have formed their triumphal partnership, and formed it so early.
For Jacobs set up Cummings's first book of poems, *Tulips and
Chimneys,* and discovered to his delight, among other beauties in
that book, six poems, under the heading of "Orientale," which must
have awakened racial memories. For these poems might have been
written by a Persian poet—in them are emperors and elephants, in-
cense, fountains, and "a flutter of stars," a queen dancing and the
jealousy of the harem:

> they are
> alone
> he beckons, she rises she
> stands

a moment
in the passion of the fifty
pillars
listening

while the queens of all the
earth writhe upon deep rugs

6

No one seems to know how the manuscript of Cummings's
first book of poems found its publisher. Cummings was abroad when
Thomas Seltzer, the head of a small, distinguished house, accepted
Tulips and Chimneys for publication. Mr. Seltzer is dead, his publishing house long defunct, its records gone. Albert and Charles Boni,
nephews of Seltzer, who took over what remained of his business, and
who became publishers in their own right, have no information on
the subject. Dos Passos wrote me, "It's my recollection that Stewart
Mitchell had something to do with getting the manuscript to
Seltzer."[1] Mr. Mitchell died in 1957 before I could ask him about
this. Dos Passos himself once had the original manuscript in his
possession, and his friend, John Peale Bishop, has left an account
of the excitement he felt when he read it:

"It is impossible for me as I reread the poems of E. E. Cummings
not to recall the emotion with which I first read *Tulips and Chimneys.* Their freshness and grace have not been lost, but to these
qualities there was then added a rare excitement of discovery. This
was early in the summer of 1922; John Dos Passos had loaned me
a copy of the manuscript which Cummings on going abroad had
left in his hands that he might arrange, if he could, for its publication. The following year, Thomas Seltzer was persuaded to bring
out *Tulips and Chimneys,* but only in a much shortened form. About
half the poems I had read in manuscript did not appear in print
until much later and then scattered through volumes which wore
other titles" (review of *Collected Poems* in *The Southern Review*).

[1] Despite Dos Passos's modest disclaimer, it was in fact he who placed the manuscript with Seltzer. Cummings wrote to his sister from Guéthary, France, July 28,
1923: "Dos is a 'lovely gentleman' . . . he is wholly responsible for the bringing out
of my poems by a Mr. Selzer [sic] next fall" (from *Selected Letters,* Harcourt, Brace
& World, Inc., 1969).

In 1924, after selections had been made for XLI *Poems,* published by Lincoln MacVeagh: The Dial Press, Cummings sent Jacobs two lists—of MacVeagh's selections and "my own list (43 poems) of remaining material in the original T & C MS." He added: "On rereading, I was ever so pleased to discover that my most personal work had been carefully omitted by both Thomas&Lincoln. I hope that you will publish this,under your own coatofarms. Nobody else in the world can set what I like best of my own poems—for 1 thing. . . ." A "PS" to this letter declares:

> I haven't,in the least,abandoned idea
> of an eventual publication of the
> original T & C MS as such— . . . . —
> my ancestors are hereditary optimists

In 1925, Jacobs printed, in a limited edition, the volume entitled &, the major portion of which consists of the poems left out of the compilations by Seltzer and MacVeagh, and in 1937 he published the "Archetype Edition" of *Tulips and Chimneys* from the original manuscript.

The Seltzer edition of *Tulips and Chimneys* appeared in 1923. One has only to examine the anthologies of that time, crowded with mediocrities now mercifully forgotten, to perceive the revolution the book wrought. How fresh, how lovely, was the new voice amid the "melancholy trillers":

> the hours rise up putting off stars and it is
> dawn
> into the street of the sky light walks scattering poems

It was a book of enormous surprises. The lower-case "i" and the typographical acrobatics—

> a tall
>
> wind
> is dragging
> the
> sea
>
> with
>
> dream
>
> -S

—were the least of them. In it came to dwell forever "the Cambridge ladies who live in furnished souls"; in it appeared the now much-loved "All in green went my love riding," the (afterwards) much-anthologized "when god lets my body be," and "in Just-spring" with its magical ending. There was also the versification of a master:

> it is the autumn of a year:
> When through the thin air stooped with fear,
> across the harvest whitely peer
> empty of surprise
> death's faultless eyes

Above all, it was the book of a poet dealing from a fresh deck, who offered a way of writing which was peculiarly his own, and which his imitators, who have been legion, have never quite got the knack of; it said only what had to be said, while other poets were "busy stitching images together" (as Edmund Wilson remarked in his review of *Him*):

> into the strenuous briefness
> Life:
> handorgans and April
> darkness, friends
>
> i charge laughing.
> Into the hair-thin tints
> of yellow dawn,
> into the women-coloured twilight
>
> i smilingly
> glide.   I
> into the big vermilion departure
> swim, sayingly;
>
> (Do you think?) the
> i do, world
> is probably made
> of roses & hello:
>
> (of solongs and, ashes)

In the light of contemporary reactions, it is interesting to note that the book opens with a poem—"Epithalamion"—of twenty-one eight-line rhymed stanzas, and ends with seventeen sonnets, including "it may not always be so." The book contains, as well, the long, rhymed and beautifully cadenced "Puella Mea."

7

Matthew Josephson reviewed *Tulips and Chimneys* in the New York *Tribune,* Sunday, November 25, 1923, under the heading "A New Poet." He took cognizance of the fact that "many good people felt seriously outraged, and even scandalized, upon the appearance of Cummings's poems in magazines several years ago." He added that *Tulips and Chimneys* "is the somewhat confined first volume of his poems, selected by his publishers with one troubled eye on the Vice Society. This must be mentioned in fairness to the author, although the book does greatly aid in shaping for us the prodigious hero of 'The Enormous Room.' "

Mr. Josephson gives high praise to "Puella Mea." "Further on," he wrote, "the bizarre, bristling exterior is really incidental to the great values present. I do not claim for his punctuation and typography that they change to any extent the essential possibilities of the language. I can simply venture that Cummings is a fertile and irreverent fellow; out of his great insolence and enthusiasm he is prone to try his 'stunts' in public, nay, in holy places. His penchant for sheer invention leads him into such fine, skillful mischief as this:

> when over my head a
> shooting
> star
> Bur   s
>
> (t
> into a stale shriek
> like an alarm-clock)

"It is interesting to speculate upon where such experiment will lead. I feel that Cummings is simply being clairvoyant in deciding to employ the technique of effective advertising, which hurls phrases and superstitions into your memory like shot."

The book was reviewed by Herbert S. Gorman on the front page of the New York *Times Book Review,* December 9, 1923, under the heading, "Goliath Beats His Poetic Breast, Whilst Critics Gape —Verses From the Left Wing of American Poetry." Two other books of verse were reviewed at the same time—*Birds, Beasts and Flowers,* by D. H. Lawrence, and *After Disillusion,* by Robert L. Wolf. It is from the second of these that the heading came. Both were also published by Seltzer.

Mr. Gorman, after noting there were divergent views in the critical field, wrote: "In the case of Mr. Cummings the answer is in the affirmative. He does write poetry, and often he reaches a high and concentrated pitch of emotion that even his mannerisms cannot hide. . . . There is beauty and melody in the long 'Epithalamion,' which opens the book. The color and movement of the 'Orientales,' which are often so directly based on the biblical Song of Songs of Solomon, are undeniable. The wistfulness and delicate traceries of some of the sonnets should be apparent to even a prejudiced reader. Ignoring those pieces in which the mannerisms are so extreme as to trouble the eyesight, what could be more melodic or charming than his poem entitled 'Of Nicolette'?" He did not care for "Puella Mea."

He found "meat in Mr. Lawrence."

Mr. Wolf had attracted some attention to himself by a sonnet, included in his collection and quoted by Mr. Gorman:

> Goliath beat his breast and curled his beard,
> Disguised his egotism with small i's,
> Wrote free verse for the *Broom,* so I have heard,
> Press-agented himself in every wise.
> One hairy ear cupped in a hairy paw,
> Alert for every veer or passing whim,
> Goliath painted blue his lower jaw—
> It made the editors stare after him.
>
> Colossally he strode, while critics gaped;
> Reluctant artists hurried home, revised
> Their outworn methods, imitated, aped.
> Goliathisms everywhere were prized!
> But David, unsophisticated youth,
> Sat polishing a rounded pebble smooth.

"This sonnet," wrote Mr. Gorman, "obviously refers to Mr. Cummings and, as in most things, there is a measure of truth in it. Still there are times when these hairy giants reform and become respected pillars of the community. And in the case of Mr. Cummings, if anybody takes the trouble to wash the blue paint off his poetic jaw he will discover a rather charming visage that is neither glowering nor repulsive."

Perhaps Wolf saw himself as David. He was a charming and handsome man, very boyish in appearance, and he was married to one of the most beautiful women ever to appear in Greenwich Village—Genevieve Taggard. Miss Taggard wrote better verse than her husband, and her views about Cummings were quite different. It would appear that her influence and Wolf's own good sense and generosity finally made a convert of him. For in the *World* of November 18, 1923, Wolf reviewed Cummings's book.

"As to 'Tulips and Chimneys,' a book of poetry by E. E. Cummings," he wrote, "it is a very disconcerting thing to be compelled to admit, reluctantly, that it is good, that it is extraordinarily good, that it contains, in its own individual and unprecedented style, as beautiful poems as have been written by any present-day poet in the English language.

"When I first read Mr. Cummings's poetry, some years ago, in magazines, it inspired me chiefly with rage and scorn; from which it appears that disgust is a half-way station on the road to admiration, and that only indifference is uncomplimentary and secure. For those of more swift and sensitive penetration this review will be a superfluity."

For those for whom it was not, he explains Cummings's technique and how the poems should be read—"with extreme nimbleness and in almost a mental undertone." He praised "Puella Mea" as the most beautiful poem in this "long and lovely book," and quotes the whole of "in Just-spring."

Miss Taggard reviewed Cummings several times, and always with unstinted admiration and praise. Example: "When reading the poetry of Mr. E. E. Cummings it is the eye that first comes awake. The eye opens, then the ear hears—and somewhere between the streaks of Mr. Jacobs's beautiful type the imagination gets a little drunk. Mr. Cummings is a sensuous poet with an obsession for getting the darling FACT on the page before it entirely wilts" (review of *is* 5, *Tribune Books*).

Mr. Jacobs can also be instructive. Concerning the book, *&*, he wrote me:

> "*and*
>   implies to:
>   OVERTONES, as for example, in
>   TULIPS and CHIMNEYS, where
>   the overtone AND is the
>   basis of the author's technique."

The *Nation*, "Books in Brief," declared (I give the entire review):
"Mr. Cummings is a poet. One deduces that from his language, his observations, and an occasional idea that struggles across his pages. But he is also a pedant. His typography is so perverse that the reader is scared off before he has gone very far. The puzzle of his punctuation is not even an amusing one; it certainly is not worth solving."

Let us see if it is not.

8

Is a poem really "recollected in tranquillity" as Wordsworth held? Perhaps not every poem.

A poem is the culmination of a poet's experience, and is itself part of that experience. Cummings communicates his experience by means of language and forms that *dramatize* it, so that the experience is still taking place so far as the reader is concerned. Andrew Marvell's "To His Coy Mistress" is too well known for me to quote more than a few lines; but I believe these lines will illustrate the difference between a poem that is *read* and a poem that is *happening:*

> An hundred years should go to praise
> Thine eyes and on thy forehead gaze;
> Two hundred to adore each breast,
> But thirty thousand to the rest;
> An age at least to every part,
> And the last age should show your heart.
> For, Lady, you deserve this state,
> Nor would I love at lower rate.
>   But at my back I always hear
> Time's wingèd chariot hurrying near;
> And yonder all before us lie
> Deserts of vast eternity. . . .

And this is Cummings:

> since feeling is first
> who pays any attention
> to the syntax of things
> will never wholly kiss you;
>
> wholly to be a fool
> while Spring is in the world
>
> my blood approves,
> and kisses are a better fate
> than wisdom
> lady i swear by all flowers. Don't cry
> —the best gesture of my brain is less than
> your eyelids' flutter which says
>
> we are for each other: then
> laugh, leaning back in my arms
> for life's not a paragraph
>
> And death i think is no parenthesis

Not to labor the obvious, both poems are addressed to ladies, but while the first lady needs persuading, which demands wit, the second wants reassurance, which calls for feeling. In the second poem, the reader becomes, as it were, a spectator at a lovers' quarrel and hears the reassurance proffered. (In miniature, "since feeling is first" is like the talk of the lovers in the play *Him.*) Marvell wrote "To His Coy Mistress" in his study; but so far as a reader is concerned Cummings is still in the moment he has memorialized. So is his lady. His poem is different from Marvell's, and different from the kind of poem he wrote when he took Marvell's theme and tried persuasion by wit (Shakespeare's Sonnet 19—"Devouring Time blunt thou the lion's paws"—was also in his mind):

> (ponder,darling,these busted statues
> of yon motheaten forum be aware
> notice what hath remained
> —the stone cringes
> clinging to the stone, how obsolete
>
> lips utter their extant smile . . . .
> remark

a few deleted of texture
or meaning monuments and dolls

resist Them Greediest Paws of careful
time all of which is extremely
unimportant) whereas Life

matters if or

when the your- and my-
idle vertical worthless
self unite in a peculiarly
momentary

partnership (to instigate
constructive
            Horizontal
business . . . . even so, let us make haste
—consider well this ruined aqueduct

lady,
which used to lead something into somewhere)

Another example of his dramatization is the poem about a
mouse. The mouse has not come and gone: we are in the room
with the poet and his lady *and the mouse* (whose eyes peer out of
a parenthesis). Abruptly:

here's a little mouse) and
what does he think about, i
wonder as over this
floor (quietly with

bright eyes) drifts (nobody
can tell because
Nobody knows, or why
jerks Here &, here,
gr(oo)ving the room's Silence) this like
a littlest
poem a
(with wee ears and see?

tail frisks)
                        (gonE)
"mouse",
            We are not the same you and

i, since here's a little he
or is
it It
?   (or was something we saw in the mirror)?

therefore we'll kiss; for maybe
what was Disappeared
into ourselves
who   (look).   ,startled

Cummings's love poems are devoid of literary devices, as opposed to technique. Only by an extraordinarily accomplished and controlled technique could he have communicated so much intensity. Everything is fresh, new, and deeply moving:

> i go to this window
>
> just as day dissolves
> when it is twilight (and
> looking up in fear
>
> i see the new moon
> thinner than a hair)
>
> making me feel
> how myself has been coarse and dull
> compared with you . . .

This is the expression of a lover who happens to be a poet; it is not the same thing the other way around.

Twilight and the moon are very important, and appear frequently, in Cummings's poems as do other natural phenomena. Is it because his background is suburban and country? In another poem, twilight hesitates, the moon *emerges,* over the

> street
> where
> you will come,

```
                    at twi li ght
          s(oon & there's
          a                m oo
      )n.
```

Max Eastman wrote in *Enjoyment of Poetry:* "Years ago, before
Mr. Cummings was known as the inventor of the punctuational gym-
nastic, I sat with him and some others in a room where a cat was
purring. In a pause of our conversation—which was a rather chilly
one, he being a poet and I for the moment an editor—he suddenly
exclaimed: 'I have it—it's milking the cow, it's the milk scudding into
the foam in the pail!' The emotional incongruity of this remark to the
prevailing atmosphere was so great that everybody, as I remember,
was a trifle embarrassed. But as a pure matter of auditory sensation it
was so accurate that it remained in my mind—John Stuart Mill to the
contrary notwithstanding—as the sure proof of a poet."

It was logical for Cummings, when he came to write a poem about
a grasshopper, to make it *hop*; it hops out of the first line, grass-end
first:

```
                    r-p-o-p-h-e-s-s-a-g-r
              who
      a)s w(e loo)k
      upnowgath
              PPEGORHRASS
                          eringint(o-
      aThe) :l
              eA
              !p:
      s                                a
              (r
      rIvInG              .gRrEaPsPhOs)
                          to
      rea(be)rran(com)gi(e)ngly
      ,grasshopper;
```

This is the poem that traumatized Stanton A. Coblentz, publisher
of *Wings* and head committeeman for the League for Sanity in Poetry.
"No, we have not here the work of a drunken typesetter," he wrote in
the New York *Times Magazine* in an article on modern poetry entitled "What Are They—Poems or Puzzles?" No, certainly not—it

was by "E. E. Cummings, who has been widely credited with being
one of our leading American poets—the author of 'Is 5,' '&,'
'CIOPW,' '1/20,' '1 x 1' and other volumes." In *Wings* Mr. Coblentz
some years ago inaugurated a new department containing facing pages.
Under the heading of "Not Poetry," there was a quotation from Cummings in almost every issue, which indicates a fixation I leave to others
to define; opposite, under the heading of "This Is Poetry," were
proudly set execrable lines which not only scan but rhyme. But Cummings had the last word long ago, when he ventured to suggest

> that certain ideas gestures
> rhymes, like Gillette Razor Blades
> having been used and reused
> to the mystical moment of dullness emphatically are
> Not To Be Resharpened.

Mr. Coblentz, in the article referred to, concludes that most of the
modern poets are "(1) Sheer exhibitionists, never far from the 'luna-
tic fringe' and never better than literary clowns delighting in verbal
acrobatics. (2) Tricksters who, having found the newer methods to
pay dividends, prefer visible rewards to scruples." As for the first
indictment, I rather like the idea of "literary clowns delighting in
verbal acrobatics"; as for the second, Cummings told me long ago:
"I have been poor a long time but, you know, I have never gotten
used to it."

The truth is he has cared very little whether an audience existed for
him or not. He told me: "The relation of an artist to his audience is
neither positive nor negative. It's at right angles. I'm not writing
'difficult' so that simple people won't understand me. I'm not writing
'difficult' for difficult people to understand. Insofar as I have any conception of my audience, it inhibits me. An audience directs things its
own way."

His resistances are many and, like his language, special. An editor
to whom he sent five poems returned two; Cummings returned the
check and asked for the other three. (The editor used all five.) An
anthologist wrote him:

"If posterity could know your work only by one single brief poem,
what poem of yours would you choose to represent you?"

Cummings replied:

"I do not know nor can I tell what I should care or not care to not have or have per(un)sist but my favorite poem is A Grave by Miss M. Moore."

What Cummings felt like publishing at this time was a drawing of an elephant, and he sent a drawing of an elephant. The anthologist reproduced it and also used Marianne Moore's poem (*Fifty Poets,* edited by William Rose Benét).

9

In addition to his instinct for drama, Cummings magically communicates atmosphere—

> when light fails and this sweet profound
> Paris moves with lovers, two and two
> bound for themselves

—and constantly surprises by the *mot juste*. It is intensity that he is after. I take two examples; one early, one late. The first occurs in the poem which begins

> beyond the brittle towns asleep
> i look where stealing needles of foam
> in the last light
>
> thread the creeping shores

Here, "stealing," "thread," and "creeping" are used with precision; but it is when he selects the word to describe what the sea itself does that he achieves a master stroke—the sea

> *pours* its eyeless miles

In the second, exegesis is superfluous:

> (did you kiss
> a girl with nipples
> like pink thimbles)

He once said to me: "You know, I ought to like Frost. After all, we're both New Englanders. But I've never been able to read him. Why do you like him?" I tried to explain. He said: "I have four or

five collections here; would you read me some of the poems you like?"
He got the books down and I read "My November Guest," the last
stanza of "Reluctance," "To Earthward," and "Acquainted with the
Night." He listened with eyes closed. There was a long pause.
"Would you like to know what *I* think?" he asked. "They lack
intensity."

Cummings continues to experiment with language—the Picasso of
poets—often excitingly, always interestingly, sometimes obscurely.
There is in his work a series of "private" poems which appear cryptic
because they deal with persons unknown to his readers (I include myself). A simpler example of these "private" poems is the one about
Miss Gay, previously cited. Another is such a passage as

                            2 boston
            Dolls;found
            with
            Holes in each other

            's lullaby

No reader not familiar with the sensational "double suicide" of
Harry Crosby and Mrs. Josephine Bigelow might be expected to
understand this nevertheless vivid passage (there is an excellent account of the incident in *Exile's Return*).

Cummings's technical range has enabled him to write both light
and dark, to compress a romance into three minuscule stanzas, as in
"myself, walking in Dragon st," and to achieve the highest degree of
excitement in a poem equally brief (conveyed in part by the extraordinary *caesura* which occurs between the first and second stanzas, in my
opinion one of the most remarkable examples of it in the whole range
of English poetry) :

            no time ago
            or else a life
            walking in the dark
            i met christ

            jesus) my heart
            flopped over
            and lay still
            while he passed(as

> close as i'm to you
> yes closer
> made of nothing
> except loneliness

Cummings wrote this poem after a walk one night. He told me he started up West Tenth Street, and as he neared Greenwich Avenue he saw "a little person who now is dead and who lived by begging." He had known this man well; but now he suddenly saw him as "someone else."

It was Joe Gould.

Chapter 9

THE TWENTIES: PARIS

1

Paris; this April sunset completely utters
utters serenely silently a cathedral
before whose upward lean magnificent face
the streets turn young with rain,

spiral acres of bloated rose
coiled within cobalt miles of sky
yield to and heed
the mauve
              of twilight(who slenderly descends,
daintily carrying in her eyes the dangerous first stars)
people move love hurry in a gently

arriving gloom and
see!(the new moon
fills abruptly with sudden silver
these torn pockets of lame and begging colour)while
there and here the lithe indolent prostitute
Night, argues

with certain houses

Cummings went to Paris in the spring of 1921 and stayed until 1923. He went there in the company of John Dos Passos, who had just received an advance on *Three Soldiers* and was eager to get to Persia. Cummings wrote me: "Dos & I took the diminutive freighter Mormugao from New Bedford(Mass)to Lisboa(Portugal)via the Azores—a 23day voyage—& later wandered up & down & again up Spain;which fascinated me." But not Portugal. As Dos Passos tells it in *The Best Times:*

"I couldn't interest Cummings in Lisbon. A New Englander to the core he was repelled by the rankness of the Manueline style. When I tried to rub his nose in the great panels of Nuno Gonçalves' São Vicente he said he'd rather look at Rembrandt. At Coimbra some ancestral phobia against popery came to the surface. The students all looked to him like plainclothes Jesuits."

Cummings, he relates, "didn't feel himself again until we climbed off the train at the Gare d'Orléans."

It is not surprising. Paris was the foreign city for him, as New York had been and would be for the rest of his life the American one. He never could get enough of Paris:

"Pounds, progress, dollars and morals have assailed and still assail her, but in vain. At any *bistro,* a *bordeaux blanc* is still a *bordeaux blanc* and *un demi* is still *un demi* and *fine* is *fine,* for all the attacks of 'whiskey,' gin, 'pal-al,' and *grog américain*—not to mention the *Ligue Nationale Contre l'Alcoölisme* (*O, mores!*). Albeit employed nightly as an advertisement for Citroën automobiles, that ultra-Freudian symbol which is known as *la tour Eiffel* smites the sunlit heavens as aforetime. A *foire* goes full blast at Porte Vincennes, with its 'toboggan' and its 'steam swings' and its games and shooting galleries and wrestlers and stomach-dancers and bodiless ladies and lion tamers. The *Tout Est Bon* café of *Porte Sainte Denis* still observes the *Tout Va Mieux* café, just across the street, with a scornful smile. At Auteuil and Longchamps there are still hooves and colours. Defying uncounted *films américains,* the ancient and honourable *théâtre du Châtelet* promulgates its honourable and ancient brand of three-dimensional melodrama—the Fratellinis have moved to the *Cirque d'Hiver,* but a *cirque* is still a *cirque* and they are still the Fratellinis. 'Miss' appears in a super-Follies concoction, but still does the sacred Mistinguette stuff—the *Moulins* are all turning. Always the *Jardin du*

Luxembourg has its wooden horses to ride and its tiny ships to sail; and in the Elysian Fields *guignols* twinkle like fireflies. Barges and *bateaux mouches* glide (and will forever glide) through the exquisite river; from which old gentlemen, armed with prodigious poles and preternatural patience, will forever extract microscopic fish. Beneath 'Paree,' beneath the glittering victory of 'civilization,' a careful eye perceives the deep, extraordinary, luminous triumph of Life Itself and of a city founded upon Life—a city called 'Paname,' a heart which throbs always, a spirit which cannot die. The winged monsters of the garden of Cluny do not appear to have heard of 'progress.' The cathedral of Notre Dame does not budge an inch for all the idiocies of this world.

"Meanwhile, spring and summer everywhere openingly arrive.

"Lovers capture the *Bois*.

"In crooked streets young voices cry flowers."

Thus did Cummings pay homage to Paris in poetry and prose, distinguishing between the "Gay Paree" of the tourists and "Paname," *argot* for the inner city. The article from which I have quoted was one of a series he wrote for *Vanity Fair* in the Twenties, of which more later. Meanwhile, there were some things he held onto from his land across the sea:

"Thanks a million times for the K Kats!" he wrote Slater Brown. "The batch which G. Seldes brought over he wanted to put with his own collection, so I let him—keeping the later arrivals myself, as you direct." In another letter to Brown: "thanks much for letters plus immeasurable KK!" A final accolade—thanks "for a Kat of indescribable beauty."

(Years later, when a publisher decided to issue a selection of George Herriman's panels, Cummings was asked to write the Introduction. He wrote it with love, and love is his theme: "A lot of people 'love' because, and a lot of people 'love' although, and a few individuals love. Love is something illimitable; and a lot of people spend their limited lives trying to prevent anything illimitable from happening to them." Not Krazy Kat—she is overwhelmingly in love with Ignatz Mouse, and suffers ecstatically. "She has no fear—even of a mouse.")

He appeared in *Secession* Number Two, July 1922 (Director: Gorham B. Munson, Temporary editorial office: Berlin, Germany) with four poems—"on the Madam's best april the," "(and i imagine," "life hurl my," and "working man with hand so hairy-sturdy," all of which afterwards appeared in *is* 5 (1926). Among the notes about contributors on the inside front cover of the magazine was the following:

> E. E. Cummings. Candidate for the mayoralty of Paris, the present literary capital of America. Indorses *Secession* campaign against Louis Untermeyer, an anthologist best known for the omission of William Carlos Williams and Marianne Moore from his *Modern American Poetry.*

(Williams and Miss Moore were included in the "Third Revised Edition," 1925, as was Cummings.)

In Paris, and in his wanderings around Europe, Cummings followed his usual practice of painting in the daytime and writing at night. On December 28, 1922, he shipped fifty-nine watercolors to Slater Brown, who was then living on the top floor of *The Dial* building (by a coincidence of sorts Hart Crane lived on the top floor of the *Little Review* building). "By all means," he wrote Brown, "send for me to the Pittsburgh or other shows if convenient. Some of the 59 are amusing." He sent them registered but not insured, "with the idea that you won't have to pay duty."

It was during this first of his many sojourns abroad that he met Pound. He thinks it was at the Hotel Meurice, where Scofield Thayer was staying. It was then that Mr. Thayer asked Pound to become the Paris correspondent of *The Dial.*

2

After the "Black Knight," after the "Hell Hole," after the Columbian saloon; after the whispered password in the half-opened door, after the metallic hooch, the needled beer and the bathtub gin, the young men from Prohibition America slaked their thirsts in the open, at the round-topped tables with the carafes and the leaning-tower-of-Pisa saucers, the world in free and pleasant motion around them.

On a spring night in 1923 Cummings, in company with Gilbert Seldes and John Dos Passos, left the Café de la Paix and drove in a fiacre to the Left Bank. In the neighborhood of the rue Gît-le-Coeur, near the Place St. Michel, the fiacre stopped and the men got out. Cummings went to the rear of the fiacre, and Seldes began an oration on the advantages of pantheism over monotheism—how much more imaginative the Greeks were, if only because of this, while modern man has contented himself with only one deity, which showed up his dullness; and so forth. At that moment a gendarme seized Cummings and placed him under arrest.

For many years the story was that Cummings asked the gendarme why he was being arrested, and the gendarme replied, "For pissing on Paris." Cummings pointed out that he had merely pissed on the fiacre. "Le fiacre—c'est Paris!" exclaimed the gendarme, and took him along—Seldes and Dos Passos following.

Dos Passos wrote me:

"Gilbert and EEC and I (was there somebody else? I don't remember) had had one of our long bibulous and conversational dinners and were walking, maybe noisily, through one of the dark little streets near the Place St. Michel when Cummings decided to take a leak in a corner. As I remember it he was set upon by a whole phalanx of gendarmes who carried him off to a *poste de police.* We followed protesting. I tried to get in to argue with the authorities in what I considered my very best French and was thrown out bodily a number of times. C. did some funny drawings of this scene. Gilbert went off to call up his acquaintance Paul Morand who, as a fellow literateur— he was fairly highly placed at the Quai d'Orsay—had Cummings sprung sometime before morning. It was an idiotic but fairly comic incident and much laughed over by all our friends."

Although the incident has its amusing aspects, there was a serious side to it: Cummings, with 1917 in mind, was naturally apprehensive that he would be thrown out of France. The same thought had occurred to his friends—Seldes told me that never in his life had he seen three men become sober so quickly. As he, too, was being ejected, Seldes overheard this colloquy between the arresting gendarme and the officer behind the desk:

"Un Américain qui pisse."

"Quoi—encore un pisseur Américain?"

Cummings told me the dialogue that took place inside.

"Would you do that in your own country?" asked the officer behind the desk.

"Yes," replied Cummings.

"Menteur!" screamed the sergeant of police.

"Why do you call me a liar?" asked Cummings.

"Because I know about America— I have a relative there."

"Where?"

"In Brook-leen."

Cummings was asked where he lived, and a gendarme went outside to check with Seldes and Dos Passos. When it was found that he had told the truth, he was permitted to leave, but with orders to report to a magistrate the next morning. This was alarming. It was then that Seldes decided to enlist Morand. He told Cummings to come by on his way to the magistrate's court, and the three men separated.

Seldes was living in Lewis Galantière's apartment on the Quai de Béthune, Ile St. Louis, where he was writing *The Seven Lively Arts*. When Cummings showed up, he was greeted by several hastily drawn posters announcing, "Reprieve Pisseur Américain!" Seldes had called Morand at the Quai d'Orsay and explained that, whatever happened, it was essential that Cummings be permitted to stay away from the magistrate's court. Morand, although naturally reluctant to involve the Foreign Office in a police matter, gave Seldes his word that it would be arranged.

Burton Rascoe and Stewart Mitchell provide two other glimpses of Cummings at this time. In *We Were Interrupted,* Rascoe has recounted how Ford Madox Ford sent him a *pneumatique* inviting him and his wife to dinner.

"After dinner," he wrote, "we went to a *bal musette* near the Panthéon where Ford introduced us to Nancy Cunard, E. E. Cummings, Robert McAlmon, and a number of other people whose names I did not catch—and to Mrs. Ernest Hemingway. Hemingway was there, but he and Ford were not speaking. Hemingway came up to me and introduced himself. After Ford had asked my wife and me and Mrs. Hemingway to sit at a table with him, Hemingway said to Mrs. Hemingway, 'Pay for your own drinks, do you hear! Don't let him [nodding toward Ford] buy you anything.' "

Here, Rascoe gave the explanation—Hemingway's attack on Eliot in the *Transatlantic Review,* and Ford's apology in print to Eliot, which incensed Hemingway. He had "ceased to speak to Ford, although night after night they met in the same gathering places; and Hadley Hemingway and the Fords remained on good terms."

Stewart Mitchell, on his way to Spain in 1923, called on Cummings in the rue St. André des Arts, and was much struck by a self-portrait, the first Cummings had ever painted. The background of this oil is the tiny room in which Cummings was living. Mitchell told me that when he expressed his admiration, Cummings gave him the portrait, and when he sent a check from Spain to pay for it, Cummings returned the check. Mitchell thought this the best self-portrait Cummings ever made. Back in Boston, he showed it to Dr. Cummings who said:

"Well, Stewart, I'll never be known as anything but the father of my son."

It is now in the Berg Collection.

3

Cummings returned to New York and moved into a studio on the top floor of 4 Patchin Place, which he still uses for his writing and painting, and which his friend Watson had rented to protect the occupant of the adjoining room, John Cowper Powys. One of Cummings's most read, most marked-up books—sentences copied out on flyleaves and underscored on pages—is Powys's *Visions and Revisions: A Book of Literary Devotions.* On the front flyleaf Cummings wrote "truth-joy," and directly beneath is a quotation from Powys: "the truth of truth is not in labor and sorrow, but in joy and happiness." As this is basic in Cummings's philosophy, and as the book itself happens to be smooth and exhilarating reading, I examined it further. It is a collection of essays on writers reflecting Powys's enthusiasms or "devotions," from Rabelais to Dostoievsky, taking in Milton, Lamb, Dickens, Goethe, Shelley and Keats on the way, and two Americans, Poe and Whitman. I choose for quotation a passage from the essay on Shakespeare, which is heavily scored by Cummings:

"No one can read Shakespeare with direct and simple enjoyment without discovering in his plays a quite definite and personal attitude towards life. Shakespeare is no Absolute Divinity, reconciling all oppositions and transcending all limitations. He is not that 'cloud-capped mountain,' too lofty to be scanned, of Matthew Arnold's sonnet. He is a sad and passionate artist, using his bitter experiences to intensify his insight, and playing with his humours and his dreams to soften the sting of that brutish reality which he was doomed to unmask. The best way of indicating the personal mood which emerges as his final attitude is to describe it as that of the *perfectly natural man* confronting the universe. Of course, there is no such 'perfectly natural man,' but he is a legitimate lay-figure, and we all approximate to him at times. The natural man, in his unsophisticated hours, takes the universe at its surface value, neither rejecting the delicate compensations, nor mitigating the cruelty of the grotesque farce. The natural man accepts *what is given.* He swallows the chaotic surprises, the extravagant accidents, the whole fantastic 'pell-mell.' He accepts, too, the traditional pieties of his race, their 'hope against hope,' their gracious ceremonial, their consecration of birth and death. He accepts these, not because he is confident of their 'truth,' but because *they are there*; because they have been there so long, and have interwoven themselves with the chances and changes of the whole dramatic spectacle."

Of the three phrases here italicized, only the third is so printed in Powys's book, the other two having been underlined by Cummings.

Shakespeare, of course, is *the* poet for him. His favorite plays are the great cluster of tragedies—*Antony and Cleopatra, Lear, Hamlet, Macbeth, Othello,* and *Romeo and Juliet.*

"Shakespeare's tragedies never end in gloom—there is always an upward surge, of life to be lived," he said. *Romeo and Juliet* he called "an incredible *tour de force,* the greatest love story ever written." In his notebook he wrote: "Of course Bacon wrote Shakespeare; but so did everybody else, including (luckily) Shakespeare."

4

The expatriates were also returning from their haunts abroad. Back and forth across the sick but for them joyful Continent they had shuttled, strangers in strange lands who had joined the "new race of tourists, the *Valutaschweine,* the parasites of the exchange," as Malcolm Cowley termed them in a new-fangled version of *ubi bene, ibi patria*—

> Following the dollar, ah, following the dollar, I
> learned three fashions of eating with the knife.

On a trip to Vienna Cowley had carried the material for the third issue of *Secession,* now edited by Munson and Matthew Josephson. "Five hundred copies of the magazine could be printed in Vienna for twenty-five dollars." At Imst, in the Austrian Tyrol, he was asked if he knew "Herr Braun von Amerika." Yes, to be sure: William Slater Brown. In Berlin he was met at the station by Josephson and Harold Loeb (Robert Cohn in *The Sun Also Rises*); *Broom* was to be printed there—a dollar bought "two thousand paper marks or an all-wool overcoat."

"Farther than Atlantis is my land," Cowley wrote in his excellent poem,

> but I shall return to it never,
> never shall wed my pale Alaska virgin,
> in thine arms never lie, O Texas Rose.

Nevertheless, he returned, and the others returned, for they were never of Europe—the nostalgia in his poem alone would prove it— they were never really happy, they hankered after ham and eggs, and the checks stopped coming. It was all a frenzy. There were, of course, other kinds of Americans abroad—I remember one, a retired professor from Columbia who, when the franc was falling, never took more than the pre-war exchange and shoved the rest back over the till, as patriotic Frenchmen were doing to bolster the country's gold reserve.

Cowley returned, and Matthew Josephson, and together they resumed publication of *Broom* on West Twelfth Street, William Slater Brown assisting.

Burton Rascoe, the first critic of reputation to hail *The Waste Land* as a great modern work, which he did immediately after its publication and was much belabored for it, published an interview with Josephson in his column, "A Bookman's Daybook," in the New York *Tribune*. Rascoe was a slender, eager (so eager that he seemed at times to be trembling), generous and well-read columnist from Chicago where he had tasted to the full the intoxication of the Midwestern renaissance. Now he had descended on New York, bringing with him his insatiable curiosity about writers and writing. No literary tea, no publisher's cocktail party, was overlooked by him; and he made his daily literary gossip live because to him it was life itself. His columns were liberally sprinkled with names, but it was not mere name dropping, as often the names he dropped were of unknowns. He wrote in his column, Monday, September 17, 1923:

"Matthew Josephson, one of the editors of the modern review,

Broom, came to see me today and was kind enough to explain to me the aesthetic concepts formulated by him and his confrères in what is perhaps the youngest articulate generation.

" 'First of all,' he told me, rather abruptly, 'we are against all the dead lumber which critics like you have been touting. We think that Anatole France, Thomas Hardy, Joseph Conrad, Sherwood Anderson, Sinclair Lewis, Willa Cather, Joseph Hergesheimer, Edna St. Vincent Millay, Elinor Wylie and all these writers voicing a worn-out, conventional, sentimental, romantic despair and disillusion are all bad writers.' "

On this, a tolerant Rascoe commented: "From what I could gather, Mr. Josephson's ideas and aims and the ideas and aims of his confrères are salutary as well as interesting. They have the iconoclasm of youth, and that is the best sign in the world.

"On one point I found it necessary mildly to reprove Mr. Josephson, or at all events to disillusion him. He, like Mr. Seldes, of *The Dial,* has just discovered the comic strip, the American vaudeville, Charlie Chaplin, Al Jolson, Fanny Brice, Eddie Cantor, Joe Cook, Ed Wynn, Paul Whiteman, Ring Lardner and the Ziegfeld Follies, and he thinks, like Mr. Seldes, that this is a brand-new discovery; he is in enthusiastic haste to familiarize the good people of America with these artists through the agency of *Broom,* which has a circulation, I believe, of 1,500. He thinks they have been neglected.

"I reminded him that, far from neglecting these artists, the appreciative American public has for ten years or more so roundly applauded their work and paid good money to enjoy it that some of these artists are millionaires."

At the time Rascoe published this, Seldes was writing his famous book on the Ile St. Louis. A new edition of *The Seven Lively Arts* appeared in 1957.

5

Picasso
you give us Things
which
bulge:grunting lungs pumped full of sharp thick mind

you make us shrill
presents always
shut in the sumptuous screech of
simplicity

(out of the
black unbunged
Something gushes vaguely a squeak of planes
or

between squeals of
Nothing grabbed with circular shrieking tightness
solid screams whisper.)
Lumberman of the Distinct

your brain's
axe only chops hugest inherent
Trees of Ego,from
whose living and biggest

bodies lopped
of every
prettiness

you hew form truly

In 1924, Cummings was again in Paris. In Lewis Galantière's apartment on the Quai de Béthune, talking with him and Louis Aragon, poet and a leader of one of the two Dada factions of Paris, Cummings praised Cocteau's *Les Mariés de la Tour Eiffel;* as he wrote afterwards in *Vanity Fair,* "having been more amused by *Les Mariés* than by anything else in Paris—more, even, than by the police—I entertained a wish to meet the author of this excellent satire." Aragon, "a militant *superrealist* writer and one of the most charming of people," discouraged him. Aragon, in fact, "made several enormous assertions; the smallest of which was, that the renowned poet and author of such novels as *Thomas l'Imposteur, Le Grand Ecart,* etc., etc., did not know how to write French."

(According to Galantière, Aragon attacked, chiefly, the homosexual "tone" of Cocteau's prose.)

"My surprise," Cummings wrote in *Vanity Fair,* "when Aragon uttered this very superrealist statement was by no means negligible;

but I was infinitely more surprised to learn that Jean Cocteau—doubtless overhearing, from the Eiffel Tower radio station, or in some even more obscure manner, those terrible words—had been moved to produce a volume, not of poems, nor yet of prose, but of drawings. My third surprise came when I opened this book and read the first words of the dedication to Picasso: 'Poets don't draw.'

"Cocteau continues: 'They [poets] untie writing and then tie it up again differently. Which is why I allow myself to dedicate to you a few strokes made on blotters, tablecloths and backs of envelopes. Without your advice I'd never have dared to put them together.'

"Judging by this profound and brittle bow to the greatest living draughtsman, and knowing Cocteau's predilection for satire, I anticipated a mass of imitative pretense. And once again I was surprised. For *Desseins* (as this collection of more than 200 of Cocteau's drawings is modestly entitled) reveals itself as a rather lengthy and random concoction of portrait sketches, scenes, caricatures, scrawls, imaginings—or what you will—strictly by a 'poetic ironist' of this day and time, and possessing so much originality that if M. Picasso be to blame for its publication the world owes him a new debt of gratitude."

Here Cummings, taking his cue from Cocteau's drawing, which he termed "the person with the pipe, called *Picasso*," proceeded to describe the Spaniard:

"Nobody, I am sure, will deny one thing: meeting him for the first time, the flesh-and-blood Picasso is a troll who has just sprung out of the ground. He is not a man. Picasso himself, I reiterate, is a troll—tightly made, genial, clinched, eyeful, and moreover (as E. O. once remarked, descending the Elysées with me one fragile and immortal evening) 'with little velvet feet such as dolls *should* have.' Returning now, to what I shall call this portrait of Picasso by Cocteau—let me assure any interested person who has not found him- or herself face to face with the original, that what Cocteau's drawing expresses, first of all, is an uncouth aliveness which Picasso's actual presence emanates. In other words, this sketch apprehends—in a spontaneous, acutely personal way—the tactile stimulus which a glimpse of the Spaniard, creature, or genius, called 'Picasso' involves: the feathery jolt or, so to speak, shock, of confrontation."

He had been taken to Picasso's studio by Seldes; and later met the "troll" chez lui, thanks to Larionov of the Ballet Russe.

His admiration did not last.

One evening, years later, Larionov and Cummings were sitting on the Café Flore terrace. "A few yards away," Cummings recalls, "we noticed an aged louche-looking lump of arrogance, ringed with fawning Villagey acolytes. 'There he is,' Larionov murmured—and I almost dropped my drink. The shock would have been even greater if Picasso hadn't already issued his pronunciamento, 'we know now that art is not truth. Art is a noble game.' When I saw these words," said Cummings, "I felt that the person who wrote them was no longer alive; he was merely undead. But it took a recent all-out supershow at New York City's socalled Museum of Modern soi-disant Art to reveal the erstwhile Satanic Santa Claus of painting as a poor devil of a millionaire, who'd wasted most of his life trying desperately to persuade himself that he wasn't a born illustrator."

On another day, on the Right Bank, at four o'clock in the afternoon, Cummings saw a Communist demonstration. The police broke it up— "50 (fifty) flics for every one (1) communist"—the enormous room in little and in the open:

> 16 heures
> l'Etoile
>
> the communists have fine Eyes
>
> some are young some old none
> look alike

while, on the other hand:

> all the flics are very organically
> arranged
> and their nucleus (composed
> of captains in freshly-creased
> -uniforms with only-just-
> shined buttons
> tidiyum
> before and behind) has a nucleolus:
>
> the Prefect of Police

with the result that

> the
> communists pick
> up themselves friends
> & their hats legs &

arms brush dirt coats
smile looking hands
spit blood teeth

the Communists have(very)fine eyes
(which stroll hither and thither through the
evening in bruised narrow questioning faces)

It will be observed that Cummings pays his compliment typographically, too—that is, with a sudden capital letter. The Left-wing
literati in the United States liked it.

6

Burton Rascoe was indefatigable. In Paris, on a chilly fall
Sunday afternoon in 1924, he and his wife took a train at the Gare
St. Lazare and rode to St. Cloud. As they stood on the ridge of St.
Cloud in thick mist three figures approached and "There you are!"
said a voice in the mist. "We won't take a cab, for the house is
only up the road a step. Mrs. Rascoe, allow me to present Mr. Cum-
mings and Mr. MacLeish. Mr. Rascoe, Mr. MacLeish; you've met
Cummings."

The speaker was Lewis Galantière. He was referring to MacLeish's
house, to which they now set forth, Cummings beside Mrs. Rascoe,
who was suddenly heard remarking, "I like your *lyrical* poetry";
"which," commented her husband, "is like saying to a poet 'I like
your *left* ear' and implying that his right ear leaves much to be
desired."

But when Rascoe came to write an account of this visit in *A Bookman's Daybook* he admitted: "Strange though, she said just what I
feel, though perhaps less felicitously and more directly than I, in my
brashest and most cock-sure mood, should be able to express it. Coming out on the train I had been counting up our lyric poets of the first
order since Poe—Emily Dickinson, yes, on the evidence of two or
three lyrics alone—Sara Teasdale, darn near it, darn near first rank
anyhow, maybe first rank—Edna St. Vincent Millay, absolutely, because she is one of the few poets who have been able to breathe life
into the sonnet since Shakespeare; Arthur Ficke is another, and Cummings! But we'll come to him—.'"

Rascoe came to him after finishing his catalogue: "Wallace Stevens
for a certainty . . . Conrad Aiken, when you excavate . . . T. S. Eliot,

poet-laureate and elegist of the jazz age . . . Ezra Pound, a talent, but has he written more than one lyric (you know, we're talking about lyrics not epigrams after Martial and Catullus, valuable and worthy as they are)? Put him down anyway . . . Comes then who? Sandburg, Bodenheim, Lindsay, Masters, Lowell (Amy), Kreymborg?—let's keep Kreymborg in, if only in memory of the tightening about my heart and the expansion about my head when I heard 'Earth Wisdom' recited for the first time with the accompaniment of the mandolute; the others are among my favorites but they are, as Herbert Gorman would say, cerebral; so let's keep them out of the lyrical group. Robinson, Wheelock. . . .

"Who remains? Who indeed, but the chap we're to meet this afternoon. If there is a lyricist finer since Keats and Swinburne (I include them both), forgetting Yeats, in the English language I wish you would introduce me to him. Uneven? Yes, I grant you! So was God—look at Ben Turpin and the Siamese Twins! Even He is always experimenting and sometimes turning out things more fascinating than tasteful. Even He is more radical and revolutionary and whimsical than that of printing the first person singular with a lower case 'i'—look at His turning out a man like Volstead. Take it all in all, or all in little, Cummings's poetry, the best of it, is beauty like a lark's song or the Ode on a Grecian Urn or any other danged thing you please."

At this point, Rascoe began to soar like his lark:

"I won't argue the case any more. When our myopic literary birchmen finally gutter out in the grease of their own stupidities, when the geoffreys have left their parsonage and all the reeds are broken and the putnams have ceased to put—then milady, my dear lady, America will have discovered that it has some poets and Cummings will be highty-tighty among the lot."

In the MacLeish living-room, in the mansion flamboyantly decorated by an ex-Russian prince for his former mistress, the six Americans conversed. Rascoe has described them: MacLeish, "a clear-eyed, deferential young man, with an extremely Nordic head, quiet manners . . . and a wife who is charming American 'quality' "; Galantière, wearing thick-lensed spectacles and plus-fours; Cummings, sitting by the fire. "His mouth was taut and sullen under a blond toothbrush mustache. His head was thrown back challengingly as always except when he is being courteous to a lady. There was the fire of passionate conviction in his eye." Cummings was about to talk, and Rascoe has done a pretty good job getting it down, all things considered; for Cummings's monologue lasted eight hours.

Cummings (according to Rascoe): "Poets and artists, especially in America, make me sick. What right has such a beggar to take on airs? I have no more interest in or respect for a man because he can write a poem or paint a picture that will hang in the Louvre than I have for a man because he can fix the plumbing or design a beautiful motor car. Crossing the Place de la Concorde this morning I saw a Rolls-Royce car with a body that was a thing of grace, beauty and utility. Someone designed it. Someone who is a genius, an artist, much more an artist than I am, because it is not only a beautiful thing, it runs, and not only does it run, but it is useful and in demand, and the man who designed it can make a living out of his design.

"I am a poet, true enough; but what right have I to be proud of my disease? It's such a shabby, idiotic disease. You know what I want? Money, comfort, love, ease, luxury, the price in my pocket for theatre tickets and good wine. What do I do to go about getting them? I sit up in a shabby room, shivering with the cold, and use my imagination to keep me warm, thinking about the South Sea Islands and the tropical swamps. Your plumber wouldn't do that. He has more sense. He would go out and get some coal and wood to make a fire. He wouldn't sit there and freeze and try to imagine he was warm. I make poems because it is the thing I know how to do best. In fact, it is about the only thing I know how to do. America doesn't want poems badly enough to make it a profitable business to be engaged in. That's America's privilege. If you don't need something you would be a fool to buy it. If a fellow comes to my door and tries to sell me a handmade butter churn, I send him away because I don't need a churn. What do I want with a churn? I haven't any cow or any milk and I buy my butter at the dairy store around the corner. I am in the position of a fellow trying to sell flat-dwellers butter churns which they have no need for.

"But I'd be a fool, a worse fool than I am, if I imagined that I was a superior and precious sort of being because I went around trying to peddle butter churns that nobody wanted. Poets and artists are unfortunate persons trying to capitalize their neuroses. They get a shabby sort of satisfaction out of thinking themselves superior to people who are able to adjust themselves to life. I know, because I used to be that way myself. Since I got hep to myself, I have seen what an ingrown, puny lot poets are. I'd rather listen to a group of paper-box manufacturers talk about their business than to hear poets talk about theirs—the box manufacturers at least know their business from the ground up."

"I have caught here only the gist of it," wrote Rascoe. "The monologue itself was brilliant, elaborated with the most startling images and the most laughable conceits. We roared with laughter."

Mrs. MacLeish suggested dinner "at a little restaurant about a quarter of a mile away. Cummings suggested another round of cognac." When they set forth, Rascoe and Cummings, arms linked, took the middle of the road. Over dinner, Cummings "continued, a coruscating cascade of unrelated or only slightly related images, poetic tags, remembered lines in Greek, French, Latin, German, and English. At one point he convulsed us with a recital of a whole episode from 'Hiawatha,' with a sententiousness which made the banality of that banal poem insupportable."

After quoting Sappho's "Ode to Aphrodite," says Rascoe, Cummings remarked: "Noblest poem, messieurs, noblest poem ever written." He quoted Laforgue, Verlaine, Catullus, Amy Lowell and Shakespeare, and resumed his monologue.

MacLeish told Rascoe: "His memory is astounding. I've heard about Swinburne memorizing and declaiming whole Greek tragedies and Hugo knowing the Iliad by heart and all that. What a bore it must have been to listen to them! I'll bet there was a rush for the exits at the Savage Club whenever Swinburne looked as if he might burst into a recital of Oedipus Rex in the original any moment. But Cummings is different. I have never been so royally entertained in my life. His mood changes. One melts into the other, tenderness into comicality, burlesque into profundity, snatches of Heine alternating with Rimbaud, advertising catch-lines tied up with Catullus and Longfellow. Funny thing—he knows yards and yards of Tennyson and Longfellow by heart."

Monologue, dialogue and dinner came to an end, and the Rascoes, Galantière and Cummings returned to Paris. The hands of the clock in the tower of the Gare St. Lazare semaphored one-thirty. "I was a rag from listening," Rascoe commented; "but Cummings wanted to go somewhere and dance."

"Count me out!" said Galantière. "I have to be at work at nine in the morning. Paris for you fellows is a pleasure resort. For me it's where I earn my living." Galantière was employed by the International Chamber of Commerce, and worked six days a week. He was also translating Cocteau.

They all got into a cab.

"It's funny I never thought of that," said Cummings. "Somehow you never seem to associate Paris and a job. Think of having a job in Paris! What a quaint idea! But having a job anywhere would be a quaint idea for me, least of all in Paris. Did I say an idea? Why, it would be a godsend! Do you know where I can get a job, any little job—in Paris, Andalusia, New York, or Hong Kong? I hereby apply for any little job that may be floating around. All I require of the job is that it shall not be eleemosynary. It must pay me enough for a bed, cognac and cheese—and, oh yes! a ticket fortnightly for the Bal Tabarin and two sous for the vestiare. Vestiares must live. Two sous for the vestiare. That's all I ask."

Rascoe has also recounted, in *We Were Interrupted,* that the night before he left Paris, "Cummings, Galantière, Morris Gilbert, Morris Bishop, my wife, and I had dinner at the Café de Paris and, having consumed much champagne, we made a night of it, going from one bar to another and landing up finally at a restaurant in the market amusingly named *Aux Pères Tranquilles."*

This restaurant, *Au Père Tranquille* (Les Halles), afterwards became the setting for Act III, Scene III, of Cummings's play, *Him.*

7

According to the announcement of the Dial Award for 1925, Cummings had been living in France "for reasons of economy." He now returned to New York, and got a job. It was not, however, one for which he had to report at nine in the morning or six days a week. He began to write for *Vanity Fair,* which left him free to go abroad again. All he remembers about this roving assignment is, "I talked with Frank Crowninshield." It sufficed.

One of his pieces was entitled "How I Do Not Love Italy." He had made three trips there at the time he wrote it. He did not care for it the other times, either. "Shocks, however, cannot discourage really inquisitive people," he wrote. But he begs to opine "(1) that the ceiling of the Sistine Chapel is worth all the rest of *Italia* dead and undead (2) that we love Venice much but that we love Coney

Island more (3) that one small church at San Tomé (Spain), which contains El Greco's *The Burial of Count Orgáz*, houses more aesthetic intensity than does the whole *Galleria degli Uffizi* and (4) that the world is still looking for an unidentified man who disappeared after partially expressing a desire to show us the coliseum by moonlight."

Of the country, he wrote:

"*Italia,* without any doubt the most overestimated country in this world, consists of a peninsula which is shaped like a leg that has been caught in the act of kicking Sicily. This naughty leg, whose chief industries are ruins, religion and automobiles, is technically a monarchy ruled over by a king (S.M. Il Re) but he is actually a pawn in the hands of the *onorevole* Benito Mussolini. The king nevertheless retains two extremely important functions, which are (a) to be photographed with Mussolini and (b) to pose for postage-stamps."

Mussolini, Cummings wrote, "was, just a few years ago, a wicked radical. But one day this wicked radical turned a complete backward somersault and landed an ultra-conservative. Shortly afterward he bought up all the black shirts in sight, hurriedly put a great many young men into them and captured Rome without difficulty. He then informed everybody that *Italia* had been dead for some time and that his program, *il fascismo,* consisted of nothing less than a revivication of the corpse. If *Italia* swallowed the dictatorship pill, Mussolini positively guaranteed that she would rise from the dead and be alive even as she was alive in the days of the Caesars. In other words, she would be alive at the expense of everybody else and would rule the modern world very much as Rome ruled the ancient world.

"After a number of Mussolini's former comrades, the Italian bolsheviks, had been beaten up, compelled to drink castor oil and sent to other planes, the corpse took her medicine and Mussolini was acclaimed as 'Ceasar.' But Mussolini was no ordinary man. He could not possibly be satisfied with being merely Caesar. He also wanted to be Napoleon. This was easily arranged. A photographer 'shot' him in Napoleonic costume, the photograph was printed on thousands of postcards and the postcards were circulated all over *Italia.*"

It is as Napoleon that Mussolini appears in Cummings's play.

Cummings was back in Paris in 1926, when John Carroll made a drawing of him. Cummings kept up a rapid-fire of talk while posing; "he was a witty sonofabitch," said Carroll admiringly. The drawing was transferred to stone and became a lithograph. Everyone wanted a copy. The last of them, Carroll's own copy, is reproduced in this book.

Carroll told me that he drank champagne with Cummings at the Rotonde while Cummings talked about "the significance of WAS" [such was Carroll's recollection after thirty-one years; I suspect IS] and when they tired of the Rotonde they went to a place on the Right Bank where they continued to drink champagne, and finally returned to the Rotonde, but it was "too early for us to be served, the sun was just coming up."

Carroll said "Cummings was painting a lot—he was very interested in painting." He looked surprised over this.

8

It was Morrie Werner who called my attention to Cummings's humorous articles in *Vanity Fair,* many of which appeared under pseudonyms. Werner dwelt with particular pleasure on an article about Edna St. Vincent Millay, a good-natured piece of spoofing which also contained imitations of her verse style. Miss Millay had herself written a series of satirical articles for *Vanity Fair* under a pseudonym. Much of her early poetry had appeared in this magazine and had helped to establish her enormous reputation, and Frank Crowninshield, the editor, was naturally anxious to have her sign her pieces with her own name, offering her more money if she would do so. But this she refused to do. In time, of course, the literary world and many readers knew the true identity of the writer signing herself "Nancy Boyd."

Cummings used several pseudonyms. His piece about Miss Millay, entitled "Helen Whiffletree, American Poetess," was signed "P. H. Dunkels, N. G." and appeared in November, 1925. An editor's note states:

"The unexpected demise of Helen Whiffletree, the American poetess, who was accidentally shot by a *gendarme* while she was picking violets in the *Bois de Boulogne,* has saddened poetry lovers all over the world and deprived *Vanity Fair* of one of its most valued contributors. Wishing to give a slight token of our profound grief at Miss Whiffletree's tragic disappearance from the field of letters, we asked the internationally known authority on literature, Professor P.

H. Dunkels, of Colgate University, to write a brief biographical sketch and appreciation of his illustrious contemporary, Helen Whiffletree. It is our conviction that Professor Dunkels' article, which we publish herewith, is fraught with comfort and happiness for the host of this poetess's admirers, both here and in Europe. They number countless thousands."

Cummings alias Professor Dunkels happily sketches Miss Whiffletree's parentage: "Her mother, Gertrude Magee, was descended from a long line of brewers. Giusseppi Paladini, her father, rose to the position of first assistant dish-washer in the local automat restaurant, but apparently failed to make good." This, enshrined in his first paragraph, triggers the salvo in the last, in which Professor Dunkels describes his first glimpse of Miss Whiffletree, which took place as she alighted from a taxicab in Montmartre: "The poetess (for it was indeed she) was attired in a red tamashanta, a white *cache-nez* and sky-blue pyjamas. True to her ancestry, she carried under one arm the *Decameron* and under the other a nearly empty quart bottle labelled *Hennessy Three Star*."

This is what he wrote about her verse:

"Early in her career, in fact while still in her teens at college, Helen Whiffletree wrote verse in which *naiveté* is carried to a pitch of unheard of poignancy. As an example, I can do no better than quote eight lovely lines which appeared, over the signature 'H. W.', in the literary magazine of her *alma mater,* and which are entitled 'Conversation':

> Quoth a busy bee,
> To a butterfly
> "Honey make I
> And what maketh thee?"
> "Go ask a lily,"
> Was the sage reply
> Of the silly
> Butterfly.

"To this, her collegiate period, belong also such lilting lyrics as 'Sodom and Gomorrah,' 'A Sparrow's Christmas,' 'Under the Mistletoe,' and the inimitable 'Day-Dream'—her first experiment in the Petrarchan sonnet form; which, besides showing the influence of Keats, caused three leading New York critics to compare her to Mrs. Browning, Shakespeare and Sappho, respectively. Readers of *Vanity Fair* will doubtless pardon me for reminding them of the exquisite sextet:

I ope my windows to this April eve,
Letting sweet twilight whisper o'er my soul
Its wondrous secrets without more ado.
Night from day's sentence now doth seek reprieve,
While—from the summit of yon wooded knoll—
A final whippoorwill the ear doth woo.

"Alexander Woollcott is said to have remarked, when the last line was recited to him for the first time by a friend in the course of a camping trip in the Canadian Rockies: 'It hurts, it is so fine.' "

Perhaps Mr. Woollcott remembered this for a later occasion.

Cummings's *Vanity Fair* pieces, whether serious or spoofing, appear now like kaleidoscopic views of the Twenties. His own stance is everywhere expressed.

Item: "That the recent exhibition of abstract sculpture by Ivan Narb proved the big aesthetic event of 1926 is far from surprising—given the overwhelming originality of the sculptor's conceptions and the bewildering variety of the media employed (tin cans, sealing wax, hay wire, candlegrease, birchbark, bottle glass, gingerbread, chewing-gum, etc.), as well as the quite preposterous mastery of his materials which Narb displays at every turn" (from "Ivan Narb: Abstract Sculptor of the Cosmic, by Gwendolyn Orloff").

Item: "From a thousand adjectives which fairly clamour for a chance to describe the Great American Mentality, there immediately stands forth one adjective in which our epoch finds its perfect portrait, in which our civilization sees itself miraculously mirrored, in which the U. S. A. shimmers in all the unmitigated splendour of its great-and-only-ness. This adjective is: infantile" (from "The Tabloid Newspaper"). However, in another of his signed pieces six months later, entitled "Why I like America," he noted: "France has happened more than she is happening, whereas America is happening more than she has happened."

Continuing to report on the American scene, he wrote articles in praise of Coney Island (a "fusion of the circus and the theatre"); about the Aquarium's most distinguished inhabitant, the Penguin; and the zoo: " 'Zoo' originates in that most beautiful of all verbs, *zao*, 'I am alive'—hence a zoo, by its derivation, is not a collection of animals but *a number of ways of being alive"* (and by inference, aspects of ourselves).

In addition to the piece on tabloids, he did one on sex and confession magazines, signing it "John F. Rutter," which sounds suspiciously like John S. Sumner, onetime Secretary of the Society for the Suppression of Vice and the terror of booksellers who had long ago decided—I think in the infancy of the trade—that a little pornography don't hurt none; but Mr. Sumner disagreed, sometimes very efficiently. The byline of the piece—entitled "I Confess!"—is adorned with an asterisk which, when collated below, reveals that Mr. Rutter "was formerly President of the Society for the Contraception of Vice." He discovers the pleasures of sex magazines, if not of sex, and concludes "they are one of the three greatest blessings which our civilization has produced, the other being the player-piano and the radio." Mr. Rutter, in his more militant phase or role, reappears in Cummings's play *Him.*

Cummings wrote for *Vanity Fair* for approximately two years. He also wrote occasional pieces for other magazines. One of these, "Mr. X," appeared in *The Bookman* for September, 1927. It seems, on a rereading, to have suggested, as it preceded, Chaplin's "Modern Times." Mr. X works for Drof, "the greatest industrial genius of the twentieth century." He works in a Wheel Mine. Cummings explains: "If you can imagine wheels, and if you can imagine but, and if you can imagine nothing, then you certainly ought to be able to stand on your head and imagine nothing but wheels; and if you can do that, you can get some idea of what Model Wheel Mines are like. In my opinion, they are like a novel by Mr. Dos Passos, only different." Cummings returned to the subject in his morality, *Santa Claus,* described in "The Poet as Playwright."

Burton Rascoe was editor of *The Bookman* at the time "Mr. X" appeared. He had recently purchased an unfinished story—really the beginning of a novel—by Joseph Conrad (*The Sisters,* found among Conrad's papers) and he decided to ask Ford Madox Ford to complete it. Ford had collaborated with Conrad, and Rascoe saw "a literary coup" if he could "engage Ford to complete the story in the Conrad manner." He wrote in *We Were Interrupted:*

"I was of the belief that Ford knew nothing of the existence of the manuscript of *The Sisters,* but that if I could implant in his mind the idea that *I believed* he did, and that I thought he knew how Conrad intended to develop the story, he would say that of course he knew all about the story and would consent to finish it, or at least tell the *Bookman* readers how Conrad intended to develop it. If I let Ford disclose that he had never heard of the story before I spoke of it, my plan would fall through; Ford could not pretend to know how a Conrad story was to develop if he had never heard of it.

"I phoned Ford at the Brevoort and invited him to lunch, asking him to come to the office of the *Bookman*. Meanwhile E. E. Cummings had dropped in and I not only invited him to lunch with Ford and me but told him my plan and asked his help in carrying it through."

The three men went to Jack & Charlie's where they had cocktails, filet of sole Marguery, "a good dry sauterne," and brandy with coffee. Over the second brandy, Rascoe brought up the subject of the story. He spoke rapidly. "Of course you are familiar with it and know how Conrad meant to develop it. I should like you to finish the story for us or at least tell us what Conrad intended to do with it." Ford said he was familiar with the story and that "Conrad had discussed it thoroughly with him."

Afterwards, while Ford was putting on his topcoat, Cummings whispered to Rascoe: "Good work! He swallowed it hook, line, and sinker." But, Rascoe wrote, "Ford turned in such an interesting and plausible article about Conrad's intentions that I have never been able to decide to this day whether what he wrote is true or imagined."

The three men walked down Fifth Avenue. At Forty-fourth, Ford excused himself and went into the Guaranty Trust Company. "Cummings expressed astonishment to me," Rascoe wrote, "that Ford should have business with the bank. He asked Ford, when he came out, if he had an account there. Ford said, no, he didn't, but that he had once gone there with John Quinn and had discovered that the bank had an *urinoir;* since then he had often used it, because, he said, 'American cities are not so solicitous of man's comfort as Paris is.' Cummings said, It *would* take Ford to find an *urinoir* in a bank on Fifth Avenue and have the courage to use it without having an account there."

Edmund Wilson has given us another glimpse of Cummings in New York at this time. It was in a Village speakeasy, where each had dined alone. Wilson wrote in *The Shores of Light:*

"He stopped at my table, and I asked him where he had spent

the summer. 'I thought of going to Boston,' he ejaculated, 'to see
the machine-guns!—but we've all seen plenty of machine-guns!—
commonest thing in the world!—so I walked around New York, ex-
pecting to be blown up at any moment—be a fine thing to blow the
subways up!—of course, my attitude toward this whole thing—I
mean, it's just unfortunate—it's a bore, like somebody losing his
pants—embarrassing, but it oughtn't be a surprise to anybody—
what surprises me is that they managed to stay alive for seven years!
—why, I've seen them shoot people first and search them afterwards
—and if they've got any bullets in them, they arrest them for carrying
concealed weapons!' He slipped away with his spirited crest of hair
and his narrow self-regarding eyes."

A footnote by Wilson states: "Sacco and Vanzetti had been executed in Boston on August 23, 1927."

Cummings was in Paris again in 1928. His return to the United
States is celebrated in

> myself,walking in Dragon st
> one fine August
> night,i just
> happened to meet
>
> "how do you do" she smiling
> said "thought you
> were earning your living
> or probably dead"
>
> so Jones was murdered by
> a man named Smith and
> we sailed on the
> Leviathan

Cummings's visit to Soviet Russia in 1931 is the subject of a
separate chapter. He went abroad again for most of 1933, much of
1937, part of 1951, and from March 17 to May 19, 1956. On the
last-mentioned trip he went to Spain. It was his second visit. He
wrote Willard Trask from New Hampshire after his return:

> Marion & I almost froze in Europe. But
> we saw Christian idols borne through the
> streets of Cordoba by starlight;& adoring

> pilgrims worshipping El Greco's sublime
> Burial of Count Orgaz at Toledo;& that un-
> imaginable miracle, the Alhambra—not to
> mention Madrid Roma Firenze Venezia Paris.

I had observed over the years that—latterly—whenever he returned from Europe he was more chauvinistic, regionalist even—an
unreconstructed Yankee. Now it was American virtues that he praised,
the New England landscape that he preferred. After the trip to Spain
his pro-Americanism was more evident than ever. It was only by
chance that I learned that part of his feeling of frustration abroad,
that year, was due to the fact that he had missed the blossoming of
the crab-apple tree in Washington Square.

Chapter 10

THE POET AS PLAYWRIGHT

1

"The poet who is both lyrical and dramatic usually turns to drama." Thus Edna St. Vincent Millay to the present writer.

"The best plot is a man," said John Galsworthy, not to the present writer.

Cummings turned to drama in 1927. His play, *Him,* is about a man and a woman. He tells her: "I am an Artist, I am a Man, I am a Failure." He also tells her—and shows the audience—by means of the play he is writing everything else that is of consequence to him: everything that is lowdown and earthy, everything that is lyric and magical; circus, burlesque, and vaudeville; love, and the anarchy and pathos of the modern world. Him, in "reality," gives Me (and you) a thorough self-analysis. But she does not understand, because she feels. The woman Me is at once indefinable, being beautiful and tender; and more commonplace, being the victim of emotions and experiences she cannot share.

> ME: You mean I'm no good to you and that we should
> have ended everything long ago; because—not being in-
> terested in all the ideas you're interested in—it's obvi-
> ously silly of me to pretend.

HIM: To pretend?

ME: —because with part of you I think I'm in love. What can I do?

HIM: Well now let's see . . . here's a bright idea; you can advertise in the Paris edition of the New York Herald for a new lover, thus—"By a freckled fragile petite brunette incapable of loneliness and cooking, wanted: a tall strong handsome blond capable of indigestion and death (signed) Cinderalla Van Winkle."

ME: (*Involuntarily*): Who's she?

The idea for his play must have germinated swiftly in Cummings's mind. He had taken over the theatre department of *The Dial* for two issues, April and May, 1926. In August, 1927, *The Dial* published six scenes from the play, and *Him* appeared the same year.

As a writer on the theatre, Cummings had his own views of what constituted entertainment. Writing in April he gave high praise to the Moscow Art Theatre Musical Studio performances at the Lyric: "as in the case of any authentic experiment, there is not much failure and much invincibility." He criticized "an exhibition of a different sort," the Quinn collection of modern art which "reveals a total absence of Lachaise, many merely fifteenth-rate things, and a fatuous sought negligible unthing by Augustus John, but also a structurally sumptuous irrevocably itself coloured vibration by John Marin." At the conclusion of his article he recommended the National Winter Garden as "a singularly fundamental institution, whose Scratch is a noble clown, whose first wink is worth the struttings of a hundred thousand Barrymores, who are the unmitigated bunk: since the direction of all spectacle lives in Aristophanes and the 'theatre' has a great future behind it, said 'future' being The Circus."

In May, he reviewed three productions—*Little Eyolf,* at the Guild; the International Theatre Exposition "occupying two floors of the Steinway Building"; and the Harry Greb-Tiger Flowers middleweight championship fight at Madison Square Garden. The first had "a more than creditable performance; a performance far more than creditable, or even than excellent, in so far as Clare Eames was concerned." Of the third, he wrote:

"On February 26, '26, in a circus-theatre bulging with incredible thousands of human and nonhuman unbeings and beings, a negro deacon named Tiger Flowers won the middleweight championship of the world. Mr. Flowers (who moves pleasantly, fights cleanly, and plays the violin) said: "Harry stuck his thumb in my eye once, but it may have been an accident for he fought a clean fight after that. The only thing I didn't like was that he used some profane language at times. But I guess he was a little excited.' " (Cummings made an oil painting of the fight, reproduced in *CIOPW*.)

Of the International Theatre Exposition, Cummings quoted with approval from the program note by Friedrich Kiesler, who criticized the contemporary theatre as "a peep-show stage . . . appended to an assembly room. This box owes its form to technical considerations; it is not the result of deliberate artistic purpose."

From Kiesler's note, as quoted in *The Dial*, I take a passage which appears to me to have been significant for Cummings: "The elements of the new dramatic style are still to be worked out. They are not yet classified. Drama, poetry, and scenic formation have no natural milieu. Public, space, and players are artificially assembled. The new aesthetic has not yet attained unity of expression. Communication lasts two hours; the pauses are the social event. We have no contemporary theatre."

So far as Cummings was concerned, the real contemporary theatre was what he had been viewing—unofficially—and writing about for years: burlesque, vaudeville, the circus. From this came his basic concept: a writer for hero—or as Cummings prefers to term him, "nonhero"—who is writing a play in which elements from the "lively arts" would appear. Instead of a "peep-show stage," the static space in which actors act out their roles, Cummings visualized a room for his lovers to converse in which has three visible walls; the fourth is invisible—that is, it faces the audience, although for the occupants of the room it is a real wall, solid and functional. In successive scenes, the room turns clockwise, so that the invisible wall is different each time. For the scenes from the play Him is writing, Cummings utilized either depth or the "flats" of vaudeville and burlesque. The least that can be said for his conception is that he introduced some dynamism to the "peep-show."

I have said that Him shows Me—and the audience—what he believes in; but it is Him seen through the mind of Me, who, when the play opens, is being anaesthetized for an abortion. It is interesting to note that Cummings had made use of a vaudeville device for the scene: "A flat surface on which is painted a DOCTOR anaesthetising a WOMAN. In this picture there are two holes corresponding to the heads of the physician and of the patient, and through these holes protrude the living heads of a man and of a woman." In this crisis of her life Me reviews her relationship with Him, projecting in the ensuing scenes all that has meaning for her lover, but not always for herself.

"A poet sees the metaphor in all things." It is at once his triumph and dilemma. Him reads from his notebook: "I do not stroke edges and I do not feel music but only metaphors. Metaphors are what comfort and astonish us, which are the projected brightness of ourselves—a million metaphors times or divided by a million metaphors constitute a moment or a coatsleeve—here is what we call smells and flavours, the difference between this face and another, god, never, tomorrow, love, yesterday, death or whatever yourself and myself agree to entitle that minute indestructible doll which only the artist possibly may endow with a carefully passionate gesture." She comments: "Maybe you mean something, I don't know."

Cummings, as I have said, is an eavesdropper of speech. As regards English speech, in all its fearful and wonderful manifestations, particularly American, his range is very great. He is a supreme reporter. But unlike Professor Higgins, he is not a snob: he makes no strictures, draws no conclusions. He reports. *Him* projects many of the transmogrifications that have befallen the American language since Samuel Adams told the royal (lieutenant-) governor in Boston: "the night is falling, the country is rising." A poet is also a man, when "he" is not something else, and *Him* is a treasury of tender and lyric utterance.

From Act III, Scene I. Him and Me are seated at opposite ends of the sofa:

> ME: Where I am I think it must be getting dark: I feel that everything is moving and mixing, with everything else.
> HIM: I feel that it's very dark.
> ME: Do you—feel?
> HIM: Terribly dark.
> ME: Are you a little afraid of the dark?
> HIM: I've always been. (*The room darkens rapidly*) May I sit beside you?

ME: If you don't very much mind. (*He does so*)

HIM: A hand. Accurate and incredible.

ME (*to herself*): The dark is so many corners—

HIM: Here life is, moves; faintly. A wrist. The faint throb of blood, precise, miraculous.

ME: (*As before*):—so many dolls, who move—

HIM: Curve. And they talk of dying! The blood delicately descending and ascending: making an arm. Being an arm. The warm flesh, the dim slender flesh filled with life, slenderer than a miracle, frailer.

ME:(*As before*):—by Themselves.

HIM: These are the shoulders through which fell the world. The dangerous shoulders of Eve, in god's entire garden newly strolling. How young they are! They are shy, shyest, birdlike. Not shoulders, but young alert birds. (*The figures of* ME *and* HIM *are almost invisible*)

ME: (*Almost inaudibly*): Darker.

HIM: A distinct throat. Which breathes. A head: small, smaller than a flower. With eyes and with lips. Lips more slender than light; a smile how carefully and slowly made, a smile made entirely of dream. Eyes deeper than Spring. Eyes darker than Spring, more new.

ME (*To herself*): We must go very carefully . . .

HIM: These, these are the further miracles—

ME (*Almost inaudibly*): . . . gradually . . .

HIM: —the breasts. Thighs. The All which is beyond comprehension—the All which is perpetually discovered, yet undiscovered: sexual, sweet. Alive!

ME (*Faintly*): . . . until light. (*Complete darkness. After a few moments her voice whispers with a sort of terror.*)

VOICE OF ME: What are you saying.

VOICE OF HIM (*Subdued, intense, trembling*): Not saying: praying . . . (*The voice hardens*) . . . now I lay you down to not sleep—. (*Silence. Then a scream: the room suddenly opens into total visibility.* ME *stands—terse erect panting—beside the sofa on which* HIM *sprawls.*)

ME: No!

HIM (*Slowly collecting himself rises slowly*): Are you sure? Are you terribly, wonderfully sure?

ME: Sure. Yes. (*A pause. She walks upstage to the mirror.*

He crosses the room to the table; takes and lights a cigarette.)

HIM (*Standing at the window, laughs briefly*): Mademoiselle d'Autrefois, purveyor of mental meanderings and bodily bliss to Ahsh E. M. His Imperial Majesty, the Man in the Mirror!

ME (*At the mirror*): What do you mean.

HIM: I mean——. (*Twirls the match out*)—That you have been the mistress of someone.

ME: Are you terribly, wonderfully sure?

HIM: Of that? Yes. I am sure.

ME: I gave him everything, you mean?

HIM: I mean just that. Once upon a time.

ME: How extraordinary—and who were you, once upon a time?

HIM (*Flicks the ash*): Why do you ask?

ME: Because—shall I tell you?

HIM: If you wish.

ME: The more I remember, the more I am sure it never happened.

HIM (*Simply*): Dead.

ME (*Turning from the mirror, walks toward him slowly*): And now everything changes. And I can distinguish between things. O, I begin to see things very clearly. —You are just as you were.

HIM: I understand less and less.

ME: Do you? It's clear now—can't you see?

HIM: My eyes are very bad today as the blind man said.

ME: That's what he said. (*Stands before him*) And this is what you say: "May I kiss you?"

HIM: I say that to whom? . . . Excuse me; will you have a cigarette?

ME (*Refuses with a curt gesture*): You simply say it.

HIM: I am very dull. . . . May I kiss you?

ME: No. Because I'm not, any more—this isn't me. But somewhere me is, and it would be jealous if you kissed somebody else.

HIM (*Cutting a laugh in two*): "Jealous!" Why not the truth?

ME: You are making a mistake.

HIM: Probably.

ME: There's nobody else. Really: so far as I know.

HIM: I should prefer that you did not lie to me.

ME: Yes?

HIM: I should.

ME (*She looks entirely at him*): I'm not lying.

HIM (*looking intently at her*): No, you're not lying.

ME (*Quietly*): The snow did it, or it was the rain—Something outside of me and you: and we may as well let Something alone. (*She walks toward the sofa*)

HIM: That would be pleasant to believe.

ME (*To herself*): Which moves quietly, when everything is asleep; folding hands . . . I don't know. Shutting flowers I guess, putting toys away. (*She sits, in one corner of the sofa*)

HIM: This is the end?

ME: Do you like to call it that?

HIM: Tell me, what is it, if it isn't the end?

ME: This might be where we begin.

HIM:To begin hurts. (*A pause*) Do you think that this folding and shutting Person, who moves, can take memories away?

ME: No. (*A pause. She smiles.*) —I feel as if we'd never lived: everything is so sure, so queer. (*Another pause*)

HIM: Everything will be queerer perhaps.

ME: Do you think?

HIM: When everything has stopped.

ME. Stopped?

HIM: When I and you are—so to speak—folded, with all our curves and gestures.

ME: —In the earth?

HIM (*Strolls toward the sofa*): Anywhere.

ME: Somewhere, in the Spring, you and I lying . . . together. . . .

HIM: And so exceedingly still.

ME (*Smiles, shaking her head*): No: there'll be things.

HIM (*Sitting opposite her*): Things?

ME: Trees pushing. And little creatures wandering busily in the ground, because everywhere it's Spring. (*Smiles*)

Rebecca Haswell Clarke   Rev. Edward Cummings

The birthplace: 104 Irving Street, Cambridge, Mass. *(Henry W. and Albert A.*
Berg Collection, The New York Public Library, Astor, Lenox and Tilden Foun-
dations)

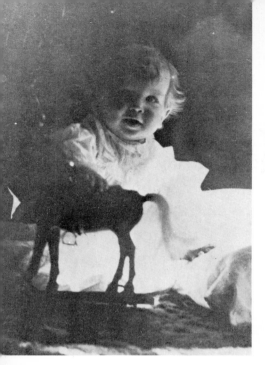

LEFT: Edward Estlin Cummings and toy *(Berg Collection)*. RIGHT: Estlin's tree house, built by Dr. Cummings

ABOVE: A young poet at Joy Farm, photographed by Dr. Cummings *(Berg Collection)*

OPPOSITE BOTTOM: Estlin, with Elizabeth Cummings on Jack, a donkey

BELOW: Dr. Cummings sharpens an ax, audience of one, camera set and placed in position by Dr. Cummings

LEFT: "B" in *The Enormous Room*: William Slater Brown, Paris, 1917, before leaving for Front with Cummings. ABOVE: Pass from Enormous Room to "immortal sunlight"

BELOW LEFT: The soldier, Cambridge, 1918 (*photograph by Dr. Cummings*). RIGHT: E. E. Cummings, Patchin Place, 1925 (*photograph by James Sibley Watson*)

Patchin Place in the Thirties; No. 4 is last house on right looking toward gate (*photograph by Boris Haytin, courtesy of Ethel Haytin Koff*)

BELOW LEFT: Elaine Orr, first wife of the poet. RIGHT: Anne Barton, second wife of the poet

Joe Gould, with notebook of his "Oral History of the World" *(photograph by Boris Haytin, courtesy of Ethel Haytin Koff)*

Anne Barton, Lorna Dietz, Hart Crane at Joy Farm

LEFT: Anne Barton and E. E. Cummings, Silver Lake, summer. RIGHT: Anne Barton and E. E. Cummings, Joy Farm, winter

Sam Ward and wife at Joy Farm—in background, Cummings's 1929 Ford

Cummings's mother,
watercolor by her son

Marion Morehouse and Cummings, Paris, 1937 *(photograph by Gloria Braggiotti)*

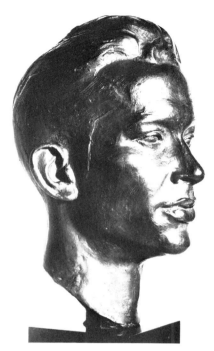

Head of Cummings by Gaston Lachaise,
New York, 1924

BELOW LEFT: Portrait by John Carroll, Paris, 1926 *(lithograph, 10¼ x 7¼ in.)*
RIGHT: Portrait by Hildegarde Watson, Rochester, 1957 *(pencil, 15 x 22 in.)*

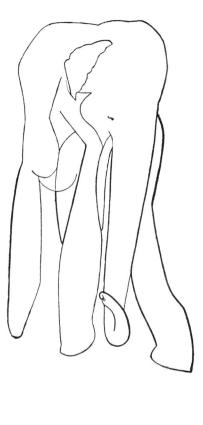

"My own totem is the elephant" *(ink, 19 x 25 in.)*

Portrait of Marion, Tucson, spring, 1946 *(oil, 12 x 16 in.)*

They will go wandering into me and into you, I expect
—roots and creatures and things—but I shan't mind.

HIM: No.

ME (*In a low voice*): If I'm with you.

HIM (*In a low voice*): It will be all gone then; then it will
be too late. Think.

ME: . . . I don't want to think.

HIM: Lips, which touched—at first how lightly! What
were lips distinctly slowly coming against more than
lips; mouths, firmly living upon each other: the focussed
Ourselves (alive proud deep bewildered) approaching
gradually. Nearing, exquisitely and scarcely. Touching.
And then—heartily announced by miles, by years, of
strutting light—the minute instant, the enormous Now.
. . . (*Pauses; smiles*) Only think, dear, of you and of me
gone, like two kites when the string breaks, positively
into nowhere. Shut like umbrellas. Folded like napkins.

ME (*Looking at him and away, speaks softly*): Only think,
dear, that you and I have never been really in love.
Think that I am not a bit the sort of person you think.
Think that you fell in love with someone you invented
—someone who wasn't me at all. Now you are trying to
feel things; but that doesn't work, because the nicest
things happen by themselves. You can't make them
happen. I can't either, but I don't want to. And when
you try to make them happen, you don't really fool yourself and certainly you don't fool me. That's one thing
about me. I'm not clever and I don't try to make things
happen.—Well, you made a mistake about me and I
know that. But the fact is, you know you made a mistake. Everybody knows it. . . . Think what is: think that
you are now talking very beautifully through your hat.

Him was written partly in Paris and "chiefly" in New York City,
Cummings recollects, and adds that "the book was probably published soon after the play had finished itself." The book appeared
October 25, 1927. He says that "whoever wrote a thumbnail-analysis
of *Him* which was printed on the jacket of the book's 1st edition did
an A1 job." On the inside flap of the jacket was printed the now

well-known *Imaginary Dialogue Between an Author and a Public as Imagined by E. E. Cummings:*

> AUTHOR: Well?
> PUBLIC: What is *Him* about?
> AUTHOR: Why ask me? Did I or didn't I make the play?
> PUBLIC: But you surely know what you're making—
> AUTHOR: Beg pardon, Mr. Public; I surely make what I'm knowing.
> PUBLIC: So far as I'm concerned, my very dear sir, nonsense isn't everything in life.
> AUTHOR: And so far as you're concerned "Life" is a verb of two voices—active, to do, and passive, to dream. Others believe doing to be only a kind of dreaming. Still others have discovered (in·a mirror surrounded with mirrors), something harder than silence but softer than falling; the third voice of "life," which believes itself and which cannot mean because it is.
> PUBLIC: Bravo, but are such persons good for anything in particular?
> AUTHOR: They are good for nothing except walking upright in the cordial revelation of the fatal reflexive.
> PUBLIC: And your play is all about one of these persons, Mr. Author?
> AUTHOR: Perhaps. But (let me tell you a secret) I rather hope my play is one of these persons.

Not to be outdone, the publishers, on the back flap, offered *A Statement to a Certain Public by a Certain Publisher* (the "thumbnail analysis"):

"There is good reason for Mr. Cummings's crypticism in his description of HIM. We do not remember any book that more baffles an attempt to describe it.

"You may think you know what to expect in a play by Cummings —and you will find out that you don't know the half of it. Such lucid madness, such adventurous gayety, such graceful irreverence, such abounding novelties—squads of characters firing broadsides of wit—interpolations of American folklore, extravagances that astound the imagination. It is a play that satisfies the five senses, and every corner of the intelligence—a play full of revels for the grown-up mind."

This was written by Isidor Schneider, the poet in the advertising department of Boni & Liveright previously mentioned. The entire back of the jacket was given over to Colonel Lawrence's praise of *The Enormous Room*.

Nothing is so autobiographical as a piece of writing about someone else. I therefore choose to believe that the protagonist of *Him* is E. E. Cummings, *circa* 1927. I also believe that while "ME" could be any woman, she is a particular person, and the central "fact" or "experience" of the play happened to her. But as nothing is so creative as writing about one's self and a friend, as all great poetry proves, the reader of *Him* who is ignorant of Cummings's other books, but not ignorant of poetry, would know the author to be a poet.

The title-page of *Him* carries the following epigraph:

> looking forward into the past or looking
> backward into the future I
> walk on the highest
> hills and
> I laugh
> about
> it
> all
> the way
> ANNE BARTON

Anne Barton was Cummings's second wife. There were no children. Her first husband was Ralph Barton, a famous caricaturist of the Twenties, by whom she had a daughter. It was Edward Pierce Nagle who first brought her to the upstairs studio in Patchin Place to meet Cummings, she told me. She used to bring him bouquets of flowers and paints to paint them; and she also posed for him—his portraits of her are among the most joyous of his creations, and her loveliness glows in them. She was a most beautiful and gallant lady.

2

The most important review, and the most comprehensive, appeared in the *New Republic*. It was by Edmund Wilson. It did what a good review should do—it threw light on the author and his subject. It may be read at large, in revised form, in *The Shores of Light*.

At the other end of the scale was a review headed "Drama in Extremis," by John Hyde Preston. It appeared in the *Saturday Review of Literature*. Mr. Preston was terribly outraged by Cummings's effort; why? He wrote:

> This new play (which is not a play at all, but a mess of formless talk with a not very clear idea behind it) is the *reductio ad absurdum* of his talents and his highly modernistic Symbolism. Cummings knows no more about playwriting than I know about Hungarian wild-flowers; and it evidently pleases him to think comprehensibility is the first of the Seven Deadly Virtues. Take this stage-direction, for example:
>
> > A Plainclothesman, his entire being focussed on something just offstage to the audience's left, stalks this invisible something minutely.
>
> I suppose I am obligated to consider this as delicate comedy; but if I were a stage manager I think I should have some difficulty in explaining to the Plainclothesman just what he is expected to do! Or take this speech (at random) from the text:
>
> > Horseradish will not produce consequences unless cowslips which is unlikely so be not daunted tho' affairs go badly since all will be well. The cards say and the leaves admit that enough is as good as a feast which will cause you some flatulence which you will not mind as long as Gipsy continues to remain a diurnal watering pot but beware of a woman called Metope who is in the pay of Triglyph disguised as either an insurance agent or I forget which it doesn't matter and whenever a stuffed platitude hits you in the exaggerated omphalos respond with a three-fisted aphorism to the precise casazza.
>
> You will have to draw your own conclusions. But if you can make any suggestions as to the possible significance of the foregoing, it may help matters out considerably. I rather fancy that Mr. Cummings, also, would be interested to know what it means. . . .

As for the essential idea (whatever little of it there is here), Calderon treated it, centuries ago, with considerable more intelligence and dramatic force, in *Life is a Dream.* In *Him* life is something of a nightmare, with a quantity of excellent horse-play and large doses of bad taste (*vide* especially Act II, Scene VIII, which is no better than cheap, tenth-rate vulgarity).

So much for the man who once had the promise of an American Keats.

On January 21, 1928, Slater Brown wrote the *Saturday Review of Literature* from Bernardsville, New Jersey:

Mr. John Hyde Preston, who reviews E. E. Cummings's *Him* in a recent issue of the *Review,* confesses with indescribable modesty that he and Mr. Cummings don't know what *Him* is about. A lot of it, Mr. Preston declares, is very, very difficult, and though he can understand all the vulgar parts quite well, there are some passages of 'crazy stuff' that makes his head whirl. Mr. Preston quotes two of these 'crazy' passages, and suggests that he and Mr. Cummings would be grateful if some thoughtful soul would explain them. Perhaps I might be of some help.

The first passage . . . is simply an accurate description of a plainclothesman creeping furtively across the stage toward some invisible objective concealed in the wings. I am sorry I have been unable to paraphrase the passage in words of fewer syllables than Mr. Cummings uses, but if Mr. Preston will look all the hard ones up in the dictionary, I am sure the meaning will be cleared up for him nicely.

[The] second passage, if I remember correctly for I haven't the book here, is uttered by one of the three Fates and is a travesty on the idiom and vocabulary of oracles and fortune telling. If Mr. Preston will read the first act of *Macbeth,* he will find the witches there talking in similar lyrical nonsense. But of course Shakespeare is very enigmatic too.

And by the way, Mr. Preston and I would like to know

what 'Symbolism' as Mr. Preston uses the word in his review, means.

"What are years?" asks a modern poet. Thirty years later, I and
possibly Mr. Brown, perhaps the *Saturday Review,* would like to
know why Mr. Preston dragged in Calderon. Did he ever read *Life
is a Dream*—truly read it? I have just read it, in the translation by
Edward Fitzgerald—not the early version, which does not contain the
"dream," but the later one which does. And I wish to report that
Calderon not only did not treat the theme of *Him* "with considerable
more intelligence and dramatic force"—he simply did not treat it at
all. My friend, Willard R. Trask, read the play in Spanish at my request, and writes: "I don't see any resemblance either." Such are the
risks run by a reader of old—and possibly new—reviews.

A second salvo came from Providence, Rhode Island, from the pen
of S. Foster Damon; it provides an excellent commentary on Mr.
Preston's text:

> Historically, *Him* belongs in the tradition started by
> Strindberg's Dream Play, adapted by Joyce for the Hell
> scene in *Ulysses,* and again remodeled for the *Beggar on
> Horseback* and Dos Passos' unappreciated *Garbage Man;*
> yet so many other elements impinge (Dada and O'Neill, I
> believe), and the auctorial personality is so strong, that the
> result is wholly new. One could discuss the play as another
> manifestation of the Literature of Nerves, established by
> T. S. Eliot's *Waste Land.* But no one of any of these an-
> cestors contains at once the raucous laughter, the realism
> brutal to the height of lyricism, the shameless and unex-
> cused bawdry, the sudden symbolic vistas, and the pro-
> found poignancy of some scenes.

3

Playwriting is a profession in which it is possible to achieve
success without being a writer. That is, it is possible to be a very
successful playwright without being a good writer. Fortunes have been
made in the theatre, and will continue to be made, by men and women who are not even middling good writers, whatever other qualities
they may possess. This is because they and their audiences, and the

critics who are part of their audiences, are not interested in language and the emotion that springs from language when it is literature; they are interested in plot, preferably in three neat servings.

In April, 1928, the following were the plays or "current attractions" that had achieved the longest runs: *The Ladder, The Ivory Door, The Trial of Mary Dugan, Command to Love* and *The Shannons of Broadway.*

This was the situation which confronted Cummings when *Him* was offered for production, and produced. It was not produced on Broadway.

Henry G. Alsberg, an associate director of the Provincetown Playhouse, afterwards National Director of the WPA Writers' Project, told me that he took a number of play scripts with him when he went to Europe in the summer of 1927. Among them was *Him.* When he returned, he said, he told his fellow directors, James Light, M. Eleanor Fitzgerald, and Eugene O'Neill, that "whatever they did or did not produce the next season, *Him* had to be done." (One wonders what O'Neill thought of the take-off on *The Great God Brown* which occurs in Cummings's play.) Cummings, however, dogmatically affirms: "*Him* was only produced by the Provincetown Playhouse because Fitzi(Eleanor Fitzgerald)insisted it should be;she thought 'twas humanitarian;& she sent the Ladies Garment Woikuz down to see. Boy were they bawd!" What is certain, in any case, was that Alsberg had an immediate ally in Miss Fitzgerald; or perhaps it was the other way around.

Neither was blind to the difficulties involved—the script was long, staging presented many problems, and the expense, they foresaw, would be greater than for any previous production. An average of $2,000 had been spent on Provincetown plays, including O'Neill's; *Him* called for an estimated expenditure of $6,000, which was raised; (among the important contributors were Mrs. Harry Payne Whitney, Felix Warburg, and James Sibley Watson). But even this sum, as it turned out, did not suffice, and there was a constant scurrying for more money, chiefly on the part of Miss Fitzgerald.

There were also technical problems.

The play consists of twenty-one scenes. There are 72 roles, not counting "crowds, cripples, beggars, black figures, jazz dancers, shapes," which raised the total cast to an estimated 105. By means of charts which were the joint work of Cummings, Light—who directed the play—and Eugene Fitsch—who designed the sets—it was found that the multitudinous roles could be played by thirty actors. There still remained the problem of scene-shifting. The Provincetown stage had no wings and no overhead flies. As Light recounted later:

"The problem was to rig the stage. Cummings had a designer's sense; by his direction, the room was turned out—a really magical thing."

Cummings repays the compliment:

"Only the ultramagic of Jimmie Light could have persuaded Him's 21 scenes to chase each other smoothly over the infradiminutive Provincetown Playhouse stage."

It was magic, and something more mundane. The cast assisted the stage hands in lowering scenery "flats" through a trap-door to the cellar. The slot through which the scenery was lowered was a narrow one, but finally shifting was down to a flat ten seconds. Alsberg recalls: "The actors · rehearsed scene-changing like a military drill." This work, of course, was in addition to rehearsals, and afterwards to performing. As the Helen Deutsch-Stella Hanau history of the Provincetown states: "Few who saw that production ever realized what thought went into the shifting of scenery." Alsberg told me: "The self-sacrifice of the kids in the cast was something to remember. Some of them were married, most of them were broke; yet no one withdrew, even after salaries were pared down to keep the production going." The actors' budget was "frozen" at length at $800 a week. But emergencies kept occurring. One actor came to Alsberg for an "advance" of $5. Alsberg, who was keeping a tight rein on the purse strings, asked him why he needed the money. "Well, you see, my father died and I need the fare to Philadelphia so I can go to his funeral." He got the $5. Finally, says Alsberg, the production was operating with a deficit of $50 every week, and every week, Miss Fitzgerald—and sometimes Light—went forth to raise it. "When the play closed because of budget difficulties, it closed to full houses," Alsberg said.

It was at first thought that the play would be done in two instalments, on successive evenings. When it was decided that that was not practicable, the suggestion was made that some of the scenes be eliminated. Cummings, however, would not agree to this; he had a reason for the succession of scenes, all of which were important in the projection of Him's character. He agreed to cut; Alsberg thinks that as a result "a few scenes lost something of their richness." Cummings, he recalls, "was around all the time, but didn't interfere with the rehearsals." They all ate in "The Black Knight," the speakeasy across the street from the Provincetown, where Cummings entertained his companions with his talk. He once complained that he couldn't keep it up, that the excitement of the theatre and all the talk was preventing him from getting anything new written; but he found it impossible to stay away.

Light recalls: "When actors wanted a reading of a line, they went to Cummings. They found out more from him than I could ever give them in direction. His greatest characteristic, of course, was his cheerfulness. After the second week of rehearsal, he began to cut the script to tighten it. He's a dramatist—he could see where he had overproved his point, and cut. It was four hours long at the start."

A comparatively unknown actress, Erin O'Brien-Moore, a former model known as "the Benda Girl," from her portraits by W. T. Benda, got the feminine lead. She says that Light was desperate, as all the uptown actresses had turned the role down. She thinks she got $80 a week. She says she suggested a young actor friend, whose name was Franchot Tone, for the male lead; but Light had already decided on William S. Johnstone.

Johnstone was only twenty years old when he was cast for the role of Him. Previous to that he had played as an extra in Theatre Guild productions. Five feet ten and a half inches tall, and weighing only 135, he portrayed the part with an intensity that he now admits he did not always quite understand. He had gray-green eyes, dark brown hair with some gray in it, and a "broken" aquiline nose ("I fell as a child, and the doctor just gave it a twist"). Like Cummings, he is Scotch.

"I read for Light and Cummings," he told me. "I have often wondered why they cast me in the part. I wasn't prepared to meet the challenge of this play. The experiences in it were very foreign to me. I can't say I completely knew what Cummings meant. I was trying to get to know my own part without troubling too much about the play. I guess I was too young to appreciate any of the values. But I soaked up some of Cummings's character to some extent by listening to him. And I began to think in symbols rather than words.

"Light and Cummings were wonderful to me. They were spending as much time with me as they could, taking me to the places where they went and where I listened to them talking. I have never done anything since that has given me quite the same satisfaction as an actor. It required all your concentration. As a consequence, you felt you had accomplished something every time you got through a performance."

I asked him what he thought of Miss O'Brien-Moore. He said: "She was voluptuous, she was sultry; I have no reason to believe she wasn't just right. Maybe she brought out in me the innocence and immaturity that I myself had at that time and that the character of Him felt in his relationship to Me."

I asked him what he thought of the reviews.

"The critics felt the power of it," he told me, "but didn't understand it. It was very depressing, because I would have liked to play the part longer. It wasn't a question of money."

The doctor was played by Lawrence Bolton, who told me that Cummings had given him "long, detailed information" about the part. But sometimes, he confessed, he had to ask himself: "What am I doing here—what is it all about? To this day, frankly, I am baffled." He had eighteen changes of costume in Act I; in Act II he walked on "with all four costumes, one under the other, for quick changing." Nevertheless, "It was a romp."

Cummings wrote me from New Hampshire:

"William Johnstone made a marvellously attractive unhero,& lovely Erin O'Brien-Moore proved an absolutely perfect Me; while the vivid versatilities of Lawrence Bolton as The Doctor more than amazed everyone (including perhaps himself). Let me only add that Lionel Stander's gargantuan impersonation of a Fairy in Act II, Scene 8 brought the house to its ankles."

Stander, croaking swish talk with his concrete-mixer voice amid the short togas, was indeed memorable. Stander was six-foot one, and had played football. He had never acted. He was nineteen. He had just been fired from his job. A minor member of the cast, Stanley Zipser, brought him to the Provincetown during a rehearsal. The rehearsal was going badly—it was the crap-shooting scene with which Act II, Scene VIII opens. The actor rolling the dice did so without conviction; he had never shot craps before. Light kept shouting, "No! No! No!" but the rolling got no better. At this point, Zipser leaned over and whispered to Light that by sheer chance and happenstance "an actor friend" of his was in the house. Stander was introduced.

He told Light: "I am a crap-shooter by training, environment and tradition." He was not lying. He picked up those dice and rolled, and Light said: "The job is yours." But higher things were in store for him: he became the First Fairy. Picture this man speaking *soprano,* for such is the stage direction. When he said, "O dear O dear—I could just cry," there was not a dry eye in the house; it was, in fact, simply divine. Stander afterwards played the role of the poet Maxwell Bodenheim in *The Scoundrel,* the memorable film about Horace Liveright. In this, as in his many Hollywood roles, his voice and his scowl were his fortune.

Zipser, a six-footer, was the Third Fairy. In the second week of the run some deviltry in Stander made him speak a line which had been eliminated by the author during rehearsals. It called for two others. These were the lines (from the printed text) about a recently departed friend:

FIRST FAIRY: How did he die?
THIRD FAIRY (*Proudly, with solemnity*): Choked to death.
FIRST FAIRY (*Rolling up his eyes and clasping his hands murmurs rapturously*): What a b-e-a-u-t-i-f-u-l death!

Miss O'Brien-Moore told me that a great gasp went up from the audience, followed by a storm of laughter. Several front-rowers got up noisily and indignantly, and stalked out; others shushed them down the aisle.

The lines stayed in.

Act II, Scene VIII, is sheer, delicious nonsense; I might have said "pure nonsense," except for its bawdry. Its ingredients are simple and basic:

"The Old Howard's conception of a luxurious Roman villa, columns 'n' everything."

Crap-shooters.

Fairies.

Mussolini caricatured.

A final ingredient: a pun, drawn out and lingering, on the name of a famous and unabashed homosexual comedian, recently struck dead by lightning, an event much discussed at the time, which gave Cummings the opportunity for a happy invention: lightning rods for fairies. The scene opens with two centurions shooting craps in front of the "villa"; an Ethiopian joins the game. Enter two Fairies "in scarlet togas, with lightningrods." The centurions and Ethiopian exit, the latter remarking:

"If daze anything worse dan Christians, it certainly am peddyrasts."

Two more Fairies with lightning rods join the other two, after which trumpets sound, and "enter majestically the onorevole BENITO MUSSOLINI, more or less in the costume of Napoleon and with the traditional pose of that hero—'hands locked behind, As if to balance the prone brow Oppressive with its mind' (Browning)—but also wearing, at the end of a lightningrod, a halo, probably in token of his Christlike role in raising Italia from the dead."

Despite the "honorable" before his name, his costume and his pose, he is as queer as the others.

> VOICE OF HIM: On the whole, how did that scene strike you?
> VOICE OF ME: Not very favourably.
> VOICE OF HIM: Really?
> VOICE OF ME: You can see for yourself how silly it is to try to make a critic out of me.
> VOICE OF HIM: I shall confine myself, however, to stating that your disapproval comes as a surprise; considering the all-pervading atmosphere of inherent spiritual nobility—not to mention the profound, deepspread, underlying religious significance of the thing. Possibly you didn't realize that those lads in the passionate nighties were Ecce Homos: the only lineal descendants of the ancient and honourable house of Savoy?
> VOICE OF ME: I hate history.

Cummings wrote me in reply to my "queery" (his word) anent the lightning rods:

> (1) the great comedian killed by lightning was Bert Savoy; of the Savoy & Brennan team,which appeared in B'way musicals at e.g. The Winter Garden uptown(not the National Winter Garden, 2nd Ave & Houston St).
>
> (2) a favorite fascist slogan in the "onorevole BENITO's" early days was *sempre avanti Savoia* i.e. forever onward(& upward with) the house of Savoy.
>
> (3) Him Act II Scene 8 is thus built on a pun—SAVOY equals (a) Italian royalty,temporarily rescued from soidi-

sant socialism by Mussolini;& (z) the unbelievably hideous incomparably obscene & excruciatingly funny Female (pour ainsi dire) Impersonator Bert S.

(4) that's why the fairies have lightningrods. It's also why Him talking with Me on page 73, describes these "Ecce Homos" as "the only lineal descendants of the ancient and honourable house of Savoy."

(5) But, in my experience, enthusiastic advocates of any form of totalitarianism are inclined to be nothing-if-not-queer, mentally if not otherwise (Henry Wadsworth Longfellow Dana, the Virgil of EIMI, is a good illustration of the otherwise).

There is a good picture of Savoy, female impersonator extraordinary, in Gilbert Seldes's *The Seven Lively Arts*. Savoy is dressed as a demi-monde, one black-slippered foot on a stool, and a froth of petticoat rippling like ocean in a cove. Out of a puffed sleeve one white-gloved hand rests on his hip, the other nestles coquettishly under his chin. A bird on a rakish hat is falling as the sparrow falls, nose downward over his left eye. Only his right can be seen, but that one is all leer stuck in a chubby face on which an eager grin floats lasciviously.

Cummings's attitude toward homosexuals is frankly "against." He simply doesn't like them. For him life is a totality—men, women and children; it is significant that he always writes this phrase as "children, women and men." But this is not to say that he is not often amused by homosexuals, which keeps him from being openly hostile. To a friend who wrote him in alarm from an artists' colony, after finding himself surrounded by men in shorts in vibrant pursuit of the arts and each other, he replied: "let me suggest that you purchase (don't rent) a *made-to-measure* chastitygirdle from your local blacksmith;& be sure to throw away the key when same arrives."

4

Him opened at the Provincetown Playhouse on Wednesday night, April 18, 1928. Copies of the play were on sale in the "lobby." Just before curtain time William C. Johnstone managed to get off a telegram to the author, care of the playhouse:

AS ONE FATHER TO ANOTHER I CLAIM THE HONOR OF
WISHING YOUR OFFSPRING A PROSPEROUS CAREER

To this, Cummings replied (after seeing the show) :

MY PLAY RECIPROCALLY SALUTES YOURSELF BEGGING
THAT YOU WILL ALLOW MYSELF SINCERELY TO CON-
GRATULATE YOU ON ITS HERO

In contrast to other openings, Alsberg says the performance was smooth from the start. Miss O'Brien-Moore told me:

"I felt the first night was right, so I was shocked by the reviews the next day. You got an exaltation from the play. Cummings created a great poignancy without begging for it. And it was the audience that did it; he did not set a trap for them."

In the audience were the drama critics.

The drama critics came to the Provincetown Playhouse, that shabby little place dear to many people not without talent or sensibility, bringing with them the squad-drills of the mind they had learned on Broadway and in the places where Broadway, like the Village, is a way of life. In this they were like the critics of literature, forever bringing something to the work under consideration, instead of being prepared to "take" something from the work which the creator had generously provided. They came in the expectation of seeing something, of which a general concept—three acts, three or four scenes—had stood them in good stead before, and has since, and always will; but they did not come prepared for what was to be offered. They had certain preconceived notions in their minds, and they came prepared only to measure what they were going to see with those notions, not to behold what a new playwright had in *his* mind. They journeyed to Macdougal Street, from their homes and haunts uptown, and after looking at what was offered, they were angry and resentful. But first they were baffled.

Perhaps it was unfortunate that the long handbill, which served for program, and on which both the title and the author's name were printed in lowercase, contained the following note, written by Cummings:

"WARNING: *him* isn't a comedy or a tragedy or a farce or a melo-drama or a revue or an operetta or a moving picture or any other convenient excuse for 'going to the theatre'—in fact, it's a PLAY, so let it PLAY; and because you are here, let it PLAY with you. Let it dart off and beckon to you from the distance, let it tiptoe back and snap its fingers under your nose, let it sweep up at you from below or pounce down on you from above, let it creep cautiously behind you and tap you on the back of the neck, let it go all around and over and under you and inside you and through you. Relax, and give this PLAY a chance to strut its stuff—relax, don't worry because it's not like something else—relax, stop wondering what it's all 'about'— like many strange and familiar things, Life included, this PLAY isn't 'about,' it simply is. Don't try to despise it, let it try to despise you. Don't try to enjoy it, let it try to enjoy you. DON'T TRY TO UNDER-STAND IT, LET IT TRY TO UNDERSTAND YOU."

But strange, strange and pitiful, were the attempts to turn this back on the author and the production. One can only wonder why the effort proved so irresistible to the majority of the drama critics, except that in quoting it, they filled up space which otherwise would have required thought to fill. But I have no wish to be entirely ungenerous, for it should be borne in mind, as I have noted elsewhere, that every-one was young in those days.

Brooks Atkinson wrote in the *Times* the next day:

"Sitting at one of the high stools in an abstract celestial realm, lower case e. e. cummings has written a facetious cerebration entitled 'him' and played with spirit and vertigo at the Provincetown last evening. Apparently (though seeing is no longer believing) mr. cummings is portraying this mundane sphere as it looks to him, or to his central character 'him,' from his microcosm—his exalted, un-qualified state of being. As he explains on the jacket of the neatly printed text, here speaks 'the third voice of "life," which believes it-self and which cannot mean because it is.' To us sensual-minded play-goers, so unaccustomed to abstractions, the frigid chastity of such a metaphysical concept comes devilishly hard.

"But no matter! The program absolves us from blame. At the head of the broadside stares this beneficent proclamation—"

Mr. Atkinson thereupon quotes the program note. Then, turning devilishly easy to the third person, he continues:

"Resolving himself into an ectoplasmic essence the above-named playgoer accordingly drifted off into a state of Nirvana and projected himself across the footlights, hoping to be understood. It was no use. Then, standing up on his seat and bending down, he carefully inspected the play through his legs, but even so the overtones and the nuances of beauty eluded him. For life regarded from mr. cummings's state of being appeared to be (1) the familiar tragedy of the man who had married a dumb wife and (2) a sophomoric burlesque show."

Oddly enough, Mr. Atkinson's review was headed "A Play Misunderstood." I wonder who the deskman was who composed that. Perhaps he had been present at the opening. Be that as it may, Mr. Atkinson had given the Provincetown an opening, and the Provincetown drove on through; for Alsberg immediately inserted an ad in the *Times* which appeared the following Sunday. In it, the third person was transmogrified to the first, so that it now read:

THEN STANDING UP ON MY SEAT AND BENDING DOWN
CAREFULLY I INSPECTED THE PLAY THROUGH MY LEGS.—
ATKINSON, *Times.*

This pleased nobody at the *Times,* including perhaps Mr. Atkinson. In the same issue, Sunday, April 22, appeared a long letter from John Dos Passos, from which I quote the opening and the conclusion:

> Parallel with modernism in painting and with the psychology of Freud in the field of science there has grown up in the half-century since Rimbaud a style of writing that might be called oblique in the sense that it attempts to generate feelings and ideas rather than put them immediately up to the understanding, and direct in that it aims to express sensations rather than to tell about them. People trying to "understand" such writing according to the method of plain narrative are likely to get seized with a sudden panic, to close their eyes tight and say it's all nonsense. . . .
>
> [*Him*] is not built, like a detective story, out of a succession of events hung on the plot like a string. Its method is much more that of a Freudian analysis of a dream. It is the method of a scientist rather than of a story-teller. The tricks by which the successive discoveries are imparted to the audience are the tricks of a review [revue] rather than of a continuously plotted entertainment. How well it is

done, how great a play it is cannot be decided until it is measured with others of its kind. I think, in the Spring of this year 1928, that it's a pretty darn good play. At any rate, it won't do you any good to curse at it for not being like "Broadway."

Meanwhile, the other reviewers were having a field day.

Alexander Woollcott, afterwards excoriated by the management for leaving the theatre before the play was over, sat on the curb outside the Provincetown during an intermission, with his head in his hands, and was excoriated on the spot by Muriel Draper. Mr. Woollcott wrote in the *World* the next day:

"Fatiguing, pretentious and empty, a play called 'him' was unfurled last evening on the patient stage of the Provincetown Playhouse. It is the work of that intermittent poet named E. E. Cummings, who once wrote a war book called 'The Enormous Room'—a malign and fascinating narrative, with curious overtones.

"It was somehow characteristic of his contribution to the drama that the management should have been at such pains to print both the title of the play and the name of the author in lower case type —should, with one bold and splendid gesture, have flung off forever the debasing tyranny of capital letters.

"The author of 'him' is one of those playwrights south of the deadline—cousins to the surgeon who needs no knowledge of anatomy and to the architect who really couldn't be bothered with anything so Victorian as specific gravity.

"I have a suspicion that the author of a piece like 'him' spends a good deal of leisure idly thinking what odds and ends would be nice to have in a play some time and even, on great occasions, jotting them down. Then some fine day someone asks him just once too often how he is getting along with that play he is supposed to be writing, and in a burst of bravado he says it is finished. The next thing he knows it is being taken seriously in Macdougal Street."

At this point, Mr. Woollcott quotes the program note up to "let it go all around and over and under you and inside you and through you." It was, of course, made to order for someone absorbed in his own deathless prose:

"Well, friends, I did just that. I let mr. cummings's drama sit on

my knee and tickle my ear and play paddycakes with me, but the result
was only an inexpressible boredom except for that all too brief interval
when, for reasons which escaped me even at the time, a great many
people seemed to be up there on the stage singing 'Franky and
Johnny' at the top of their lungs.

"That was the only bright moment up to 10:30, when, as second
watch, I was relieved by Alison Smith, who was settling down to let
the piece play peek-a-boo with her as I fled into the night."

Percy Hammond of the *Herald Tribune* was bewildered:

"Consultation with Mr. Nathan, Mr. Mantle, Mr. Winchell and
other keen clairvoyants of the Drama revealed a similar state of
bewilderment, though all of them have studied the play with their
usual thoroughness."

Having studied the play with his usual thoroughness—the
thoroughness with which he was to review *Eimi* before it was published or in galley form—George Jean Nathan wrote in *Judge,* May
12, with keen clairvoyance:

"For utter guff, this Cummings exhibition has never been surpassed
within the memory of the oldest play-reviewer operating in Manhat-
tan. It is incoherent, illiterate, preposterous balderdash, as completely
and unremittingly idiotic as the human mind, when partly sober, can
imagine. The author may be identified as a young man without any
thus far revealed talent of any sort who has sought to attract attention
to himself by composing verse rid of all sense, rhyme and punctuation,
by declining to use capital letters and printing his name in lowercase,
and by confecting a war novel the big kick of which consisted in the
use of a word hitherto more intimately associated with the lavatory
than with literature. Professing to detect genius in these obvious
monkeyshines one or two dubious commentators have spilled some ink
in celebration of Cummings's gifts, but all that the majority of critics
and laymen have been able to detect in him has been a sub-Gertrude
Stein in pants, a ridiculous adolescent in revolt against literary tradition with a hair-pin."

Mr. Nathan, it will have been observed, not only had keen clairvoyance, but was doubly fortunate in having a set of readers equally
gifted, for he has not yet said a word about the play he was reviewing
under the general heading "Judging the Shows." And he said not a
word.

Burns Mantle was too tired from his thorough study of *Him* to write a review of it; readers of the *Daily News* were given, instead, the following news item:

"HIM" IS TRIED
AND FOUND GUILTY

> Continuing its experiment with the weird and unusual drama, the Provincetown theatre last night offered a play in three acts and twenty-one scenes called "Him."
>
> It was written by e e cummings, a lowercase dramatist who would put the blame for the life force and what springs from it upon something, but is still undecided as to what.
>
> This reporter left after the second chukker, remembering Erin O'Brien-Moore as a befuddled but attractive leading woman, William Johnstone as a youth with an amazing memory for words and a colored singer, Goldye Steiner. Miss Steiner sang the Frankie and Johnnie legend with excellent effect.

Walter Winchell wrote in the Evening *Graphic:*

"E. E. Cummings, one of the stylists of the drama and the literary field, provided last evening's puzzle for the Provincetown Playhouse frequenters and the innocent passerby—the critic. The followers of this corner may have suspected already that the author of this report this morning will eagerly read what his confreres have chronicled about last night's preceedings, for it was all incoherent to him.

"Mr. Cummings, who fathered the piece called 'him,' is better known for his tome 'The Enormous Room,' which was inspired by the war, and his contributions to the *Dial.* In the magazine, his specialty was the sort of prose and verse which was not punctuated, and was written on one of those typewriters which had capital-letter trouble. At any rate, Mr. Cummings is said to be popular with the alleged 'thinkers' who enjoy their text in the so-called highbrow manner."

He was, as always, omniscient:

"At the Provincetown, last night, there were frequent outbursts of handclapping approval here and there over a scene or the play-acting. It was not sincere approval, if one may be permitted to pass judgment on audience response, but it was approval."

He remembered the face, but not the name:

"More interesting than the manuscript was the playing of a young woman whose name is difficult to locate in the confusing playbill. She may best be described, however, as a pretty young thing who officiated as the wife of a young playwright-madman."

Erin O'Brien-Moore's name heads the long cast of characters; but Mr. Winchell's eye was concentrated on the author's "WARNING":

"Perhaps the playbill's own confession that *him* is an experiment at incoherency will suffice to keep the reader informed. It follows."

Robert Littell, of the *Evening Post,* quoted from the play:

" 'Anything, Everything, Nothing and Something were looking for eels in a tree, when along came Sleep pushing a wheelbarrow full of green mice.'

"This is a pretty fair sample of Mr. Cummings' attempt, in twenty-one scenes swarming with 107 characters, to chew up *Professional* and Frank Sullivan and Ring Lardner and Mike Gold and Jean Cocteau into one great loony quid and squirt the juice at us. At rare intervals there are brief verbal gleams through the fog, but most of 'him' is tired, willful nonsense, a feverish sort of dramatization of the curlicues people scrawl in telephone booths while they are waiting for a wrong number.

"And every now and then it is exactly like stepping on something extremely nasty in the dark."

Alan Dale wrote in the New York *American:*

"To quote the programme is all that is necessary, and I herewith educe this chuck entitled 'Warning.' "

He educes it.

Gilbert W. Gabriel of the *Evening Sun* devoted his entire column to it.

Variety summed up:

" 'Him' is the most incoherent play ever mounted. Under the mantle of hobohemian art, the Provincetowners are getting away with murder at their converted Macdougal street stable theatre.

"The tip-off on the program sums it up as follows:—

"WARNING"

(and the expected follows).

I asked Lionel Stander what he and the other members of the cast thought of the reviews. He replied: "You must remember we were Villagers and ardent Bohemians. If the uptown critics had praised the play, we would have thought there was something wrong with it."

Despite the general panning, audiences filled the little theatre nightly.

"The Provincetown had again found itself," wrote the historians of the playhouse on Macdougal Street. "Audiences of a new kind were filling the theatre, made up no longer of old ladies who thought the tiny playhouse quaint, or of sightseers and pilgrims to an historic landmark, but of people who were able to select their own plays. The men and women in the lobby looked more sophisticated and amused than any Provincetown audience had looked for years. Students and professors of psychology, esthetics and drama came to see the play not once but three or four times." Light still recalls how "college boys always filled the back rows, from which came gales of laughter over Cummings's classical puns."

One of the college boys was Jacques Barzun. In the "Cummings Number" of the Harvard *Wake* he wrote, eighteen years later: "Those of us whose rich wisdom numbered twenty winters nudged each other and said, 'Here is something.' We went not once, but three times; we disregarded the author's injunction in the multi-typographical handbill and 'interpreted' the play in our undergraduate journals; and we shot barbed arrows over the college walls at the downtown press."

Light told me: "I am very proud of doing this play. The Provincetown was the place for poets. We were off Broadway in two senses—it was located at 133 Macdougal Street, and it was 'off' Broadway spiritually. We gave the bird a chance to sing, and when he sang, we asked for his next work." A new play by Cummings was actually announced.

The two men became good friends. They were encountered together in Sheridan Square on a day in May by the *Daily News* "Inquiring Photographer." He asked them: "What do you consider has been the outstanding accomplishment in President Coolidge's administration?" Their answers appeared with their pictures, Light in a fedora, Cummings bare-headed. Four other men replied:

"His budget reductions."

"The economy regime which the President initiated."

"The progress already made toward flood relief in the Mississippi Valley."

"Giving the soldiers their bonus."

"James Light, Provincetown theatre, stage director: 'Getting away with the oil deal. Much influence, no doubt, was used by those in power to soft-pedal the investigation, so that the Republican party could face the voters at the next election with a clean slate. It was a wonderful piece of political engineering.'

"E. E. Cummings, Patchin pl., playwright: 'The most wonderful thing that President Coolidge did was to confuse the whole country about the true meaning of a simple English sentence. 'I do not choose to run' sounds simple, but nobody in the country except the President knows what it means.' "

5

The critics did not like the play, but audiences did. The late Barrett H. Clark suggested that the Provincetown print a brochure contrasting the favorable reviews of the book by distinguished writers with the hysterical chorus from the drama critics. The 16-page brochure, measuring 6⅛ inches by 3¼ inches, shortly appeared. It was entitled

him AND the

CRITICS

a collection of opinions on

e e cummings' play at the

provincetown playhouse

The typography was by S. A. Jacobs. Gilbert Seldes, who provided the introduction, dedicated the pamphlet to John Anderson, of the *Journal*. "It will perhaps be one of the pleasantest circumstances of the production of 'him,' " he wrote, "that its only illuminating review should have been addressed not to the super- but to the substandard audience, and that no critic addressing an audience supposedly intelligent and sophisticated should have given them one-tenth as accurate an account."

Anderson wrote:

"Since the hero proposes to write a play the middle section of 'him' consists of some rowdy and often hilarious burlesques of the current dramas. Mr. O'Neill, a director of the Provincetown, is kidded cruelly in a sketch on 'The Great God Brown,' the Theatre Guild and the New Playwrights for their negro folk plays, and the Messrs. Shaw and Sherwood for their up-to-the-minute versions of ancient history.

"These scenes are interspersed with devilish episodes showing three old women whamming away in rocking chairs, their backs to the audience, and reeling out the tag ends of stencilled and meaningless conversation—that have been chewed upon all the front porches of the world.

"Hear Mr. Cummings' caricature of their idiocies:

"One woman: 'Four out of five will get wedlock.'

"Another: 'I held my husband up to the light yesterday and saw through him.'

"A third: 'But have you ever tried standing on the third rail?'

"Behind the eloquent delirium of such writing there is fierce sanity flaring out across parts of 'him' and making them memorable. It is vivid, confused and bawdy, with the reckless exuberance of a fantastic imagination, which sees a cockeyed world and tries to set it down to make some sort of scatter-brained sense. It doesn't quite come off. . . . but none of its flaws quite destroy the sharp perceptions behind it, and the quivering intensity of its writing. Some of it, indeed, is lyrically lovely, with a felicity of phrasing that is often superb.

"A huge cast struggled with its cantankerous movements, and tried to compass its capricious moods within the narrow limits of the Provincetown stage.

"Most of it, including speeches of interminable length and incredible variation, fell upon Mr. Johnstone and Miss O'Brien-Moore, who did excellently.

"Though it can have little popular interest, 'him' is a provocative event in the theatre, and if these notes have disobeyed orders and tried to understand the author, I hope he will do them a reciprocal courtesy."

On Monday, April 30, Anderson returned to the subject of *Him* in his column, "Footlights and Spotlights." He wrote:

"I submit, as the only extant attorney for the defense, that it is a shrewd and believable scheme for reducing a 'stream of consciousness' to a dramatic form. In other words, it attempts to do in the theatre what Joyce does in 'Ulysses,' what Virginia Woolf does in 'Mrs. Dalloway' and 'To the Lighthouse,' what O'Neill has partly achieved in 'Strange Interlude.' "

The pamphlet renewed interest in the production at the Provincetown, and audiences continued to fill the little theatre. But the persistent deficit finally closed the play. It had run six weeks. In its announcement of the 1928-1929 season, the Provincetown pointed with pride to O'Neill, Paul Green, Cummings and Virgil Geddes as "aptly illustrating the purpose of the Provincetown Playhouse and its achievement." On December 14, 1929, the Provincetown Playhouse closed its doors forever.

This, however, was not the end of the theatre, or of *Him*. The old stable continued to be used by other groups; in time it even got air-conditioning, without ridding the place of its familiar musty smell. In 1948 *Him* was again given on its stage.

Erin O'Brien-Moore told me: "I think *Him* was ahead of its time." She added that at the opening of a play by William Saroyan, when her husband, Mark Barron, drama critic of The Associated Press, praised it in enthusiastic terms, she told him: "Cummings did it years before." To me she said: "Saroyan owed a great deal to *Him*. Saroyan was more saccharine; Cummings avoided sweetness and light."

Saroyan wrote me:

"Will you believe I have never read (or seen a production of) E. E. Cummings's *Him*? But let's not pretend his work has not exerted an influence on mine, on that account, for I am willing to believe it has, and maybe I can tell you how. I heard about him (per-haps) before I was twenty. I read around in *The Enormous Room* about that time. Later on I read around in *Eimi*. I read straight through a few of his poems—the ones I ran into in various small and big magazines. From what I read, and from what I heard, I knew he was out there all alone and aloof, and I was grateful. That was how he and his work influenced me and my work. I'm not saying there weren't other influences. There were. A lot of 'em. He didn't influence my early writing for the theatre alone: he had, and has, a share in all of the influencing that went on, and is still going on. Cummings is one of the truly great writers of our time for the reason that he is one of the truly great men of our time—and in my book if a man is both great and knows how to write, he has got to exert an influence on anybody else who is alive at the same time, and not just on others who are great, or not, or who know how to write, or don't."

6

Although the Provincetown, in its 1928-1929 announcement, stated that "E. E. Cummings is now writing his second play," and scheduled it unseen, Cummings did not deliver. It would have been too late, in any case. I do not think that the "critical" reception of

Him had any influence on his theatrical thinking or ambitions, whatever effect it may have had on his feelings at the time. He has worked for many years on a play about Joan of Arc, speeches from which have appeared in various publications.

In 1930, Cummings contributed a short one-act play to a symposium entitled *Whither, Whither.* The play, *Anthropos: The Future of Art,* was afterwards printed in a limited edition by Jacobs at the Golden Eagle Press. The scene is a cave. Three "uncouth infra-human creatures smothered in filthy skins" are conferring around a dying fire. To the right, "a naked man (his back to the trio) is cautiously, with a few crude painting tools, outlining some monster on the upcurving wall before him." While the three creatures are trying out slogans on each other, to indicate progress and civilization, hideous noises rain down on them, including that of planes. The chief noise, "a sequence of rattling gushing hissing rumbling clanking noises repeats itself without interruption." It comes from the modern mastodon, a steam shovel, which is revealed by the cave artist, who draws the curtain aside.

In 1935, Cummings published *Tom,* with a frontispiece by Ben Shahn. The book carries the following dedication, "To Marion Morehouse who suggested that I make a ballet based on 'Uncle Tom's Cabin.'"

Tom is a poetic choreography, a dramatic narrative that can be read as well as used as the basis for a production. George Freedley, curator of the Theatre Collection, New York Public Library, wrote in *Stage Magazine:*

"The knowledgeable quality of his directions for movement will give the proper *régisseur* the keynote of the production. It presents the dancers and actors with a demand that they must strive to meet, for certainly *Tom* is meant to be staged. Marry the American ballet to the inspired group of Negroes who made *Four Saints in Three Acts* a minor masterpiece. Then add a full symphony orchestra, a group of understanding actors, a designer as imaginative as Donald Oenslager or Stewart Chaney. To all these must be brought a director who acknowledges the varied and cunning arts of the modern theatre, and can master them. Then it would make a performance that would thrill not only a New York but an American audience from the first tiara to the last standee. Mr. Cummings has made a working script which challenges the theatre to produce its best."

The challenge, so far as *Tom* is concerned, has not been taken up; it will be recalled, however, that a ballet about Uncle Tom was one of the most enchanting episodes in the Broadway success, *The King and I,* some fifteen years later. A complete score for *Tom* exists, the work of the composer David Diamond.

Santa Claus, published in 1946, is sub-titled *"A Morality"* and reveals Cummings in a didactic vein. It is a one-act play in five scenes, its basic line being iambic pentameter, but so varied for the purpose, presumably, of dramatic speech that it loses some of the intensity of blank verse. This defect, if defect it be, applies of course only to reading; in the presentation everything would depend on the speaking. The idea is ingenious—Death and Santa Claus, who is a young man under his mask, exchange appearances; nevertheless, a child knows Santa Claus even with his death's head disguise:

Santa Claus.   Do you like me this way?
Child.   I guess . . . I like you any way—if you're you.

The didactic vein, to which I have referred, appears with greater force in this play than in individual poems, for its entire motivation, or reason, springs from Cummings's view that love and individuality are scarce commodities in the modern world, a view familiar to readers of his verse. Santa Claus complains to Death that he has "so much to give; and nobody will take." Death knows why:

You're speaking of a true or actual world.
Imagine, if you can, a world so blurred
that its inhabitants are one another. . . .

Cummings also equates Science with Death which, considering the times we live in, is far from an odd concept. Death advises Santa Claus to become a Scientist. "Or, in plain English, a knowledge-salesman":

once people hear the magic name of "Science"
you can sell people anything—except understanding.

and

the less something exists, the more people want it.

Santa Claus thereupon sets forth to sell people "preferred stock in a giltedged wheelmine." A wheelmine, it will be recalled, is what

Mr. X worked in, in the story, "Mr. X." It is, of course, non-existent; but after buying stock the people are persuaded that there has been a disaster in the wheelmine, and are looking for the promoter to wreak vengeance on him. Their cry is now "Down with Science!" To save himself from lynching, Santa Claus has to prove he is not Science, although he looks like Death, because they have exchanged masks:

Santa Claus.   all men and every woman may be wrong;
but nobody who lives can fool a child.
—Now I'll abide by the verdict of that little girl
over there, with the yellow hair and the blue eyes.
I'll simply ask her who I am; and whoever
she says I am, I am. . . .

Child.   You are Santa Claus.

The final scene deals with the reunion of Santa Claus, the mother of the child, and the child. The drawing of Santa Claus removing his mask, in the first edition of the play, is a self-portrait. In his notebook Cummings wrote: "It takes three to make a child."

He had not seen his daughter by his first wife for many years, and did not in fact see her again until she came to Patchin Place while attending college. He appears to have passed through a troubled period following his second divorce, and with thoughts of his daughter ever-present to enlarge his remorse and guilt. *Santa Claus* is dedicated to Fritz Wittels, an eminent analyst who, Cummings told me, saved his life.

Chapter 11

THE POET AS PAINTER

1

"To a large extent," wrote Wallace Stevens, "the problems of poets are the problems of painters, and poets must often turn to the literature of painting for a discussion of their own problems."

The poet who paints not only is familiar with the literature of painting: he adds to it.

In our time, the overriding concept which the new masters have assimilated, and which is reflected in their best work, stems from Cézanne: a picture is a self-contained organism—that is, it exists as itself alone and is not a "picture" of something else, or "about" something else which it approximates. Thus the good painter, like the poet, is a man of metaphors. He presents an image—not, as some suppose and many desire, an object. The camera and academicians do other things, no doubt worthy ones; but they have nothing to do with painting because they are concerned with representation or objects. What would an apple by Cézanne be worth if you could buy it at the grocer's?

Not all images are easily perceived or experienced, and most collections reflect the subjective feelings of the collector. I have suggested that there is only one way of approaching a work of art, and that is without preconceived notions. It is an easy trick to "see" all kinds of "things" and "symbols" in a work, but this being subjective, and therefore vague, can be all things to all men or become "fixed" by means of the most authoritative or most persuasive expositor. This is never the artist, and should suffice as warning.

Eugène Delacroix, a painter whom Cummings admires, and from whose *Journal* I have heard him quote, noted, on Tuesday, April 27, 1824:

"At Leblond's. Interesting discussion about genius and unusual men. Dimier thought that great passions were the source of genius. I think that it is imagination alone, or better still, what amounts to the same thing, that delicacy of the organs that makes one see what others do not see, and which makes one see in a different way. I was saying that even great passions joined to imagination lead most often to disorder in the mind, etc. Dufresne said a very true thing: what made a man unusual was, fundamentally, a way utterly peculiar to himself of seeing things."

I happen to be one of those—Cummings says "one of five"—who like his pictures. I think he underestimates his audience; or perhaps it was a figure of speech to signify that the audience is a small one. Having had the pleasure of meeting two of the "five" (in addition to his more than enthusiastic wife) I will name them shortly—and one or two others as well. I like his pictures for the reason that Dufresne gave, plus ability; but perhaps ability was taken for granted.

We know from Cummings's poetry that he has "a way utterly peculiar to himself of seeing things." I shall attempt in this chapter to show that this applies to his pictures as well, and is the reason why they are important. I am speaking here, of course, of his best pictures; it is by them that he will be judged. Yet it seems proper to add that the unrealized or incomplete works of a good artist are infinitely more interesting than the best works of second-rate men. Cummings's studio in Patchin Place—like his house in New Hampshire—is stacked with pictures that form a text, and there are innumerable sketches that provide the footnotes. Recently he showed me eighteen such sketches, in oil, of a single subject. "Every aspect of a beautiful woman is interesting," he remarked; yet what struck me at once was that he had made no effort to catch merely beautiful effects, but only what he saw, which included angles of the face no woman would see—or care to see—in her mirror.

His best pictures and portraits are the result of intense application beforehand. These pictures seem to me to have that mingling of concept, texture and form which has always pleased and probably will always please.

Despite this, however, as a painter he has suffered from his fame as a poet, for a man who paints as well as writes is usually written off as a man who "also paints." Cummings's habit of referring to his writings in catalogue forewords also has contributed its mite to misunderstanding. They are quite different from the forewords of other artists. I give one of them here, for the light it throws on him and on his approach to painting. It is in dialogue, a favorite literary device with him:

Why do you paint?
For exactly the same reason I breathe.
That's not an answer.
There isn't any answer.
How long hasn't there been any answer?
As long as I can remember.
And how long have you written?
As long as I can remember.
I mean poetry.
So do I.
Tell me, doesn't your painting interfere with your writing?
Quite the contrary: they love each other dearly.
They're very different.
Very: one is painting and one is writing.
But your poems are rather hard to understand, whereas
    your paintings are so easy.
Easy?
Of course—you paint flowers and girls and sunsets; things
    that everybody understands.
I never met him.
Who?
Everybody.
Did you ever hear of nonrepresentational painting?
I am.
Pardon me?
I am a painter, and painting is nonrepresentational.

Not all painting.
No: housepainting is representational.
And what does a housepainter represent?
Ten dollars an hour.
In other words, you don't want to be serious—
It takes two to be serious.
Well, let's see . . . oh yes, one more question: where will
    you live after this war is over?
In China; as usual.
China?
Oh course.
Whereabouts in China?
Where a painter is a poet (Foreword to catalogue, Roch-
    ester Memorial Art Gallery, 1945).

2

Cummings has drawn and painted since childhood. He was early encouraged to do so in that remarkable household on Irving Street. His father supplied him at first with large sheets of brown paper on which he drew in pencil and crayon. Many of these drawings are still in existence; one is an elephant a yard long. From drawing Cummings went on to watercolor and oil, a transition facilitated by his father, who worked in those mediums. It is clear, then, that Cummings's pictures are not the result of idle hours of daubing. The truth is otherwise: he has painted more than he has written, and he has painted—for more than half a century—with an intense, undeviating passion. His mastery in one medium has undoubtedly helped him in the other. Just as his painter's eye has helped his poetry, his poetry has helped his concepts as a painter. For a picture is also conceived; the prime factor in all works of art being imagination, or a way of seeing things.

Imagination provides the concept, and is revealed by form. Form in painting I believe to be more important than color; there are pictures without color that are supreme works of art, and works of art whose colors have faded without diminishing their total effect. This is true also of polychrome sculpture, where nothing remains of the original painting over the stone or wood. The artist's language is line plus color, but form is the triumph of line. But where there is color we have to deal with something that is in addition to pure form, for then every inch of a canvas comes under scrutiny, and there is no area where the tactile quality of the medium itself can be slighted, except at peril. Every brush-stroke counts. I am aware, of course, that there is now a universal school or academy whose sole aim appears to be to complete as large a canvas as possible with as little paint as possible. But perhaps it is only necessary to add that the manner of applying that little bit of paint leaves everything to be desired, for the application of paint reveals what the painter feels about his medium.

There is also the question of imitation. Many present-day painters can paint like anybody; which of course raises the question whether they can paint like themselves. The imitator has always had it easy.

Cummings's handling of his medium, whether in line or color, has made for individuality of style. His line drawings are different from Picasso's or Cocteau's, for example, in that they stop abruptly at the point where movement has been caught. In his drawings of hoofers and comedians, it is their characteristic stance that he is after. Thus, in the drawing of Jack Shargel, the National Winter Garden comedian, which appeared in *The Dial,* and that of Charlie Chaplin, which appeared in *The Dial* and in Seldes's *The Seven Lively Arts,* he achieves their stance with a few flowing lines, and the stance is the design.

In watercolor, which he uses profusely, he achieves—again with a minimum of strokes—an Oriental simplicity. His watercolors are deceptive, because Cummings is after an impression, sometimes so fleeting as to be gone with a change of light; but having caught what he wished, the picture remains without embellishment. For a moment it looks as though anyone could do it; but let anyone try. His trees squirm into sunlight, his leaves are like light or birds taking off joyously into blue latitudes. Delacroix noted in his journal: "The fleeting instant of gaiety throughout nature. Those so fresh leaves, those lilacs, that rejuvenated sun. Melancholy takes flight during these brief moments." Cummings has never forgotten his first encounter with "that mystery who is Nature" in Norton's Woods.

In his watercolors Cummings is not so much painting a picture as capturing a poetic metaphor in paint; that is to say, he is celebrating Nature, as he does so often in his poetry. Loren MacIver, who owns several examples of Cummings's work, told me: "He paints not in the fashion; he paints sunsets because he likes them. I do, too. He celebrates events, because he believes in honoring things. He is a celebrant; his works revere." Nevertheless, either because of their swift execution, or the limitations of the medium itself, Cummings's watercolors—with very notable exceptions—fail to satisfy Western eyes used to projection of mass instead of space. In this, as I have suggested, he is more Oriental than occidental, as though he really were an inhabitant of China "where a painter is a poet."

It is with his oils that Cummings calls for consideration as a painter wholly apart from his other, writing self. His oils reveal a mastery of his medium in which the tactile and the sensory combine, and in this combination faces, landscapes and flowers no longer celebrate life, but are a part of it. They are felt, skilfully projected, and more than skilfully executed. The best of them have an existence of their own, being caught in timelessness. I venture to suggest that only those who have examined the mass of his work in New York and New Hampshire, and the collection of Hildegarde Watson in Rochester (to which I will again refer) can appreciate his industry, let alone his achievement. Reproductions in black and white are a poor substitute, and even reproductions in color do less than justice, because of their reduced size. And yet it is possible to feel the impact of discovery by seeing the reproductions of Cummings's work in *CIOPW*. Not surprisingly, the impact is cumulative.

CIOPW is a cloth-bound volume measuring 9½ by 12½ inches. The letters stand for the mediums in which he has worked, examples of which are included: charcoal, ink, oil, pencil and watercolor. It was published in 1931 by Covici, Friede in an edition limited to 391 copies, each signed by the artist on the title-page. To sign them, Cummings used a brush. It is in the foreword to this volume that he referred to himself as "An author of pictures, a draughtsman of words." The foreword begins:

"Like many,the undersigned was found to write spontaneously or pictures before finding oneself compelled to draw or words:unlike some who are threatened with knowledge,he encouraged himself by to be. While the portraiture progressed—while a painfully hand achieved likenesses of even polysyllabic sitters,the gradually fingers overcame perspective, his clumsily wrist contrived verses—child spin-

ning on a point of chalk emits boy who rides the squirmings of a
crayon,legarms begin inhabiting bodies who are not faces,sidewalks
cohabit with notebooks and joyously always writing continues

"—for once-upon-a-time read,neither life nor living,but originally
infinitive cooling through participle into compulsion;therefore once-
upon-a-now equals 'art',When to live is."

He pays his respect to "his distinguished audience (J. S. Watson,
Jr. and Scofield Thayer)" and to S. A. Jacobs: "persianly poemprinter
predicated picturebook." (He also printed it.) Reproduced are forty-
nine oils and twenty-three watercolors, as well as drawings in charcoal, ink and pencil. The pictures range from portraits which include
the artist and his friends—Joe Gould, M. R. Werner, Gilbert Seldes,
Thayer, Watson; and Anne Barton, the painter's second wife—to
landscapes in New Hampshire and Europe; there are several still-lifes
and several nudes; and a line drawing of an elephant. The drawings
of Shargel and Chaplin, previously mentioned, are also reproduced.

What strikes one at once in *CIOPW* is Cummings's ability as a
draughtsman and his gift for expressive portraiture. One of the charcoal drawings, "Larionov dessine," shows the famous designer of the
Ballet Russe making a sketch as he is himself being sketched by
Cummings. The Russian's face is intense in its concentration on his
sketch; but this, by itself, would be mere reporting, like a photograph
in a newspaper. What Cummings has done goes beyond this and
depicts Larionov's inner radiance, that warmth and wit which his
friends knew and which he put at the service of the greatest ballets
of modern times. This ability to capture both the "portrait" and the
essence of the person portrayed is everywhere evident in the section
devoted to oil paintings. Among the best of these are the self-portraits,
particularly the one with Anne Barton and her daughter Diana
(whose father was Ralph Barton) in the background. Here, everything is luminous and fresh, and everyone is young.

There is something else that Cummings does in his paintings which
has the enchantment of certain of his poems. Just as he is able to
see with the eyes of a child, he can also draw with a child's hand
(see, for example, the two locked, dancing figures of children in the
picture entitled "merrygoround"). This kind of verve is entirely different from imitation of children's drawings, which remains imitation.
On this subject, Cummings wrote in his article on Lachaise:

"To analyze child art in a sentence is to say that houses, trees, smoke, people, etc., are depicted not as nouns but as verbs. The more genuine child art is, the more it is, contrary to the belief of those incapable persons who are content merely to admire it, purely depictive. In denying that the child 'represents' and substituting for 'representation' some desperately overworked word like 'expression,' these people are only showing their hostility to the academies, just as when they tell us (which is true) that the bad artist is the representational artist. But, as has been sometimes pointed out, the artist who represents is bad not because he represents: he is bad because he represents something which a camera can represent better. This means that he is depicting something that is second, or rather *n*th, hand, which a child most distinctly is not. Consequently to appreciate child art we are compelled to undress one by one the soggy nouns whose agglomeration constitutes the mechanism of Normality, and finally to liberate the actual crisp organic squirm—the IS."

Because Cummings has shown so little, *CIOPW* was the first indication, so far as those outside his immediate circle were concerned, that the poet was a painter. It is therefore an important milestone in his career. But the work has been for long out-of-date and out-of-print, and what is needed is a new collection, with reproductions in color of the work of recent years.

3

The work of Gaston Lachaise confirmed for Cummings many of the concepts which he had painstakingly evolved at the time the two men met in Greenwich Village. His article about the sculptor, which appeared in the February, 1920, issue of *The Dial,* was of course a labor of love; but it was also something else. It reveals his own approach to the plastic arts, and his style and stance as a critic at this period of his life. (In writing about art, and particularly the art of others, Cummings is much more impressive, or effective, than when he is writing about himself as a combination poet and painter.) The article begins:

"To get rid altogether of contemporary 'sculpture' is perhaps the surest way of appreciating the achievement of Lachaise. This coup of unadulterated intelligence has already been given by Mr. W. H. Wright in four sentences which I lift from the masterly sixth chapter of *Modern Painting*—

> After Michelangelo there was no longer any new in-
> spiration for sculpture. After Cézanne there was no longer
> any excuse for it. He has made us see that painting can pre-
> sent a more solid vision than that of any stone image.
> Against modern statues we can only bump our heads; in
> the contemplation of modern painting we can exhaust our
> intelligences.

I say masterly, because so long as the author keeps one or more eyes
on Cézanne it must be admitted by any intelligent person that his
analysis is unspeakably correct. Were the entire book devoted to a
consideration of Cézanne our own task would be confined to proving
that Lachaise does not produce 'modern statues.' Unfortunately this
is not the case. Elsewhere the author remarks that Swinburne brought
the rhymed lyric to its highest development. And at one point he men-
tions that 'the aesthetic possibilities of the human form were exhausted by' his old friend Michelangelo, with which it is a trifle
difficult to agree. How about the renowned Pablo? Or, to take two
far from colossal geniuses: Lehmbruck, in his lean girl at the Armory
Show (1913), and Brancusi, in his Princesse Bonaparte at the Independent of is it three years past, did something more than exciting.
In the first case a super-El Greco-like significance was pitilessly ex-
torted from the human form, in the second the human form was
beautifully seduced into a sensual geometry. In his feeling for his
material, moreover, Brancusi showed for some time genuine originality. But he reached an impasse very soon. Judging from the recent
bumps and buttons at the De Zayas Gallery he is at present as dead
as a doornail."

Cummings also disposed of Paul Manship: "His work is, of course,
superior to the masterpieces of such people as French, Barnard, Bartlett, the Borglums, and Bela Pratt—in so far as something which is
thoroughly dead is superior to something which has never been
alive." Of the critics of his subject he wrote: "Lachaise has, in the
past few years, made a large number of artists extremely enthusiastic,
and a great many gallery-goers very nervous, not to mention the ladies
and gentlemen who may have died of anger. But the official 'critics,'
perhaps realizing the disastrous consequences to 'criticism' of a genuine reaction on their part to a work of overwhelming aesthetic value,
have as it were agreed to risk nothing. An exception which proves
the rule is Mr. McBride of the Sun, who on Sunday (February 17,

1918) said, in the course of some hair-raising platitudes, 'I like this statue [The Elevation] immensely,' generously adding, 'If the ribald laugh at it and call it a fat woman they may.' In regard to Lachaise's personality The Dealers In Second-Hand Ideas (Strictly guaranteed. Good as new.) are content to quote from the preface which Lachaise wrote for the catalogue of the American sculptors' show (Bourgeois Galleries, Spring of 1919)."

Of Lachaise's "The Mountain," Cummings wrote (because no critic mentioned it):

"Its completely integrated simplicity proclaims The Mountain to be one of those superlative aesthetic victories which are accidents of the complete intelligence, or the intelligence functioning at intuitional velocity. Its absolute sensual logic as perfectly transcends the merely exact arithmetic of the academies as the rhythm which utters its masses negates those static excrements of deliberate unthought which are the delight of certain would-be 'primitives.' Let us as a specimen of the latter take a painter: say Zorach." Exit Zorach, which clears the stage for the true primitives: children (previously quoted). Exit "Mr. Sargent's portrait OF Some One, Mr. French's statue OF Something (to take the worst painter and the worst sculptor in America)." The stage being clear, Cummings bestows the accolade:

"To the vocal gesture which preceded grammar Lachaise is completely sensitive. Consequently, in his enormous and exquisite way, Lachaise negates OF with IS."

Wright's praise of Swinburne occurs in his book *The Creative Will,* the "elsewhere" of Cummings's distressed observation. "Willard Huntington Wright, some years ago, gave the impression of being some one important," wrote Edmund Wilson in 1926. It may be recalled that Mr. Wright, about this time, left the field of criticism for the more lucrative one of detective fiction, and as S. S. Van Dine delighted a new and larger audience. His critical writings are nevertheless rewarding; he was, moreover, at the time he wrote almost alone as an American in his esthetic approach to works of art.

Another book in the field of art criticism which Cummings has enjoyed, and which happens to be one of his most marked-up volumes —with pencilled notations and underlinings on almost every page, and a summary on the back flyleaf—is *The Meaning of Beauty,* by the English critic Eric Newman. The summary, with page numbers, includes such notes as "Nature vs. Art," "Form Content," "Fact vs. Value," "particulars→general & impersonal→personal." On the recto of the flyleaf he has copied part of a sentence from page 200: "it is not the arrival but the journey that counts." The paragraph in which this passage occurs reads (the words in italics were underlined by Cummings):

"It is impossible for Rubens, it is easy for Mondrian and the abstract painters, to travel the whole distance, for they are prepared to jettison the whole of the visible world—peacocks, clouds, women and flowers—on their journey to *their mathematical destination.* They *do not love life* enough to regret that they travel light and arrive empty-handed, so that their spheres have lost all the sensuous implications of the apple and their cylinders have none of the strength of the tree. They are *heartless theorists* [this is starred by Cummings in the margin], who do not know that *it is not the arrival but the journey that counts.* The sacrifice they have made is no sacrifice at all, for they have persuaded themselves that what they left behind them was valueless."

Gaston Lachaise died on October 18, 1935. He had lived to see a large retrospective exhibition of his work that year at the Museum of Modern Art. Ten years later, the Weyhe Gallery, preparing for an exhibition of his drawings and sculpture, asked Cummings to write a foreword to its catalogue. He wrote:

> It was many years ago that The reborn Dial saluted Gaston Lachaise. Those years comprise (among other drolleries) a complete reversal of public untaste; "nonobjective art," once anathematized, being now *de rigueur.* By contrast, the achievement of Lachaise remains passionately and serenely itself—a marvel and a mystery: the spontaneous and inevitable expression of one fearlessly unique human being.

4

Cummings has exhibited since 1919, when he had two paintings in the Independent show of that year. They were, in Slater Brown's phrase, "hard edge abstracts," and in Mrs. Lachaise's, "the sensation of the Independent." Brown told me that Cummings used "Noise" followed by a number for his titles; in the 1924 Independent show an abstract measuring 40 x 50 inches was called "Noise Number 12," perhaps the last of the lot.

In the Spring Salon of the Salons of America, May, 1928, in which 238 artists participated, Cummings showed a drawing and Dos Passos two watercolors; in the 1930 Spring Salon he exhibited "i" (presumably a self-portrait). In August, 1931, there was an exhibition of 162 works in Cleveland, which included the bulk of those reproduced in CIOPW. The show was arranged by Philip Kaplan, a Cummings admirer and collector, and Gilbert Seldes wrote a four-page article on "The Paintings of E. E. Cummings" for *Bystander*, a Cleveland publication. Not one was sold. In December, 1931, there was an exhibition of twenty-nine pictures at the Painters and Sculptors Gallery; Cummings also participated in group shows there in June and December of 1932.

Two of his most important shows were held at the American British Art Center in March, 1944 (the month which also saw the publication of his *1 x 1*) and May, 1949. In the latter show were thirty-eight oils, eleven watercolors and two drawings. Asked for a comment to accompany reproductions of a self-portrait and "Portrait in Shadow" from this show, he wrote in *Art News* for May:

Perhaps a few individuals may enjoy my pictures. Possibly a few may enjoy my poems.

And if yes, what could be better?

Equidistant from such wonderful luck—with a distance not reckonable by mere lightyears—are the naying and the yeaing of numberless televisionary unindividuals: movie-loving each blinder than radioactive any is deaf.

Were I a critic, should probably add that "academic" (i.e. un-) art resembles every good coin, which it isn't, in having two sides. One side can be called "photographic realism" or even "naturalism"; the other, "nonrepresentational" or "abstract" sic "painting." And your stupid wiseguy doing his worst to deny Nature equals your clever fool who did his best to possess Her.

Xaipe [literally "rejoice!"—a Greek mode of greeting; also, title of book of poems by Cummings, published the following year].

Stewart Preston reviewed the show in the *Times;* he also fell back on literature. Under the heading, "Poet-Painter," he wrote:

" 'into the street of the sky light walks scattering poems' (his own words) is the best description of the intense little landscapes by the poet-painter e. e. cummings at the American British Art Center. Here are 'spiral acres of bloated rose coiled within cobalt miles of sky,' nudes of Whistlerian vagueness, flowers painted with unexpected directness, all of them unpretentious, oddly moving evocations. One looks in vain for the dazzling cleverness that marks such recent cummings verse as 'one x one' but finds, instead, the romantic feeling that infuses the early work, 'Tulips and Chimneys.' "

Cummings has also exhibited in Chicago, Baltimore, and Rochester. In the last-named city he had shows in 1945, 1950 (when he combined his two professions by giving a reading at the opening of his one-man show in the Rochester Memorial Art Gallery), 1954 and again in 1957. Speaking of the famous Armory Show of 1913 at the University of Rochester in February, 1954, Cummings told his audience: "It's an odd and interesting thing that some of those who hooted at the paintings in that show are now the owners of those very paintings." The biggest privately owned collection of Cummings's pictures is also in Rochester, the property of Hildegarde Watson (Mrs. James Sibley Watson), to whom *Xaipe: Seventy-One Poems* is dedicated. It seems fair to state that no estimate of Cummings as a painter can be had without a view of this truly representative collection, which includes examples of every medium in which Cummings has worked and from all his periods, including the abstract (which, he told me, "leads nowhere" and is why he gave it up). Here are the large New Hampshire landscapes in oil, a rage of color in the foliage; the delicate watercolors, the vivid portraits and caricatures, the poetic nudes in color or ink. They are all unmistakably the work of one man.

Cummings no longer signs his work, being certain it will not be mistaken for work by someone else. Here, I think, he misses an essential point, which is that his signature can only add to the purchaser's pleasure. But perhaps his attitude reflects an unconscious desire to break away from his role as a writer.

5

During the summer of 1954, *Art Digest* commissioned William Carlos Williams to write an article on Cummings as a painter.

Cummings, who was in New Hampshire and had no intention of leaving until the late autumn, "tried vainly to discourage Williams, offering to furnish photographs of a few paintings in the Watson collection, but remarking that paintings cannot be accurately judged by photographs, and suggesting that Williams visit Rochester and see the originals. But Williams (who had received the Dial Award in 1926 from Watson and Thayer) made no move toward Rochester." Instead, he wrote:

"Years ago I witnessed an exhibition of Cummings' paintings, it was in a New York gallery. I haven't seen one since. How can I speak of them except from memory? The reproductions which I hold in my hand are misleading. The color is absent. Only the box of strawberries of which I have already spoken ["you could almost eat them"] (owned now, I am told, by the poet Marianne Moore) holds a still recognizable form. It is a box of strawberries, pure and simple, painted with realistic but poetic insight, the very scent and taste of the berries, even the feel of them in the mouth when crushed by the tongue against the inside of the cheek is there.

"A picture of a nude on a bed is no different: she is young. You want to go to bed with her. Even Rubens' women do not give you that feeling. It is not a painting of a nude by Mary Cassatt.

"Cummings himself, during his brief abstract period when the line drawing of Charlie Chaplin was made, was caught by the importance of design. But others had gone farther with the mode. He returning on himself from that venture found himself faced by pure paint again and wasn't sufficiently interested in drawing to push the matter further.

"He had, or has still, perhaps, the makings of a great watercolorist. When he faced his one great opportunity of the sea, he produced, though that is an oil, a small picture said by a competent critic to be 'The finest sea picture of our time.' With that optimistic dictum I am in sympathy but have not sufficient experience to completely agree. It is Cummings at his best as a painter and he knew it; he could not go beyond that excellence without giving it more time which he seems disinclined to do, he has other fish to fry."

Turning to Cummings's poetry, Dr. Williams wrote:

"I have had at least five of Cummings' books on my shelves for many years. I did have a sixth but I got so mad at it that in spite of the fact that my wife had made me a present of it at my request

I tore it up and burned it; at least it had that much virtue in it and
I shall never, in the present mode, cut me into small pieces and feed
me to the dogs, 'reveal its name.' "

In New Hampshire, on a day when I was looking at Cummings's
pictures, I mentioned Williams's article. Cummings gave me a concentrated look.

"Did you read the passage about the book?" he asked.

There is, alas, no such picture as "the box of strawberries" mentioned by Williams; Miss Moore owns a picture of a rose. What Dr.
Williams recollected subconsciously was a poem by Miss Moore which
begins:

>   you've seen a strawberry
>   that's had a struggle; yet
>   was, where the fragments met,
>
>   a hedgehog or a star-
>   fish for the multitude
>   of seeds. . . .

As Miss Moore has described her picture better than I can do, I
quote—with permission—her letter of April 12, 1938, thanking
Cummings for the present she had received:

>   I marvel that one can give so much, and at your te-
> merarious trust in our caterpillar-tractor post-office. After
> studying this very noble rose,—the turquoise under-leaf
> and touch of red reflected back even to the petals, I can
> surmise why botanical gardens and over-flowered shops do
> not abound in yellow roses. Yet they might, and still lack
> this one.
>   I try not to think of your loss in the fact of my having
> the painting. We say what a man has done he can do again,
> but can he; an effect is got once. But another awaits him.
> At best or at worst, please know that in having the yellow
> rose, I study and enjoy it and am grateful.

In the same issue of *Art Digest*, under a reproduction of the sea-
scape mentioned by Williams, and owned by Mrs. Watson, there is
a statement by Cummings entitled "Videlicet"—that is to say, an
autobiography in little:

For more than half a hundred years, the oversigned's twin obsessions have been painting and writing.

Several decades ago (when Academic Unart was exactly as representational as it now isn't) an eminent art critic described my most recent pictures as "hardly the sort of thing you would care to live with."

Earlier still, if memory serves, the notable promoter of a book called The Enormous Room had remaindered its first edition at thirty cents a copy; and I'd scarcely prevented the author's enthusiastic father from purchasing more than sixty copies.

Long before an epoch of disillusionment became an era of dehumanization—and about the time a play called Him, by my "lower-case" self, was dramacritically deplored as "exactly like stepping on something extremely nasty in the dark"—our prenonobjectivist realized that denying Nature's imagination meant renouncing my own; and joyfully hurdled Jehovah's anaesthetic commandment *"Thou shalt not make unto thee any graven image, or any likeness of any thing that is in the heaven above, or that is in the earth beneath, or that is in the water under the earth."* (Exodus xx 4).

Some years later Eimi—the diary of a pilgrimage to Marxist Russia—was dutifully damned by America's fellowtravelling literary gangsters. Still later, learning that fourteen publishers had refused a collection of poems aptly entitled No Thanks, my serenely confident mother requested the privilege of ensuring its unwelcome appearance.

Came the forties; and culture (lucely translated You Never Had It So Good) leaped like a weed. Education of the not educable outranked all other national rackets: college degrees, crowning any activity from stagelighting to piecrustrolling, were sold as freely as pardons during the middle ages. Television antennae blossomed from the poorest housetops; and moviestars, no longer content with a Cézanne in the toilet, hastily acquired livingroomsize Picassos. Nobody and nothing escaped The New Look: children of parents who'd honestly hated my writing were taught how to pity my painting instead. For a voice like unto the cooing of A-bombs had spoken, saying "EVERY-BODY SHALL BE EVERYBODYELSE!" and (after a period of anxiety, during which The Nonforgotten Man pretty nearly suspected that he'd been properly frigged) it was revealed—amid everybody's surprise and delight—that everybodyelse was an artist.

Let me only add that one human being considers himself immeasurably lucky to enjoy, both as a painter and as a writer, the affectionate respect of a few human beings.

Part Three

Chapter 12

THE PILGRIM IN RUSSIA

1

E. E. Cummings went to the Soviet Union in the spring of 1931. He went there from Paris. He went as himself—"peesahtel y hoodozhnik," writer and painter. To do this he needed a special passport ("byez-parteenee"—i.e., without political affiliations) which eventually arrived but was reputed to be unobtainable. Foreign visitors were not allowed to enter Russia except as members of some organization or as tourists, "since otherwise they could not easily be controlled and might discover that the real ruler of 'Karl Marx's paradise' was the universally feared and immemorially loathed—once Tzarist, now Socialist, but always inhumanly pitiless—'Gay-Pay-Oo' or Secret Police." Cummings, however, remembered the parting admonition of his distinguished friend Fritz Wittels: "look out for 'Russian Villages' (that is, communities instituted by the government to make visitors think that Marxism was not an economic as well as a spiritual catastrophe)'" and, as we shall soon see, the "comrade capitalist" writer and painter gently but firmly refused to enter Russia as anyone else.

"When Russia was interesting," wrote Ezra Pound in a review of *Eimi* to which I will again refer, "Mr. Cummings got up and went there. When one of us wants to know about Russia to the extent that Mr. Cummings once wanted to, we might perhaps show like activity."

Paul Rosenfeld, with his usual insight, offered a more intimate view in the "Cummings Number" of the Harvard *Wake:*

"Part of Communistic propaganda was the allurement of visitors to Russia with pictures ranging from the plentifulness of vintage wines from the cellars of the aristocrats to pictures of the new bloom of the theatre-arts. The latter, Cummings pretends, allured himself; probably the mirage had been drawn for him by members of the circle of his friend Louis Aragon."

That Aragon was a charming Communist there is no doubt; his wife was charming, and they had charming friends. Aragon was also a good poet, and there were things in his work which attracted Cummings (French is practically a second mother tongue to him). At the request of Mme. Aragon, Cummings took to Moscow "an extraordinary assortment of indubitably capitalist literature and trinkets" (which, to his astonishment, were passed by the Soviet customs officials) and "presented them to the lady's radiantly grateful sister" ("Madame Potiphar" in *Eimi*). Later on, when the Revolutionary Literature Bureau suggested he translate Aragon's "ecstatically marxist poem 'Le Front Rouge,' " Cummings—who by this time abominated everything marxist—cheerfully undertook the task as "a friendly gesture of farewell."

"The Red Front" appeared first in English in *Literature of the World Revolution, No. 3,* in 1931, and as a separate publication in 1933 (Contempo, Chapel Hill, N. C.). It has all the virtues of Aragon's metaphorical mind, particularly in the lines about Paris streets, and the glaring defects of all revolutionary literature. Its movement, its sparsely placed fresh images, its harsh novelties, and, above all, its fierce contempt (so close to Cummings's own) of the advertisement-product with

tissue paper around the packages

and

paper around the tissue paper

struck a responsive chord. Although Aragon wrote with revolutionary fervor—

> Fire on Leon Blum
> Fire on Boncour Frossard Deat
> Fire on the trained bears of the social-democracy
> Fire Fire I hear pass by
> the death which throws itself on Garchery—

and was afterwards arraigned on a charge of inciting to murder, he also could write with a poet's art. Time has dimmed the enchantment of the Soviet Union for many who loved it too well only a few decades ago; but Aragon's poem cannot be belittled in its entirety even today. The force of his pistoned verse remains (with a bow to Honegger's "Pacific 231") :

> The red train starts and nothing shall stop it
> UR
> SS
> UR
> SS
> UR
> SS
> No one remains behind
> waving handkerchiefs Everyone is going
> UR
> SS
> UR
> SS. . . .
>
> The past dies the moment is thrown into gear
> SSSR SSSR
> The roads spring the rail warms SSSR
> The train plunges toward tomorrow—

and so forth. But now the world would rather have yesterday or today, without benefit of commissars. For only the sickest of foreign converts to the Communist cause can still believe the lie about dictatorship of the proletariat.

Having translated the poem, Cummings proceeded to analyze certain lines and ideas in it. The analysis went into *Eimi,* pp. 142-143, and is interesting on many counts but chiefly in showing Cummings's indestructible consistency. This is his analysis:

HE PUT ON A STARCHED COLLAR

"there are cigaretteholders between cigarette and man"—. Correct. Machinemade "civilization" isolates every human being from experience(that is, from himself) by teaching mankind to mistake a mere gadgety interpretation(e.g.the weatherman's prediction)of experience for experience itself(e.g.weather)

"worldliness . . . delicacy"—. He doesn't like them; probably because they're as overrated in Europe as are pigheadedness and insolence in America(by the way,he's never visited America)

everything's "advertising"—. Right. The "modern man" equals a defenceless literate bombarded with slogans mottoes pictures and whatever else will tend to unmake him; i.e.make him need something unnecessary

"how sweet is the groan which comes from ruins"—. Bullshit

"the bursting of gunfire adds a hitherto unknown gaiety to the landscape"—. If you're not within range. If you are, you'll be apt to accept even communism rather than endure that same gaiety.

"hail to materialistic dialectic and its incarnation,the red army"—. Anciently, de gustibus;or as(anent "modern art") Professor Bliss Perry of Harvard used to chuckle "it's all right if you like it"

"spare nothing"—. Nyet. Hardboiledness is dull

dressez-vous contre vos mères—. See complex, Oedipus

"the most beautiful structure isn't worth the splendid and chaotic heap which is easily produced by a church and some dynamite"— Untrue. Dynamite, however, is an easier vocation than poetry

"abandon night pestilence and the family . . . you are holding in your hands a laughing child . . . a child such as has never been seen . . . he knows beforehand how to

speak,all the songs of the new life"—. And let's hope he
also knows that all the microtelescopically rhetorical opti-
pessimism of any premeditatedly Un(or possible)world
may not katalyze 1 spontaneously singular impossibility
or(shall we say)workof art
      "a star is born on earth"—. Very neat;the "star" being
Russia's cross
      "dawn rises over the salles de bain"—. Fact. And over
a great many other things,cher maître;for wonderfully
dawn,unlike the propagandist,and like the poet,is no snob
      "history led on leash by the third international"—. Also,
muzzled
      (and now,comrades,we come to this paean's infantile
climax: now the language,fairly wetting its drawers,begins
achugging and apuffing—"all aboard!" the paeaner now
ecstatically cries—"everybody jump on the red train!"
(alias,N.B.,the bandwagon)—"nobody will be left behind!"(and of course Prosperity is just around the Corner)
—U-S-S-R,choo-choo-choo-choo(your name's in the paper)wake up and dream(let's all get arrested)Pippa passes
the buck

                    P.S.—HE GOT THE JOB

   Nevertheless, when the poem appeared in translation, the Left-wing
literati again thought they had an ally, and again turned out to be
badly mistaken—which was resented.

2

      To prepare the reader for their reaction to Cummings's re-
port on the Soviet Union and subsequent books, I will state the general premises on which the Communist intellectuals operated—at
least, in the United States—in the Thirties.
   To begin with, they were not interested in art; if they had been,
they would not have told party members, under threat of expulsion,
what to write and what to paint. Art has never come out of organization, any organization; it can only come from artists, and artists are
individuals. Under the party *diktat* artists who were party members

lost their individuality. To judge by the writing that appeared under this scheme of things, no irreparable harm was done to American literature. Yet it is possible that some of the men and women who wrote "proletarian" books and "poems" might have written another kind of book and another kind of poetry, and having known some of them, I feel a certain regret—and contempt for those who misled them.

The Communists also thought that certain books were better—or said that they were—because these books supposedly advanced the Communist cause. For a time the brightest critical writing—and the most powerful—was by Communists; so powerful and all-pervading was it that Thornton Wilder accepted the challenge of a Communist spokesman—Mike Gold—to write about contemporary American life. He happened to be a good writer, and he wrote a good book. But what of the writers who had not yet found themselves, who might have written something original and personal if left to themselves?

"As the country plunged deeper into the slough of economic depression," wrote Philip Horton in his life of Hart Crane, "most of them abandoned the cause of 'pure' literature for a growing interest in political and social ideas; and tacitly relinquishing their first books of verse, their one or two novels to the limbo of 'early works,' dipped their pens afresh in the brilliant ink of the new thought. Somewhere, perhaps, Ernest Boyd indulged in a sibylline smile, recalling his prophecy of the aesthetes who would become journalists; for of all of them only Cummings and Crane shied clear of the new factionalism."

I asked Gold—*circa* 1932—why the *New Masses* persisted in publishing terrible poems seemingly because the "poets" had inserted the word "comrade" here and there (e.g., "comrade, the grass is green," etc.) when he could have the pick of the best, since most of the poets at the time were expressing disenchantment or liberalism, or both. He replied: "There are magazines for that kind of stuff."

But it was all false, all futile. Neither books nor anything else could "advance" the party because the party could never get anywhere in the United States, and it got nowhere. It succeeded only in making a nuisance of itself, and in creating a great deal of mischief, chiefly to the Liberal movement, which was indigenous. Many "nice" people were involved in this, including writers; but there were others. If rumor is to be believed, one of the future commissars of Greenwich

Village was, in the Thirties, making a list of those to be "liquidated" when the revolution came—the "unmitigated hate" which Cummings had noted.

It was therefore not to be supposed that the new revolutionaries would differ from the old; and the first thing the so-called proletariat does when it has weapons and its victims have none is to kill, and to kill in such a way as to make both death and life obscene and meaningless. The word "proletariat," which exerted so great a fascination over the intellectuals of the Thirties, was historically a contemptuous term, denoting the lowest class. But even supposing it stands for the laboring class, how did it come about that a "worker"—any worker— was the noblest product of civilization?

I should like, however, to add this to the melancholy history of the party and its dupes in this country: In the Twenties and Thirties —particularly during the depression—everyone had a right to believe, or not, in that party's program, while in the Forties the Russians were our allies and held at bay great armies to our gain. But by the end of this dreadful decade, when it was clear that Russia, by design or fear, was the potential enemy, only traitors and the sick in mind could remain among the enrolled.

3

Cummings spent "a fabulous month" there, before "reentering the world" at Istanbul. The first hint of his reactions to the noble experiment, soviet style, came in a front-page interview in the Paris edition of the Chicago *Tribune,* June 29, 1931. His interviewer was Don Brown, who asked one or two questions and let Cummings talk. Cummings said:

"Are the Russian people happy? They struck me like this: they just love to suffer and they're suffering like hell, so they must be happy. You know, Dostoievsky.

"They couldn't seem to understand my visit.

"They said, 'Why are you here?'

"I said, 'I don't know.'

"They are very serious. According to their point of view they are engaged in the greatest work of all time.

"They asked: 'What do you want to see?' I didn't know exactly.

They suggested the theatre; I said 'Fine.' They suggested five or six
other things. I said 'Fine.' They said: 'You won't have time to see
them all in three weeks.' I said 'Fine.'

"I kept a regular old-fashioned diary. Getting it through was just
a matter of graft. Just like in the United States. Only in the United
States it would be a matter of dropping $200 here or there while
in Russia it was small graft.

"You can't compare Russia with anything else. There is nothing
sufficiently like it. I wouldn't dream of making any thesis. Nobody
should shoot his face off about Russia. They themselves admit the
present state of affairs is temporary.

"According to their own formula Russia is like a beleaguered city;
traitors within and besieged without. This is no time to form any
judgment of them.

"There are three worlds in Russia. The first world consists in the
tourists for whom everything is fixed up. The second world is composed of sympathetic pilgrims from abroad. Naive bozos go roaring
in there and see nude bathing carried on in complete modesty and
think it is due to the system. It's not. It's just the character and temperament of the people. They are marvelous people. These people are
the third world.

"On my way to Odessa a Russian gave up his berth in the train
to me. I had been talking to him in German for four hours. At midnight I was awakened by a G.P.U., a handsome man with a revolver.
I asked him why, but he made no reply. I asked my German-speaking
Russian friend who said: 'I don't know, but you had better hurry.'
I tried to find my shoes. I found one. The friend said, 'Keep quiet.'
Then the G.P.U. changed his mind and left me alone. I asked my
friend again, 'Why?' He said, 'I don't know.' 'I don't know' is the
greatest phrase in Russia. You hear it everywhere.

"The foreigner who doesn't come in as a sort of official tourist is
isolated. No foreigner is expected to be found in a third-class carriage
talking to Russians. The amazing thing is that no one can tell you
anything. Try living a month without finding anyone that you can
trust.

"I went on to Odessa. It is a beautiful place. I was walking along
breathing in the free air and feeling good when I saw my G.P.U.
friend, still tagging along. In other words, the Soviet Government
went to considerable expense on my trip through Russia.

"Their propaganda system is great. They've got the goods on everybody. It is silly to rave about Russia if you don't know anything about it.

"People talk about the strain and tension of life in the United States. It is nothing to that in Moscow. If you said 'boo' to some of those people they might drop dead. If they are supposed to work 24 hours a day, they try to work 25. If it's 36 they try to make it 37. They are in a peculiarly nervous condition.

"The generalizers go there. Life is so soft outside Russia and so hard there. The generalizers go there and spout platitudes.

"An idealistic girl friend of mine went there to help them and work with them. She never dreamed of the fact that when you apply an ideal you may get very strange consequences. She went crazy."

"Cummings," the interviewer concluded, "is going to make a book of his impressions. He is sailing today for New York."

The interview, the references to the diary and the book, gave party members and the Left-wing generally the tip-off. When the book was published, one of them—a poet—said at a literary gathering that it was not an accurate account of Russia. M. R. Werner overheard him. Twenty-five years later, when he told me about his retort, he was still indignant. He told the poet: "If there is one thing you *can* count on, it's that Cummings is accurate."

Cummings told me: "When the book appeared, some of my 'best friends' crossed the street to avoid speaking to me."

4

Cummings worked on *Eimi* in Patchin Place. Chiefly, his labors consisted in transferring his diary notes in the preparation of his manuscript, and he refrained from expanding in recollection what he had put down on the spot. He was to admit afterwards that if he had not had his diary before him he would have been bewildered by his impressions. By and large, *Eimi* is the on-the-spot record made by a reporter who happened to be a poet and a painter—hence the extra dimension, the "feel" of things present or impalpable. It is a travel book, or diary, and as such unique, just as *The Enormous Room* is unique among war books. Some sections of *Eimi* appeared in *Hound and Horn* before the book came out.

Covici, Friede, a firm which had previously published Cummings's

book without a title (1930) and *CIOPW* (1931), announced *Eimi*
as a novel, possibly because it was thought the book would sell better
that way; and the preliminary notices in the press took up that des-
ignation, which was unfortunate. Because the editors of *Contempo*
were friends, Cummings took time out to send the following letter:

> Editors of *Contempo*
> Sir and Madam
>
> learned publishers having allowed as how *Eimi* were a
> novel, ignorant undersigned takes great pleasure in plead-
> ing not guilty: alleging (under oath)
> 1—that *Eimi's* source equals on-the-spot-scribbled
> hieroglyphics
> 2—that, through my subsequent deciphering of said
> hieroglyphics, not one incident has been revalued; not
> one situation has been contracted or expanded; not one
> significance has been warped; not one item has been
> omitted or inserted.
> "Pour l'artiste, voir c'est concevoir, et concevoir, c'est
> composer" (Paul Cézanne)
> if this be fiction, make the etc.
>   Yours
> January 27, '33   E. E. Cummings

The first edition was printed from type and was limited to 1,381
copies, representing the number of orders received up to February 15,
1933. These copies were numbered in ink and signed by Cummings.
The book carries no dedication. Instead, there is a tribute:

> The author joins the publishers in congratulating S. A.
> Jacobs who designed the format of EIMI, solved all the
> technical problems connected with the typesetting and
> printing, and from start to finish personally supervised this
> book's production.

Mr. Covici, who is now with Viking, told me that whenever Jacobs
was in charge of setting up a book he, as a publisher, ceased to worry
about it. Cummings told me that Jacobs, having seen what other
linotypers were making of the copy, snatched the manuscript away,
sat down before his own machine in the basement at 48 Charles
Street, and set up the entire book himself in 72 hours, working almost
without stopping on a diet of coffee.

Although Paul Rosenfeld wrote in the "Cummings Number" of the Harvard *Wake:* "The equilibration of the Swing to the Left, *Eimi* was met with almost total silence, and the fewest of readers know the book," the statement is not entirely true, for there were vociferous voices. *Eimi,* however, despite a new printing in 1949, and another in 1958, has had, perhaps, the "fewest of readers" of any of Cummings's books. The year 1933 may have been a "bad" year for such a book, for then the Soviet could do no wrong, and nothing that was right was being done anywhere else. But 1949 was different; things had been different from about 1945; and the Soviet now loomed with a menace that has grown instead of diminished. As it cannot be said that interest in Russia has decreased, the only possible explanation lies in a combination of circumstances for which the critics are only partly to blame.

Compared with *Eimi, The Enormous Room* appears incredibly simple and can be read with hardly any difficulty, and then only because of a foreign phrase which appears here and there, or because the author's intensity turns what might have been prose into poetry. But while Cummings drew from notes for *The Enormous Room,* for *Eimi* he drew from his diary—in fact, merely transcribed it. Different material equals a different form. Admittedly it is "harder" to read; perhaps the critics wanted a "story." But *Eimi* is not a novel—it is a book of skilfully constructed sentences which portray a time, a place, and people. The importance of sentences lies in this: They not only tell what a writer wishes to convey—even more important, they reveal how that writer thinks and feels. However, it is all a lost cause, if it ever was a cause, for only the good writer is interested in sentences. I do not think the critics ever found out what *Eimi* was, or what it was about. (If they were Leftist, they came to it with prefabricated notions.) But they have only a certain amount of time to devote to any particular book, and novels are easier to read and assess—if they are not particularly original. When Marianne Moore reviewed *Eimi* in *Poetry,* August, 1933, she termed it "a large poem."

Eimi is about a man; it is only incidentally about Russia. In this connection, I will quote Cummings himself:

> So you're thirty-eight?
> Correct.
> And have only just finished your second novel?
> Socalled.

Entitled ee-eye-em-eye?
Right.
And pronounced?
"A" as in a, "me" as in me; accent on the "me."
Signifying?
Am.
How does Am compare with The Enormous Room?
Favorably.
They're not at all similar, are they?

When The Enormous Room was published, some people wanted a war book; they were disappointed. When Eimi was published, some people wanted Another Enormous Room; they were disappointed (from Cummings's Introduction to the Modern Library edition of *The Enormous Room*).

5

Eimi opens with the words

> SHUT seems to be The Verb

and closes with

> (Who
> Loves;
> Creates,
> Imagines)
> OPENS

I have said that Cummings has only one style, and that it suffices because of its range and flexibility. Thus, to the interest in his achievements as a writer must be added a factor, or different interest, that exists independently: the development of a personality. For Cummings has only one subject: himself *vis-à-vis* the world or people. This is from *Eimi:*

> The redfox leans toward me. Why do you wish to go to Russia?
> because I've never been there.
> (He slumps,recovers). You are interested in economic and sociological problems?
> no.

Perhaps you are aware that there has been a change of government in recent years?

yes (I say without being able to suppress a smile).

And your sympathies are not with socialism?

may I be perfectly frank?

Please!

I know almost nothing about these important matters and care even less.

(His eyes appreciate my answer). For what do you care?

my work.

Which is writing?

and painting.

What kind of writing?

chiefly verse;some prose.

Then you wish to go to Russia as a writer and painter. Is that it?

no;I wish to go as myself.

(An almost smile). Do you realize that to go as what you call Yourself will cost a great deal?

I've been told so.

Let me earnestly warn you (says the sandyhaired spokesman for the Soviet Embassy in Paris) that such is the case. Visiting Russia as you intend would be futile from every point of view. The best way for you to go would be as a member of some organization—

but, so far as I know,I'm not a member of any organization.

In that case you should go as a tourist. And I'm speaking not only from the financial standpoint:do you realize that without some sort of guidance you will not see anything,let alone understand?

I realize what you mean. But—

yes? (he encourages).

Again frankly—

Well?

I'm ready to take my chances.

"In my experience," Cummings noted (see p. 221, "The Poet as Playwright"), "enthusiastic advocates of any form of totalitarianism are inclined to be nothing-if-not-queer, mentally if not otherwise

(Henry Wadsworth Longfellow Dana, the Virgil of EIMI, is a good illustration of the otherwise)."

Dana was a dyspeptic "improper" Bostonian with deepset eyes and sagging jowls. He has been described as "a combination of Baron Charlus and The Village Blacksmith" which, bearing in mind who his grandfather was, is a palpable hit. Cummings met Dana in Paris, and ran into him again at the Hotel Metropole in Moscow.

> "I like it here so much!" lyrically explains Virgil "have you noticed a particular feeling in the air—a tension?"
> "Have I!"
> and Dante has. Apparently one cubic inch of Moscow is to all the metropolis of New York—so far as "tension" goes—as all the metropolis of New York is to tension-less Silver Lake,New Hampshire:around,through,under, behind,over myself do amazingly not physical vibrations contract,expand,collide,mesh,and murderfully procreate: each fraction,every particle,of the atmosphere in which moving moves,of my moving,of me,of cityless city,of peo-pleless people,actually is charged to a literally prodigious degree with what might faintly be described as compulsory psychic promiscuity. Whereby(if in no other respect)Mos-cow of the inexorably obsessing mentality, and merely mad NewYork(not to mention most complacent Cambridge Mass and proudly peaceful New Hampshire)belong to dif-ferent universes . . . verily,verily have I entered a new realm, whose inhabitants are made of each other;proudly I swear that they shall not fail to note my shadow and the moving of the leaves.

Another talk with Dana (the "Q" of this dialogue may stand for "Question," but also may represent "Queer"):

> Q: The whole trouble with you is that,like so many people who were brought up on religion,you can't bear the idea of anything doing away with it.
> A: Can't bear the idea of any what doing away with which?
> Q: Of science doing away with religion.
> A: I see:we're supposed to suppose that the new religion,science, does away with religion,the old religion—tahk.

Q (snorts) : How can you be so perverse!

A: I?

Q: As if religion and science weren't direct opposites!

A: Right you are,colonel:every coin has two sides.

Q: Odear. There you go,utterly confusing the issue—

A: Issue? We've all tried paying with one side and keeping the other side for ourselves, haven't we?

Q: But, my dear chap—can't you possibly be serious?

A: I'm afraid I'm being much too serious,comrade.

Q: No you're not—you're being extremely trivial and very childish and rather cheaply amusing.

A: And I'm quoting Emerson.

Q: Emerson?

A: "When me you fly,I am the wings".

Q: Who said that?

A: Brahma, the sage of Concord;who(inconsiderately)went to Rome and found—

Q: O,of course . . . but to return to our muttons. What you can't seem to realise is this:religion imprisons the human mind, whereas science makes people free.

A: What I can seem to realise is that I'd just as soon be imprisoned in freedom as free in a jail—if that's any help.

Q: You simply won't be serious,will you.

Eimi, like *The Enormous Room,* is full of vivid portraits. As the foregoing dialogues indicate, Cummings's people come alive not through description but speech. But foremost, and chiefly, Cummings portrays himself: (here "T" stands for "Turk," "K" for "Kem-min-kz," that is to say, our "nonhero") :

(fervently)K: An "idea" was never "put in practice"—never is,or will be.

T(leaning across how solidly between us situated daylabouring tovarich) :Never?

K: Suppose it were even "scientifically" established that the best "idea",when "put in practice",produced the worst results;that would be 1 face of the cube.

T: Right. But disagreeable . . . probably because I sincerely tried to believe in this religion of humanity.

K: What a murderfully vast difference exists between "standing

up for an idea" (between combatting unvalues;for instance,Amer-
ican unvalues)and inhabiting the "practice" "of" an "idea",in-
habiting so-called socialist Russia!

T: Machinery came to exalt mankind. It remained to degrade
human nature. I cry shame on capitalism,for making a fetich of
machinery in behalf of personal profit. I cry doubly shame on the
5 year plan for glorifying gogetting,in behalf—if you please—of
impersonal profit!

K: This comrade feels very humble;this comrade begins to realise
that soandso enters the pigeonhole for the same "reason" that
suchandsuch doesn't. Take, for illustration, my good friend—
who will soon be my good enemy—the talented author of that
hymn of hate which I've been unbusy "translating":well,what-
ever "reason" for this conversion to communism is probably a
fair lady, which is probably whatever unreason for my own non-
conversion. Amen

On "Mon. 25 Mai," at Moscow's Museum of Western Art, having
waded through "much bourgeoise merde" plus "certainties & un-
certainties" plus "ponderous(wouldbe proletarian)unvisions of amor-
phous 'workers'—and may Marx help the cause of labour if ever
these should come to life," Cummings stood in a room completely
filled with paintings by Picasso and Matisse, "painted when these
artists were in their prime, before 'Jehovah's anaesthetic commandment' dehumanized a world." Here was "oasis"; now our pilgrim
could actually feel not merely "why comradeless Kem-min-kz made
pilgrimage to socialist soviet Russia" but "why socialist soviet Russia
made pilgrimage to Is." This realm only could be called his home;
his, and the home of all creators; and in an eloquent passage he pays
a creator's tribute to it:

> We of whom Is partakes,only to whom our deaths are
> births—savagely makers beneath docile time(and beyond
> conquerable space travellers)who are not contained or com-
> prised,who cannot fail in wonder—possibly we conceive
> dreaming and impossibly freedom:opening and mind's
> agony of first joy—stern we,the hugely forever-pitying
> genitals of spirit
>   continue not to be,arithmetic of unwish!die on, measure
> with your nonexistence our existings! Unplay,very O most

trivial marionettes,unplay—so solemnly—that gameless
game whose ignorant beginning neatly predetermines its
knowledgeable end,or which can merely be to living as an
equation to a smile . . . continue not to be,die on,unplay:
how you shall always everywhere perish! Not here and not
there shall,nor then nor now,perish;not "religion" and not
"science" shall perish,but what undreams would deny feeling shall attain the end of their beginning(always they
shall know the everywhere knowledge,which death is) . . .
whatever knows must die.

    & live—lovers of To Be!eyes of the world,relax;open
and feel,give yourselves only to the giving walls of this
single house—only whose ceilings and whose floors frame
the Self's full perfect doom of imperfection:doom untrans-
latable,doom of which all exhortations constitute unplastic
parodies—breathe in this house,makers of Is, not hope and
not despair,but timeless deep unspace,the single poem,
which builds unconsciousness:immeasurably this house only
shall live! Only these walls may not wilt;only cannot drown
with any earthquake,any wave. "Revolutions" everywhere
must perish, but not these walls:only these walls are
Revolution)

At Harvard, in "Nonlecture Six," he chose, from *Eimi,* the account of his visit to Lenin's tomb, of which this is the concluding
paragraph:

"Certainly it was not made of flesh. And I have seen so many wax-
works which were actual(some ludicrous more horrible most both)so
many images whose very unaliveness could liberate Is,invent Being(or
what equally disdains life and unlife)—I have seen so very many
better gods or stranger,many mightier deeper puppets;everywhere and
elsewhere and perhaps in America and(for instance)in Coney Island."

After several encounters with the "Gay-Pay-Oo" and a series of
fantastic experiences in Kiev and Odessa, Cummings sailed from the
"incredible but real unworld" on an "unbig" Soviet steamer, bound
for Istanbul. This is an impression of Kiev:

"The churches are drowning with stars,everywhere stars blossom,
frank and gold and keen. Among these starry miracles time stops,lives
a silence which thought cannot capture. Now(touched by a resonance

of sexually celestial forms) the little murdered adventure called Humanity becomes a selfless symbol(the doomed assertion of impermanence recoils;falters the loud insignificant intrusion) whereas these stars eternally and all their cathedrals march to some harmony beyond themselves (here the lone star of socialism dies;defeated by all stars)."

This is his welcome to returning life:

> . . .O,now everything begins
> everything expands increasing now even the air celebrates (the sky's building within the sky a steep incredible pleasure out of what far Forms unbelievable;springs a sun,but no mere world:1 atom—of blood of life of all) every-and-thing & opens lifting quietly rising growing-and-upward infinitely opening & throughout coolness alive always deepening growing beside wonder and height rising among promise and dream lifting upon immeasurable
> whereless
> silence
> whom float the unimagined swim the not guessed or at whose eternal brainlike deepness drift the shy immortal
> wanderers invisibly(and visible pilgrims fearless
> of no thing conscious except themselves moving within themselves drifting by their own light swimming a self-creating everywhere now which is against our life possibly more close than dying) now impossibly beyond our mind less than death near floating futures easily how past how indolently present voyaging toward endlessness brave (travellers wandering always always not despairing unresting visible now and now invisible & always pilgrims never tiring fearing
> swift dolls of unutterable wish dressed with mystery and hope)
> poems.
> & ghost-cries . . . ghost-gestures
>   look—
> (new Stars!Stars not-of-heaven awfully
> begin;here
> multiplying suddenly become the

very arising magically
is:looms!a
. . .now. . .
allblossoming finite Firmament of throbbing frenzied
Ifs of leaping fiercely Whys. Now insane structure of To
Be;finally sprouting terror ecstasy and semblance—now a
profound a trivial an architecture of mortality—moves at
us like a
Yes) unfaltering
& toward our ghostship comes,inhabited by thousands
upon millions of manlights, the World

6

The first, and the strangest, reviewing incident in connection
with *Eimi* occurred in the *American Spectator,* of which George Jean
Nathan was the chief editor. Mr. Nathan, for many years the associate
of H. L. Mencken on the *American Mercury,* carried with him to the
new publication some old notions of how to be rambunctious and the
clairvoyance exhibited as drama critic of *Judge.* He instituted a department headed "The Worst Book of the Month." Now it might
be supposed that before a book could be given such a distinctive label
some thought would go into the process of selection—it might be presumed, for example, that a book so designated had first been *read.*
There does not seem to be a single shred of evidence that this was the
case when the April, 1933, issue of the *American Spectator* appeared
with the following blazon:

THE WORST BOOK
OF THE MONTH

Eimi. By e. e. cummings.
6½ x 8½. Pp. 464. $3.00
New York: Covici-Friede.

An April magazine, appearing on the newsstands in March, is
largely set up in February. There were no bound copies of the book
and not even galleys at the time the April *Spectator* went to press.
Covici, Friede issued a statement which began, "The Spectator editors

are to be congratulated for discovering a unique method of book reviewing"; and the editors retorted with a statement that "their sources
of information about forthcoming books are infinite," which sounds
equivocal. Even when the publishers pointed out that "the book exists
only in manuscript, only a part of it having as yet been set up in
print," the *Spectator* literati continued their omniscient pose. The
New York *Times* reported on March 23:

"George Jean Nathan made it plain yesterday on behalf of himself
and his fellow-editors of The American Spectator that he had really
read *Eimi* by E. E. Cummings, before calling it 'the worst book of the
month' in The Spectator's current issue. He explained also that the
phrase 'worst book of the month' is by no means all-inclusive, the
only books given that title being those written by authors of reputation
whose previous books have been of a kind likely to interest readers of
The Spectator."

(The May choice of the *Spectator* for "Worst Book of the Month"
was *Lawrence and Brett: A Friendship,* by the Hon. Dorothy Brett.
This, too, had not yet appeared, and the blazon carried this additional
note: "Passed upon in galley form, Nos. 1 to 99.")

Lewis Gannett wrote in the *Herald Tribune:*

"Lincoln Steffens, who went to Soviet Russia during the Paris
peace conference, returned whispering, 'I have been into the future,
and, by God, it works!' E. E. Cummings went to Russia last summer,
and returned wondering 'why the glorious future of mankind should
consist in every one ecstatically minding every one else's business.'
He did not like it. He says so in a great variety of ways in *Eimi."*

He added: "If only Cummings would condescend to let his readers
read him!"

The Boston *Transcript* said:

"It is by no means astonishing to hear that E. E. Cummings's latest
book, *Eimi,* was put into type under the author's personal supervision,
and that its proofs were read and corrected by its author no less than
eleven times. Even with all this labor and care, however, it is difficult
for any normal mind to understand what the book is all about."

It was not difficult when the view was from the Left. Nathan Asch
wrote in the *New Republic,* April 26, under the heading, "Descent
into Russia":

"Mr. Cummings was very glad to get away from Russia; he had
found that country hell. From Paris, via Poland, he arrived in Mos-

cow, fortified by much several-weeks-learned-in-Paris Russian, stayed twenty-three days, did not go to see the cheerfully-prepared-for-tourists sights, did not get a letter from his wife, did not meet Duranty, found the males and females on the street so unindividual that they were almost not men or women, listened to arguments, went to parties, liked a certain scientist, met Americans-in-Russia, found no gayety, no laughter, went much to the theatre, did not speak to—not even meet—a single worker or peasant, nor visit a single factory, nor dam, nor workers' quarters, nor workers' clubs, nor a prophylactic station. He was made to pay in dollars, he was overcharged, the food was awful, and he had to wait, there was inefficiency, no letter from his wife, and he thought no creative art could come out of this. . . .

"The publishers say: 'Fundamentally, "Emi" constitutes the epic reaction of a human being to a transcendent experience.' It constitutes nothing of the kind. The experience may have been transcendent, but Mr. Cummings was hardly feeling epic. It is not enough to give one's guide the name of Virgil. One also has to be a Dante."

7

Pound wrote Cummings from Rapallo:

Thank you or Covici for *Eimi*.

I dunno whether I rank as them wot finds it painful to read; and if I said anything about obscurity, it wd. fare ridere polli—in view of my recent pubctns. Also I don't think *Eimi* is obscure, or not very; BUT, the longer a work is, the more and longer shd. be the passages that are perfectly clear and simple to read. Matter of scale, matter of how long you can cause the reader to stay immobile or nearly so on a given number of pages. (Obviously NOT to the Edgar Wallace virtue (?) of the oposite hurry scurry.)

Also, despite the wreaths upon the Jacobean brow, [for S. A. Jacobs], a page two or three, or two and one half centimeters *narrower* (at least a column of type that much narrower) might solve all the difficulties. That has, I think, been tested optically, etc. The normal or average eye sees a certain width without heaving from side to side. May be hygienic for it to exercise its wobble, but I dunno that the orfer shd. sacrifice himself on that altar.

At any rate, I can see
"he adds, unhatting and becoming his raven mane,"
but I don't see the rest of the line until I *look specially at it.* Multiply that 40 times per page for 400 pages. . . .

Mebbe there is wide-angle eyes. But chew gotter count on a cert. no. ov yr. readers bein at least as dumb as I am. Even in Bitch and Bugle [read *Hound and Horn*] I found it difficult to read the stuff consecutively. Which probab. annoys me a lot more than it will you.

"At any rate, damn glad to have the book and shall presumably continue taken er chaw now here n naow there.

I suppose you've got a Brit. pubr. for it? Or possibly Cov. has a Lunnon orfice by naow?

Otherwise . . . yr. opinyum re advisability of putting a few [pages] into anth. as horse d'overs or whetters. As few xmpl. p. 338.

Oh well Whell hell itza great woik. Me complimenks.

One gets the impression that Pound had merely dipped into the book, and possibly dipped again before "Oh well," etc. But one day he read it; and then he reviewed it. As his review is valuable for the light it throws on himself at the time he wrote it, as well as on Cummings, and because it is not easily available, I give it in full. It appeared in the December 20, 1934, issue of the *New English Weekly,* with the heading,

"E. E. CUMMINGS ALIVE."

Cummings seems a unique exception to the law that America tries to kill her own litter when ever it produces anything more than a hoglet. Cummings undoubtedly crashed through with "The Enormous Room." There was a war, and a preface, and there was the massed force of the Dial's approval, for E. E. was undoubtedly the white-haired boy for that outfit, although never quite of it.

There was also the mistaken idea of the New York hair-oil contingent, who boomed E. E. C. as a funny man, because of his sense of humour.

They missed his being a slow man, a man who needs

four hundred pages. That wouldn't have suited 'em. A decade ago someone discovered that Cummings "wasn't very obliging."

That was good news in the Rue Notre Dame des Champs. And New York didn't discover it, or rather, didn't uncover it. New York heard he was clever, oh crushingly clever, and sat round hoping for funniness. Some men are born snobs, others occasion snobisms in others. Cummings did and survived it.

Cummings had almost a decade to himself. Certainly in New York for a decade there can have been little other writing that would have stood foreign inspection. Hemingway and McAlmon appeared later in Paris, post war in outlook. Until the publication of "Eimi," "The Enormous Room" stood as an isolated performance, which might have been either an end, a man's one book, or a beginning of something wholly unindicated and undetermined.

"EIMI"

My more intelligent correspondents "in them partibus" write me of the pest of pinks now blowing through small streets of the wilderness. It being 17 years after 1917, after the no longer so recent events in Russia, after the Tarasov-Rodianov's "February 1917"; the half-baked little American pip-squeak has heard about communism, and has been told it is the thing to wear, and that he ought to dress it up with a "literature," the result being, mostly, deplorable.

In so far as any of 'em can be defined as *"histoire morale contemporaine,"* they are modelled on the European tradition as filtered through McAlmon and Mr. Hemingway. "Ghees! ain't it hell to be poor" or "How Mamie slept in a sewer." As necessary reports on the filthy conditions of a hypocritical country in the last staggers of liberal capitalism they are necessary. Many of them are excellent. At least six good writers are writing them. At least ten or twenty volumes of them are worth reading, though they offer almost nothing that requires any discussion by literary critics.

But all this can be very dull. Carlos Williams almost unfailingly succeeds in finding new subject matter; Farrell, Caldwell, succeed quite often, others now and again. Cummings has taken no part in this action.

On the other hand England has not yet seen him. The British publisher has not yet thought of a reverse process. He is so accustomed to SENDING his old stuff to America, that it will need some unusual dynamite to arouse him to the emergence in America, of an author.

For useful comparison with "EIMI," Europe offers only the later Joyce and Miss Stein. I hope this is going to be hard on all three. The snobism that has steamed up around Joyce's writings in regress and about Miss Gertrude Stein's Yiddish gymnastics needs a nail file and razor.

I have gone to bat for Joyce sufficiently often. And I believe no foreign writer can think of England without loathing and contempt when considering the relation of "Ulysses" and England. In that history, my own dithering and piffling fatherland shines out as a beacon light. Idiotic as was the New York suppression, blithering as were some of the American postal laws, inane as still are some of her regulations, "Ulysses" is at any rate by now recognized as a part of letters and ignorant hogs can no longer impede the book's American circulation.

On the other hand, Joyce's mind has been deprived of Joyce's eyesight for too long. You cannot say it is closed altogether, but Joyce knows very little of life as it has been in the large since he finished "Ulysses."

He has sat within the grove of his thought, he has mumbled things to himself, he has heard his voice on the phonograph and thought of sound, sound, mumble, murmur.

Three decades of life have been lived since he began writing, of the last two he has learned almost nothing. Of the dominant and cleaving ideas of the last decade he is nearly unconscious.

That either Mr. Joyce of the regression or Miss Stein have said anything that will be of any interest in itself, apart from their varieties of galimatias, I doubt without any great diffidence. Mr. Cummings on the other hand, has presented a subject. When Russia was interesting, Mr. Cummings got up and went there.

When one of us wants to know about Russia to the extent that Mr. Cummings once wanted to, we might perhaps show like activity. Most parlour Bolsheviks were not so much interested in Russia. Few of them were sufficiently interested to subscribe to that really instructive and highly stimulating periodical, "U.S.S.R. en Construction." That really did tell about Russia—Russia awake to MATERIAL civilization, to all the paraphernalia that boasting America has carried to a higher degree of bathtubbedness, of telephonedness, of nickelplatedness, of meatcannedness than even Europe.

Cummings went to see what else there might be. "EIMI." Had you or I, kind reader, gone to Russia, somewhere or other they would have got us, I mean an IDEA would have got us—for it or against it—the noble aspiration, the worthy perspiration, something would have got us. We would have forgot to be writers. We would have forgotten to take it in at the pores, and lay it there pellucidly on the page in all its slavic unfinishedness, in all its Dostoievskian slobberyness, brought up to date with no past reference, no allusion, just Russia 1920 whatever, must have been 1929. Laid there on the page not reading the least bit like Hudson, but good as "Huddy" was good about birds in the South American wilderness.

This fauna was present. This habitat was its habitat. The Kumrad saw it and smelt it, and wandered about in its darkness.

I thought I was through with introducing new writers. Heaven knows I don't want to write about literature. But here is a new piece of literature—or it was new, and I didn't expect to be called on. I thought there was enough young critical talent in both Britain and America to take care of work by men younger than I am. Or at any rate to see that such work was looked at, once it had come from its publisher.

Does any man wish to know about Russia? "EIMI!" Does any man wish to read an American author whom the

present harassed critic has read and can re-read with pleasure? Here is "EIMI" published, I forget when, in New
York and NOT published in England. Why not published in England, why not imported to England?

Young Cambridge has heard of it. For three weeks, or
three months, young Cambridge talked of it, but Mr.
Cummings wasn't there to talk to them of it.

It is not a specifically Douglasite volume. It belongs to
the Cultural Heritage. It is a *pièce justificative,* it is I
should say The *pièce justificative.* The reader who will take
it slowly (no Englishman can do otherwise if he take it in
at all) will find out why civilized Europe cannot sit
down and wait for Russia to show her.

Chapter 13

"A MAN NOW LIVING"

1

At the time Pound wrote in praise of "E. E. Cummings Alive" in the *New English Weekly,* the author of *Eimi* was without a publisher in the United States. (He was to remain without one until 1938.) His latest collection of poems went the rounds without coming to rest anywhere, and at last Cummings decided to issue the book himself. He called it *No Thanks.*

No Thanks was published April 1, 1935, by S. A. Jacobs at the Golden Eagle Press, 48 Charles Street, in Greenwich Village. There were three editions of the book, all of them limited, including the trade edition. An advertisement before publication stated that there would be nine copies of a "holograph edition" priced at $99; these were quickly subscribed. The subscribers were assured that a poem in holograph, No. 44, would never be printed; hence, the autograph and unsigned editions have a blank page where this poem should be, and there is a blank page in the *Collected Poems* of 1938 and in *Poems 1923-1954.* The poem is perhaps the starkest example of coprology in English verse. It is saved from complete coarseness by its logical structure and verve. Readers who will never see it need not repine, however, for *No Thanks* contains several poems, notably "may i feel said he," which can shock or please—or both—as the case may be.

There are two dedications in this handsome, ledger-shaped volume. The "Initial Dedication" is to

Farrar & Rinehart
Simon & Schuster
Coward-McCann
Limited Editions
Harcourt, Brace
Random House
Equinox Press
Smith & Haas
Viking Press
Knopf
Dutton
Harper's
Scribner's
Covici, Friede

This is a formidable and foolish list. It raises a moral question.

The publisher who is also a good judge of poetry is practically non-existent. He is advised by "readers." But in modern times the judgment of poetry—and indeed of any of the arts—has become one of the most difficult exercises of the esthetic faculty. This is because the "modern" artist not only is a creator, but in addition creates the laws by which his art can be judged. In poetry, a medium of constant experimentation, the requirements of trade, for which publishers' "readers" exist, can have no application whatsoever. Cummings's view, that his anti-Communist position was not welcome, fits the Thirties; but this is conjecture.

The question whether *No Thanks* was a good book or not has nothing to do with the moral issue involved. The issue is whether a poet with the achievements of Cummings in 1935 should have been denied an audience—denied, that is, the opportunity to function completely as a poet by being published. But the book happens to be a good book. The bawdry aside, it is full of inventions—for example, the grasshopper, neither intaglio nor cameo, that *hopped* so agilely into the consciousness of Stanton A. Coblentz. It contains several portraits of unpeople—

> çi gît 1 Foetus(unborn to not die
> safely whose epoch fits him like a grave)

and another who

> does not have to feel because he thinks
> (the thoughts of others, be it understood)

and a variety of "muckers pimps and tratesmen" and "mischief-hatchers," with the Communists prominent:

> kumrads die because they're told)
> kumrads die before they're old
> (kumrads aren't afraid to die
> kumrads don't
> and kumrads won't
> believe in life)and death knows whie
>
> (all good kumrads you can tell
> by their altruistic smell
> moscow pipes good kumrads dance)
> kumrads enjoy
> s. freud knows whoy
> the hope that you may mess your pance
>
> every kumrad is a bit
> of quite unmitigated hate
> (travelling in a futile groove
> god knows why)
> and so do i
> (because they are afraid to love

It leads Cummings to exclaim, in the refrain to a ballade,

> King Christ,this world is all aleak;
> and lifepreservers there are none:
> and waves which only He can walk
> Who dares to call Himself a man.

The book also contains "little joe gould," the previously mentioned "what does little Ernest croon," and the tender

little man
(in a hurry
full of an
important worry)
halt stop forget relax

wait

(little child
who have tried
who have failed
who have cried)
lie bravely down

sleep

big rain
big snow
big sun
big moon
(enter

us)

the incomparable

at dusk
        just when
the Light is filled with birds

and

be of love(a little)
More careful
Than of everything

Finally, the book contains a great number of sonnets, among them

conceive a man,should he have anything
would give a little more than it away

which serves as the epigraph to Chapter Two of this book, and
another to which Mr. Jacobs called my attention. He wrote me:
"The most interesting (for me) poem appears in the CENTER of
the book, where the poet imagines himself dead and buried."

how dark and single,where he ends,the earth
(whose texture feels of pride and loneliness
alive like some dream giving more than all
life's busy little dyings may possess)

how sincere large distinct and natural
he comes to his disappearance;as a mind
full without fear might faithfully lie down
to so much sleep they only understand

enormously which fail—look:with what ease
that bright how plural tide measures her guest
(as critics will upon a poet feast)

meanwhile this ghost goes under,his drowned girth
are mountains;and beyond all hurt of praise
the unimaginable night not known

The "Terminal Dedication" of *No Thanks* reads:

AND
THANKS
TO
R.H.C.

—Cummings's mother, who provided the money for the publication.

Louis Untermeyer reviewed the book in *The American Mercury* for August, 1935. He wrote:

"E. E. Cummings is far more incomprehensible than his poetry. He cannot make up his mind who or what he wants to be. Besides the private person—for there probably is a private E. E. Cummings —there is in him a sensitive commentator and an ornery boy, a skillful draughtsman and a leg-pulling cheapjack, a subtle musician, a silly theorist, a lyric poet, and a clown. Often he tries to be all these creatures at one time, often in the same poem. The result is as madly mixed a collection as this decade has seen."

Cummings replied in his own good time:

mr u will not be missed
who as an anthologist
sold the many on the few
not excluding mr u

(from *1 x 1*, 1944).

2

Cummings remained without a publisher between the publication of *No Thanks,* 1935, and the oddly titled *Collected Poems* of 1938. Ford Madox Ford wrote in *The Forum,* September, 1937:

"Once, with *The Enormous Room,* he swam for the moment to the surface. Today, as far as I know, he supports himself by painting portraits. And he is all the more valuable just because of his experimentalism, not merely in thought but in the minor matter of lettering. Our alphabetic characters are singularly ill-adapted for rendering shades of either rhythm or of the voice. There is no reason in the world why we should not try to make them more expressive. Yet that is supposed to be communism of the dynamitard variety. The American Ladies' Club of Paris once burned in public my *transatlantic review* simply because, tired of overcapitalizing, I printed its title as above. I printed also poems by Mr. Cummings equally without capitals at the beginnings of lines. They took that to be equivalent to advocating the decapitation of monarchs.

"Once more, all writers of any attainment whatever have, for a decade and a half at least, been conscious of the existence of Mr. Cummings—and most of the intelligentsia. Yet he has no readers among the general public. None! And no publisher!'"

Oddly enough, at the time this appeared, the first steps had been taken by a young editor at Harcourt, Brace to bring together all of Cummings's volumes of verse in a collected edition. Charles A. Pearce, now of the publishing firm of Duell, Sloan & Pearce, told me that he first broached the idea over lunch with Miss Bernice Baumgarten (Mrs. James Gould Couzzens), Cummings's agent.

In answer to specific queries, Pearce wrote me:

"I proposed a COMPLETE book, but e.e.c. made the decision to limit it, I believe. There *may* have been other factors in this, but I don't remember them and I doubt they existed.

"It must have been Cummings, not I, who omitted 'Puella Mea,' because that was one of my favorites and I was (am?) all too ready to read it aloud to anyone willing to listen. You can consult my wife on that one. Fact is that the final selection was completely in the hands of Cummings.

"One by-product of the venture always pleased me, too: the recording we made to publicize and promote the book, especially with booksellers to whom about 200 samples went at the time of publication. This was one of the first and remains one of the best of its kind."

Pearce told me that the idea for the book "met with somewhat reluctant approval" at Harcourt, Brace, "but turned out well in the long run." His proposal was made some time in the spring of 1937, and by the end of May, on the eve of Cummings's departure for London with his wife, a tentative contents had been put together. There was, of course, additional sparring. Before leaving the country, Cummings wrote Pearce:

> thanks to your extremely sporting suggestion,the enclosed
> list represents what I like,irrespective of whether it's
> obscene or unsetupable. What I don't like is,naturally,
> whatever I don't feel to be myself.
> write how much this selection disagrees with you & will
> guarantee to reciprocate;my address being,until further
> notice,3 Museum Road,Oxford,c/o Dr Solly Zuckerman

The list that Cummings forwarded with this letter specified the number of poems to be retained and omitted from each of his six previously published books. & (AND) contained 79 poems; 25 were marked for omission. XLI *Poems* contained 41; omissions, 16. *is* 5 contained 84, omissions 6. *ViVa* contained 70, no omissions. *No Thanks,* 71, no omissions, but minus the one in holograph.

On June 28 he wrote from London:

> Have wisely decided not to worry over my Introduction
> till I find out whether or not it can begin "I should like
> it distinctly understood that noone but myself is to blame
> for this selection." Perhaps your lawyer will pass on same
> one of these days.

He and his wife were now in a rooming-house in Chelsea:

> Chelsea is sad. I especially inhabit Paultons Sq &
> generally spend half my time trying to give it an apos-
> trophe. As to the sotospeak rest,games of intellectual
> chance with our pacifist landlady;presumably a frustrated
> Australian paintress,beset with continuous absence of
> domestics & otherwise resembling a Roman reproduction of
> a Greek myth or something not at all unlikely to come

floating extravagantly into one's parlor of a fine summer
morning crying halfdimly over 2 breakfasts "Mister Cummings:
all we artists shall have to go to Mars!"

A postscript states:

> we're leaving in a few hours for Paris by "British
> Airways" & are due to arrive at 17:25

On July 13 Pearce sent a proposed contents based on his earlier
list, but suggesting other omissions, and from the rue de la Bûcherie,
where Cummings and his wife were staying with friends, Cummings
wrote back:

> Leaving out of consideration "Tulips and Chimneys" and "XLI
> Poems",I count 92 ("&" 34,"is5" 12, "Viva" 21, "No Thanks" 25)
> poems which you wish to omit;of which 92,I insist on keeping
> only 14. Which doesn't mean that I insist on increasing your
> total by 14 poems: it means that 14 of the 92 happen to be
> favorites of mine which I couldn't spare without losing
> interest in the book;but that in place of these 14 I'm ready
> to sacrifice 14 others. Thus, I ask you to

keep	*omitting, instead*
"&" Sonnets Realities XV	any one of Sonnets Realities§
	VIII,IX,XII,XIII,XXI
"is 5" ONE VI,XIII,XXVII	ONE VII and two of ONE
	XXIII, TWO IV,FOUR VI
"Viva" XIII,XXXIIII,XL, ...	XI,XII,XV,L,LVI
XLI,LXII	
"No Thanks" 20,30,52, ...	17,29,39,45,62
53,70	

> (§ or leave out all these and keep in 4 poems from the
>   other groups)
> and in asking this meseems am within my rights
>
> concerning format:our hero,being poorbuthonest and(sometimes)
> wearing clothes,he is very naturally partial to something will
> fit his pocket after he's been able to pay the price. But what
> I care infinitely is that each poempicture should remain intact.

Why? Possibly because,with a few exceptions,my poems are essentially pictures. And (in my naif way) I believe that you're one of
the few people in America who can work out such a combination
of typesize and papersize as will allow every picture to breathe
its particular life (no "runover" lines) in its own private world.
A vous le dummy!

shall send, as suggested,the new poems and the introduction along
with corrected galleyproofs.

When proofs arrived, Marion Cummings discovered two poems
had been set twice—"impossibly" and "Paris; this April sunset completely utters." Pearce wrote: "I am not surprised that two of my
favorites got repeated."

Cummings and his wife returned to the United States "for autumn
in New Hampshire," and afterwards spent the winter in Patchin
Place, where copies of *Collected Poems* reached them in February.
Cummings wrote Pearce:

> being a thorow felleau,have taken my socalled
> time & space over new arrival. Verdict:
> congratulations. Marion's:ditto,Et Comment.
> A singularly perspicuous (she considers
> catalogueannouncement of CPs "a decent
> sensible straightforward account") New England-
> ess's:"I think it's your best book since The
> Enormous Room" adding proudly "they're a
> dignified lot,that Harcourt Brace". As one
> unaffiliated with headgear industry,je
> pause

To this, Pearce replied February 17, 1938:

> You are a fine fellow, and your letter of Sunday about the
> book was mighty good to have. We tried to do a decent job.
> We usually do, but in this case, I think we tried to do the
> very best we could. You wouldn't believe it, but there are
> authors who never bother to pat us on the head. In fact,
> they think it is a good thing to insult us regularly, and
> the arrival of a finished book is often the occasion for
> attempted assault.

The jacket of the first edition of *Collected Poems* states:
"Mr. Cummings has written a score of new poems and
an Introduction for this collection. In addition, he has in-
cluded in this book all of the poems from his earlier books
—'Tulips and Chimneys,' 'And,' 'XLI Poems,' 'Is Five,'
'Viva,' and 'No Thanks'—which he wishes to preserve."

The final total was 315, including twenty-two new poems. Despite
the fact that "Puella Mea" and other favorites were missing, the
collection has continuity as well as substance. The last poem in the
book, and the last of the new group, is a sonnet. It is one of the most
beautiful of all his poems:

> you shall above all things be glad and young.
> For if you're young,whatever life you wear
>
> it will become you;and if you are glad
> whatever's living will yourself become.
> Girlboys may nothing more than boygirls need:
> i can entirely her only love
>
> whose any mystery makes every man's
> flesh put space on;and his mind take off time
>
> that you should ever think,may god forbid
> and(in his mercy)your true lover spare:
> for that way knowledge lies,the foetal grave
> called progress,and negation's dead undoom.
>
> I'd rather learn from one bird how to sing
> than teach ten thousand stars how not to dance

Cummings wrote in his Introduction:

> The poems to come are for you and for me and are not
> for mostpeople
> —it's no use trying to pretend that mostpeople and our-
> selves are alike. Mostpeople have less in common with
> ourselves than the squarerootofminus one. You and I are
> human beings;mostpeople are snobs.
> Take the matter of being born. What does being born
> mean to mostpeople? Catastrophe unmitigated. Socialrevo-
> lution. The cultured aristocrat yanked out of his hyperex-

clusively ultravoluptuous superpalazzo,and dumped into an
incredibly vulgar detentioncamp swarming with every con-
ceivable species of undesirable organism. Mostpeople fancy
a guaranteed birthproof safetysuit of nondestructible self-
lessness. If mostpeople were to be born twice they'd probably call it dying—
      you and I are not snobs. We can never be born enough.
We are human beings;for whom birth is a supremely welcome mystery,the mystery of growing:the mystery which
happens only and whenever we are faithful to ourselves.
You and I wear the dangerous looseness of doom and find
it becoming. Life,for eternal us,is now;and now is much
too busy being a little more than everything to seem anything,catastrophic included.

Could anyone really quarrel with this statement?
Several did.

3

      The revived interest in Cummings resulted in several inter-
esting letters. The first was from Selden Rodman, who wrote Cummings that he was editing an anthology, "but I now find myself up
against the prices, which are higher than any other prices quoted on
any other poet living or dead. I wonder whether you will be kind
enough to intervene on my behalf, and at least give me a lower rate
on a few of them?"
      Cummings replied:

            may I somewhat tardily but most sincerely
            salute your generosity and ask it to believe
            that the present writer is as sorry to dis-
            appoint you as he is delighted to learn that
            just for a change I'm expensive?
                                    —yours for living
            P.S. no poet is dead

Pearce wrote Cummings:

      I had a pleasant interview with Carl Sandburg yesterday,
      and he tells me that he has written you a long letter that

was practically a sentence about the COLLECTED POEMS. I
am very keen to have a copy of this letter. Won't you send
me one, or won't you send me the original so that I can
have a copy made?

Sandburg's letter follows:

Dear E E Cummings
    Quite a few months ago when your Collected Poems
came out and for the first time I got at the sequence I said
I would write you a fan letter and the days and weeks
passed by and I didn't get around to it and nevertheless I
reread some of the high spots and said again I must get
around to telling this fellow he has much on the ball and I
like to watch him pitch in his own chosen world series and
he has grand blue sky and stinking prison flowers and fine
lovemaking madrigals and a compassionate identification
with conscientious objectors and the dust of very common
streets and a capacity for exquisite clowning and inexplicable effrontery and somehow he owns what is under his hat
and at some moments he himself does not know whether
he is kidding us or himself or Jesse James or the American
flag the Murrican flag extra extry uxtra mister and he has
had a rich life and is one of those isolationists requiring no
fan letters a sort of a czechoslovak who can take it with dry
tears and merge himself with twilight and darkness and
never be completely divested of his songcraft or his clowning or his adumbrant quaker speculations and some final-
ity of holiness that he would deny and deny
                                        Carl Sandburg

    Marianne Moore also wrote Cummings, after receiving *Collected
Poems:*

Dear Mr. Cummings—
blasphemous, inexorable, disrespectful, sinful author
though you are—

you received a cordial welcome at my door today. I remarked to my mother not long ago, "I wish I could write
something that people would regard with the anticipatory

confidence with which I hear of any new book by E. E.
Cummings." The Introduction to this one makes me blush
for the moderateness of the above statement. The more I
study the equivalences here of "mostpeople's" language,
the formidable use of nursery lore, and the further un-
fortuities,—known to you as technique but never known
to lookers-on,—the better, live-er, more undimmed and
undiminished they seem. Those who are deaf to the sublime, have to be without it; that is their honorarium. So,
no thanks; in the sense that thanks are too trivial.

Sincerely yours,
Marianne Moore

On March 10, 1938, Werner wrote, enclosing a review:

> The attached I clipped from the Daily Worker today. I
> send it to you because I thought you might be pleased.
> When the Daily Worker attacks one it is a badge of righ-
> teousness, for the poor, pusillanimous, doped failures who
> inject themselves with a watered hate supplied in the lab-
> oratories of the Communist International never can be on
> the right side of any issue—except by accident of juxta-
> position. Look out for the day when they praise you! I have
> confidence that that will never happen.
>
> Best of luck!
>
Morrie

> P.S. I have to get the Daily Worker these days, because it
> prints the full transcript of the testimony at the Russian
> trials, and the idiots are so dumb that they don't realize
> that the full transcript is more damaging than any reports
> in the capitalist press.

The *Daily Worker* review of *Collected Poems* began without
sparring:

"Of E. E. Cummings it might be said that he sold his poetic
birthright for a mess of punctuation marks. Unlike Keats, who
feared that his name might be writ in water, Mr. Cummings probably wants his epitaph to read: Here lies one whose name was writ
in lower case. At any rate, some bright Ph.D. might write a thesis

on the Relation between Punctuation Marks and Reaction in the
Poetry of E. E. Cummings."

The reviewer quoted from the Introduction and remarked:

"Of course we can take this as just cute, like so many things about
Mr. Cummings. But if we care to take it seriously we begin to see
the romantic roots of so many nonsensical notions in bourgeois
literature."

He also quoted two poems, with an aside to the *Daily Worker*
linotyper to "excuse and set" the first one "as is" (beginning
"brIght"). But however he may have typed it, it was not set up as
Cummings wrote it. The second one—"kumrads die because they're
told)"—appeared minus the first stanza, and in the final stanza
lines 3, 4 and 5 were omitted.

Collected Poems was also reviewed in the *New Masses* April 12,
1938. There was, of course, no difference in the point of view,
although an initial sympathy with Cummings is evident:

"His first book, *The Enormous Room,* indicated a philosophy
from which he never fled: any kind of underdog was all right with
him, any kind of government or authority impossible. He identified
himself with children, beggars, and whores; and pooped all over
Boston, Harvard, upper-class Americans, and clean, upstanding,
well-dressed boys from Yale. He would write with sympathy and
insight of a sleepless fellow at a window thinking it must be nice
never to have no doubts about why he put the ring on his wife's
finger, and really nice never to wonder whether the damn rent's
going to be paid. He would write with almost sentimental admiration of the smiles and the (very) fine eyes of Communists when
they were being outnumbered fifty to one and beaten up by French
gendarmes. But if it ever looked to him as though Communists
might stand some chance of organizing the world, he would turn
right around (though always fixed to the same base, like a weather-
vane, or a revolving statue) and say that every kumrad (sic) was a
bit of quite unmitigated hate. . . .

"This kind of anarchic philosophy, though it can be occasionally
turned to advantage by revolutionaries, is nothing for them to adopt;
in its own essence it is a counter-revolutionary principle. (At the
same time, aspirants to poetry should be warned that membership
in a responsible and disciplined political organization by no means
guarantees an automatic transfer of values, or renders them immune

to the infections of anarchy when they invade the esthetic field. Still, it ought to help.)"

It does not seem to have helped. A blight fell upon American poetry.

By way of contrast, Peter Monro Jack wrote in the New York *Times Book Review,* June 26, 1938:

"The work that Cummings has set himself to do, and has done with singular constancy, is a poet's work. It will never be remembered as current topics versified or political propaganda. It is in the tradition of romantic individualism, and Cummings is decidedly one of the few who can say 'great God' with some conviction that he'd 'rather be a pagan suckled in a creed outworn' than subscribe to the latest popular and party uses of poetry."

The Pulitzer Prize for the best book of poems published in 1938 was awarded to John Gould Fletcher. Winfield Townley Scott, book editor of the Providence *Journal,* wrote:

"According to an annual custom I am about to comment on the Pulitzer Poetry Award. My comment is, Nuts—itself rapidly becoming an annual custom. . . . Those literary editors who did vote in the straw balloting produced a much more intelligent result than the poetry awarders themselves. They voted for some unmistakably vital verse. The Pulitzer committee avoids this, so that this year— as most frequently of late years—the real news about the Pulitzer Poetry Prize is who did not get it. . . . E. E. Cummings' 'Collected Poems' did not get it—and Cummings never has had it."

He still "never has had it."

4

Cummings was not yet through with the "kumrads" and Soviet Russia; and vice versa.

The Spanish civil war gave the Communists a cause made to order for their particular ends. The cause itself was a noble one, and drew to its defense in the field the ideal-minded of many nations: the preservation of the duly elected Spanish Republican government against the onslaught of foreign invaders led by a native rebel. Many brave men, Communists among them, American as well as European, fought and died in Spain. The slogan of "Spain the graveyard of fascism" was naturally attractive to many Liberals alert to the danger of German-testing of planes and weapons south of the Pyrenees. Spain might indeed have become "the graveyard of fascism" if it had not been for the idiocy and pusillanimity of the Great Powers. The universal muddle was made worse by the Communists, until fear of them overcame the general repugnance felt for Franco.

One of the "front" organizations of the Communists during this period was the League of American Writers. The League sent questionnaires to some 400 authors, and afterwards issued a pamphlet entitled "Authors Take Sides." I quote from a news report of June 25, 1938:

"A poll conducted by the League of American Writers shows that 98 per cent of the 400 authors in this country who answered are in favor of the Spanish loyalists, 1.75 per cent (seven) are neutral and one-quarter (one reply) per cent are pro-Franco."

The item said that among those indicating a neutral stand was E. E. Cummings; but what he did was to return the form after putting in quotation marks, thus:

League of "American" "Writers"

The Communists and the Left-wing generally were all for taking sides; but they did not like it when someone took a side opposite from theirs. Curiously, a great many of those who took sides with the Left in the Thirties switched to the Right in the Forties. It would appear then that they needed a cause, and their need continued when their first choice became untenable. But in the Thirties these were the people who had everything figured out—that is, until the Forties.

5

Ezra Pound came to New York on the liner *Rex* April 30, 1939. It was his first visit to his native land in a quarter century. To ship news reporters he spoke affectionately of his friends, Mr. and Mrs. E. E. Cummings. He told William Engle of the *World-Telegram:*

"I can name one poet writing today. I mean Cummings. When Joyce was writing I ballyhooed him. Not since he retrogressed. Hemingway is a good guy, but I don't suppose we'd want to meet him personally. Spain."

He praised Mussolini: "He has a mind with the quickest uptake of any man I know of except Picabia. Picabia is the man who ties the knots in Picasso's tail."

The tall man with the pointed red beard, who had corrected the poems of Yeats and the poetry of Eliot, who had ballyhooed Eliot, Yeats, Tagore, Cummings, and Joyce, was now ballyhooing a strange subject for a poet. He told Engle:

"I regard the literature of social significance as of no significance. It is pseudo pink blah. The men who are worth anything today are definitely down on money—writing about money, the problem of money, exchange, gold and silver. I have yet to find a Bolshevik who has written of it."

Asked if he thought there would be a war, he replied:

"Nothing but devilment can start a new war west of the Vistula. I'm not making any accusation against anyone. But the bankers and the munitions interests, whoever and wherever they may be, are more responsible for the present talk of war than are the intentions of Mussolini or anyone else."

Cummings was in bed with grippe when Pound knocked at 4 Patchin Place, but sat up to welcome the visitor. He told me later that he—and his wife—had been extremely disconcerted by Pound's tirades, and were relieved when he left for Washington in a futile effort to interest members of Congress in his monetary views.

The story of Pound's broadcasts from Rome has been too often told for more than a brief mention here. A charitable view—and I think the correct one—is that he was already sick when he began to make them. Sick or not, only the most rabid of Pound's followers can continue to make believe that his broadcasts were not "contrary to his duty of allegiance to the United States," as stated in his indictment for treason by a Federal grand jury in Washington, D.C. He gave himself up on May 5, 1945, near Genoa, and was confined in a U.S. Army prison camp near Pisa. A ragged Confucius was his sole library. A guard has described how he read, "or simply sat, and combed his ragged beard, watching the Pisa road." He himself has described his miserable surroundings in *The Pisan Cantos*. On November 18 he was flown from Italy and placed in the District of Columbia jail to await trial. He was then sixty years old.

A fairly comprehensive account of his life, work, and influence, together with the views of several eminent writers, appeared in *PM*, New York's short-lived afternoon tabloid newspaper. Its author

attempted to be fair, and by and large wrote objectively. He gave
full expression to his admiration for Pound's achievements in the
realm of literature, and quoted excerpts from his poetry and letters.
He also quoted excerpts from his broadcasts. He was afterwards
attacked for "defending" Pound, and attacked for "attacking" him. In
the former category was the *New Masses,* which followed the *PM*
article with a symposium of its own, in which all the contributors
declared Pound should be executed forthwith, some favoring hanging,
some shooting, although he had not yet been tried, and consequently
had not been found guilty of anything. So much for their claim
that "Communism is twentieth century Americanism."

To the symposium in *PM* Cummings contributed the following:

> Re Ezra Pound—poetry happens to be an art;and artists
> happen to be human beings.
>
> An artist doesn't live in some geographical abstraction,
> super-imposed on a part of this beautiful earth by the
> nonimagination of unanimals and dedicated to the proposi-
> tion that massacre is a social virtue because murder is an
> individual vice. Nor does an artist live in some soi-disant
> world,nor does he live in some socalled universe,nor does
> he live in any number of "worlds" or in any number of
> "universes." As for a few trifling delusions like the "past"
> and "present" and "future" of quote mankind unquote,
> they may be big enough for a couple of billion super-
> mechanized submorons but they're much too small for one
> human being.
>
> Every artist's strictly illimitable country is himself.
>
> An artist who plays that country false has committed
> suicide;and even a good lawyer cannot kill the dead. But a
> human being who's true to himself—whoever himself may
> be—is immortal;and all the atomic bombs of all the anti-
> artists in spacetime will never civilize immortality.

This was written before Cummings had seen the broadcasts from
Rome. It was still a valid statement for him after he had seen them.
He read it at Harvard, referring to Pound as "this selfstyled world's
greatest and most generous literary figure: who had just arrived at
our nation's capitol, attired in half a GI uniform and ready to be

hanged as a traitor by the only country which ever made even a pretense of fighting for freedom of speech" (Nonlecture Four).

Cummings's generosity was not limited to this or other expressions.
Julien Cornell, Pound's counsel, wrote me (June 20, 1957):

> In the course of preparing to prove that Ezra Pound was
> mentally unfit to stand trial, I sought information con-
> cerning him from a number of his friends, among them
> E. E. Cummings. For this purpose I went to Cummings'
> home on Patchin Place, New York, in November 1945.
> He and his wife, Marion, were in their living room. They
> expressed concern over Pound's condition, which I de-
> scribed to them as a physical and mental breakdown
> brought about by his imprisonment. I also told them of my
> plan to have him examined by a leading psychiatrist, and to
> secure hospital treatment for him.
>
> Although nothing had been said about a contribution,
> Cummings went over to a desk in a corner of the room and
> came back with a check which he handed to me, saying, "I
> recently sold a painting and I don't need the money. Please
> use this for Ezra."
>
> I was, of course, much surprised and moved by this
> spontaneous generosity, and by the large amount of the
> gift. I told Cummings that the money would be used to
> secure psychiatric and medical treatment for Pound.
>
> Although this was an outright gift, with no thought of
> repayment, Mrs. Pound repaid it a year or so later after
> she had succeeded in obtaining the release of personal
> funds which had been blocked in England.

For "desk" read "table." The check was for $1,000.

6

In 1940 appeared 50 *Poems,* a volume in which Cummings
continued to express his own stance, which was and is that of an
individual who happens to be a poet. He was his own position,
which of course was and is anathema to those who "take sides." I
am tempted to use Powys's forceful phrase, "the perfectly natural man

confronting the universe," for if there is a better definition that can
fit Cummings, I do not know it. In *50 Poems* he wrote:

> wherelings whenlings
> (daughters of ifbut offspring of hopefear
> sons of unless and children of almost)
> never shall guess the dimension of
>
> him whose
> each
> foot likes the
> here of this earth
>
> whose both
> eyes
> love
> this now of the sky

   This is the volume which contains "my father moved through
dooms of love," "a pretty a day," "anyone lived in a pretty how
town," "these children singing in stone," "(sitting in a tree-),"
among other enchantments, and a sonnet which expresses his undeviating undeviated view, whether we look backward to *Tulips and
Chimneys* or forward to *Poems 1923–1954:*

> there are possibly 2½ or impossibly 3
> individuals every several fat
> thousand years. Expecting more would be
> neither fantastic nor pathological but
>
> dumb. The number of times a wheel turns
> doesn't determine its roundness;if swallows tryst
> in your barn be glad;nobody ever earns
> anything,everything little looks big in a mist
>
> and if(by Him Whose blood was for us spilled)
> than all mankind something more small occurs
> or something more distorting than socalled
> civilization i'll kiss a stalinist arse
>
> in hitler's window on wednesday next at 1
> E.S.T. bring the kiddies let's all have fun

But now, with the beginning certainty that the United States would be drawn into the war, there was much soul-searching among the intellectuals. The Communists had no such difficulty. They saw the war as a conflict that did not concern America—because it did not concern Russia—and were scathing in their denunciations of Great Britain and France as well as Germany. Their tune changed when Russia was invaded, thus fulfilling Cummings's observation: "moscow pipes good kumrads dance)"—for when this happened, they wanted everything to go to Stalin, regardless of other fronts. The embryo commissars had become generalissimos.

On June 10, 1940 the *New Republic* printed an article by Archibald MacLeish entitled "Post-war Writers and Pre-war Readers." He made two points: "The first is the attitude toward the contemporary crisis of the young generation in America. The second is the responsibility for that attitude of the writers of the generation to which I belong." The attitude was expressed in "the profound distrust of words and of principles [which] seem to characterize a considerable part of the young generation today." The writers were "men like Barbusse, Latzko, Dos Passos, Ford Madox Ford, Ernest Hemingway, Erich Maria Remarque and Richard Aldington"—all of them authors of war books. But, added MacLeish: "They were also books filled with passionate contempt for the statements of conviction, of purpose and of belief on which the war of 1914–1918 was fought. And they left behind them in many minds the conclusion that not only the war and the war issues but *all* issues, all moral issues, were false —were fraudulent—were intended to deceive." He concluded that these books were "disastrous as education for a generation which would be obliged to face the threat of fascism in its adult years."

The gist of what I have thus far presented was incorporated in a wire by the editors of *Life* and sent to a number of writers, including some not named by MacLeish, with the additional comment, "The moral and spiritual unpreparedness in arms he blamed squarely upon writers like himself and like you," and the request to "wire fifty or a hundred words of comment."

Cummings told me that when he received the telegram from *Life* he went walking in the Square. When he returned to Patchin Place he replied:

"If you will stand in the supposed fountain at Washington Square,

New York City, and look up at the so called arch, you will find yourself reading 22 words by a man now living."

The words, engraved across the back of the Arch, are:

LET US RAISE A STANDARD TO WHICH THE WISE
AND THE HONEST CAN REPAIR   THE EVENT
IS IN THE HAND OF GOD   WASHINGTON

are being published in England we are anxious to have a good introduction. We would like to use your article in the Cummings Number of THE HARVARD WAKE. Mr. Cummings himself has suggested this and I liked it immensely so we hope you will agree to let us use it. Could you possibly cable or write me airmail about this? All the proofs of the book are being sent to Cummings for correction, so you might like to look at your article again.

I hope to be coming to America in the autumn and if I do, hope I will be able to meet you.

Connolly met Frankenberg at a party given by Harvey Breit. On March 9, 1947, he wrote from London:

It was very nice meeting you, and I hope we meet again soon. It is very depressing in England now, and owing to the electricity cuts, the printers have been unable to produce the revised proofs of ONE TIMES ONE yet—an additional cause for gloom. [An addition, in ink, after this sentence: *They have just come!*]

This news was followed by Connolly's announcement that "ONE TIMES ONE will be published on 14th October—at last!"

To this Frankenberg replied:

"I'm looking forward with the greatest eagerness to ONE TIMES ONE. How auspicious that the publication date fell on Cummings' birthday!"

The book came; Frankenberg wrote:

Thank you for ONE TIMES ONE and congratulations on making such a beautiful book. It outshines the American edition in every way. The type is so much more readable. I know Cummings is enormously pleased; we admired it together, jonquil binding and all.

But neither the auspicious date nor Frankenberg's excellent introduction, neither the superior type nor the yellow binding, proved of avail in the matter of English prejudice against innovation. A book of poems whose opening line was "nonsun blob a" baffled and infuriated reviewers, some of whom returned the book unread. It might have been better if Connolly, staunch admirer of Cummings's work that he

is, had made a selection from all of the poetry, beginning with the
early traditional ones. Progression to Cummings's experiments would
have been gradual, with delight and surprise along the way. But this
is talk about another book.

3

1 x 1 contains, among its many delights, Cummings's con-
tinuous incantation to spring—

> Hills jump with brooks:
> trees tumble out of twigs and sticks;

and

> until and i heard
> a certain a bird
> i dreamed i could sing

and

> (such a sky and such a sun
> i never knew and neither did you
> and everybody never breathed
> quite so many kinds of yes)

Against the airy panorama of the natural world streaked with
sounds like invisible leaves Cummings projects his consistent philosophy,

> (blow friend to fiend:blow space to time)
> —when skies are hanged and oceans drowned,
> the single secret will still be man

for which this ending of a sonnet is summation:

> such was a poet and shall be and is

> —who'll solve the depths of horror to defend
> a sunbeam's architecture with his life:
> and carve immortal jungles of despair
> to hold a mountain's heartbeat in his hand

The book also contains a poem of more than special significance
for the student of his work.

New Hampshire has been important to Cummings. It is not only because his father was a native of that state; it was there that he met Sam Ward, caretaker of Joy Farm, whose epistolary style, by Cummings's own admission, influenced the poet.

"I remember once he wrote: 'we had a Big snow,' " Cummings said. "He'd write 'i'—not 'I'—because 'I' wasn't important to him.

"Sam Ward's way is the only way. Instead of being artificial and affected, it is the conventional way that is artificial and affected. I am not a scholar, but I believe only in English is the 'I' capitalized" (interview with Harvey Breit).

Sam Ward, New Hampshire farmer, shares with the Greeks, Elizabethans and Jacobeans the honor of influencing his neighbor Cummings. *They* have their own mighty monuments, and it is a pleasure to record that Cummings has memorialized his friend, who died a few years ago, with this poem in *1 x 1:*

> rain or hail
> sam done
> the best he kin
> till they digged his hole
>
> :sam was a man
>
> stout as a bridge
> rugged as a bear
> slickern a weazel
> how be you
>
> (sun or snow)
>
> gone into what
> like all them kings
> you read about
> and on him sings
>
> a whippoorwill;
>
> heart as big
> as the world aint square
> with room for the devil
> and his angels too
>
> yes,sir

what may be better
or what may be worse
and what may be clover
clover clover

(nobody'll know)

sam was a man
grinned his grin
done his chores
laid him down.

Sleep well

Anne Barton told me when she gave me the snapshot of Ward and
his wife which appears in this book: "Mr. Ward looks dour, but he
was a beautiful man. His smile was warm and entrancing—if he liked
you."

4

In 1944, Oscar Williams, a successful and indiscriminate
anthologist, conceived the idea of editing a collection of war poems.
He invited poems from both soldiers and civilians. He also asked
his contributors to "send along prose comments giving their ideas on
the relationship between poetry and war." Cummings replied to
Williams's letter, October 30, 1944, from Patchin Place:

I'll gladly send you a short
statement re "war";provided
you'll let me read proof(*until
I'm satisfied*) not only on my
statement but on any poems of
mine which are included in
your anthology.

On February 28, 1945, Cummings wrote Williams again, returning
proofs:

enclosed find proof with
corrections marked,also
a typewritten list of

the corrections. Please
let me have another proof
as soon as possible

The corrections, filling a page, covered the statement as well as the poems, which were: "i sing of Olaf glad and big," "my sweet old etcetera," "it was a goodly co," "all ignorance toboggans into know," "life is more true than reason will deceive," and "plato told." The statement contained this paragraph:

"When you confuse art with propaganda, you confuse an act of God with something which can be turned on and off like the hot water faucet. If 'God' means nothing to you (or less than nothing) I'll cheerfully substitute one of your own favorite words, 'freedom.' You confuse freedom—the only freedom—with absolute tyranny. Let me, incidentally, opine that absolute tyranny is what most of you are really after; that your so-called ideal isn't America at all and never was America at all: that you'll never be satisfied until what Father Abraham called 'a new nation, conceived in liberty' becomes just another subhuman superstate (like the 'great freedom-loving democracy' of Comrade Stalin) where an artist—or any other human being—either does as he's told or turns into fertilizer."

Mr. Williams's anthology, *The War Poets,* reached the Soviet Union probably around the end of 1946, and with the war over, its literary men were again free to resume their roles as stooges of the state. On January 6, 1947, the New York *Times* carried a London dispatch about a Moscow broadcast:

"American and British poets devoted their writings on war themes to 'superficial descriptions of their own emotions evoked by secondary features of the war,' a Moscow radio commentator said tonight.

"The broadcaster said such poetry had 'nothing in common with either the impassioned words of the great writer or the calm reserve and courage of the fighting man.' He added that such work could emanate only from two sources: 'a feeling of loneliness and confusion or a profound indifference to the outside world.'

"Of the American poet and novelist E. E. Cummings, author of 'The Enormous Room,' the Moscow critic said: 'He attacked the appearance of any kind of ideology in literature. But in a discussion on war poetry he did not refrain from the biggest lies about the Soviet Union.' "

There was no mention in the dispatch of the Williams book, or in the follow-up story in the *Times* the next day, which appeared on the Book Page. Under the heading, "Poets Here Scorn Soviet Attack on Work," Cummings declared:

"To be called a liar by anyone even remotely associated with the present Russian tyranny is, in my proud and humble opinion, a strictly unmitigated honor."

Chapter 15

A CONSPECTUS

1

The Spring, 1946, issue of the Harvard *Wake*—the "Cummings Number"—is, chiefly, a collection of tributes (Cummings himself contributed a fairy tale, a poem and *Santa Claus*). "It is indicative to note," said the editors' foreword, "that from so diverse a group of poets, authors and critics who contributed to this issue, so many have said essentially the same thing about Cummings. But this fact is undeniable: he is the natural gadfly to an opiated and pasteurized American public." Some of the lengthier contributions have appeared in books; for this one I choose part of a letter from Allen Tate and brief statements from John Dos Passos and Karl Shapiro. (I have already quoted from Paul Rosenfeld.) First, the letter:

"What I am about to say will sound like irony because no man should be praised for the minimum performance of his obligation as a human being, which is to remain human; and no poet deserves praise for remaining a poet. Yet in looking back over the war years I see only one American poet who kept his humanity and his poetry, and that man is Estlin Cummings."

John Dos Passos wrote:

"So few people, especially among those who make it their business to write about writing, seem to think of writing as a special skill, like the skill of a fisherman, or a farmer or an experimental chemist, that it's not surprising that after twenty years they are still telling us about the oddities of E. E. Cummings's work. To his contemporaries who have followed roughly similar occupations it's his skill that has been so continually stimulating. The oddities are a side issue. Anyway, good English writing, notably at times when there was need to deal with some fundamentally fresh aspect of life, has been full of oddities. They are a by-product of originality."

Dos Passos's view is not shared by many of those who "make it their business to write about writing." There is no room here, and indeed if there were I would see no purpose in it, to list or quote from the distinguished critics who have painstakingly examined Cummings's language to see what made his poems tick, a figure of speech that is not intended to be far-fetched, for they were left at the end with an array of chipped jewels and the main-spring missing. Some witness for the prosecution will not be out of place, however, and I choose Louise Bogan, who wrote in *Achievement in American Poetry:*

"Cummings's insistence, over a period of twenty-five years, on his youthful typographical oddities tended, as time went on, to become tiresome; and his failure to mature, emotionally and intellectually, finally introduced a note of peevishness into his work as a whole."

To this statement, made by a justly eminent writer, herself a poet, I should like to oppose two others. Horace Gregory and Marya Zaturenska wrote in *A History of American Poetry:*

"The entire question of Cummings's maturity in the writing of his poetry has been and still remains a private matter. In the light of Cummings's accomplishments and in the recognition of the boundaries or limits that they have circumscribed, it is very nearly an impertinence for anyone to tell him to 'grow up,' for one must not forget that he is one of the finest lyric poets of all time."

The second statement is from a letter by Sherwood Anderson, who wrote to Van Wyck Brooks in 1923:

"My dear Brooks, isn't there at least a chance that the fear of emotional response to life may be as much a sign of immaturity as anything else? It does seem so to me."

2

Xaipe: Seventy-One Poems, published in 1950, is the last separate volume before the monumental *Poems,* of which it is the last section. It thus offers an opportunity for discussion of Cummings's achievement as a poet and those "oddities" on which certain critics have harped. To a great extent that achievement has been presented to the reader who has followed my pages thus far. So that, even without further evidence, it must be apparent that Cummings is the author of a large body of work which, by its individuality and range, its power and influence, wears a major aspect, certainly for our time. His originality is all the more remarkable because he has functioned in an age of eclectics—Pound, Eliot, Joyce, and other synthesists (painters above all).

I have earlier referred to his experiments, and particularly to his use of *tmesis*—the separation of the parts of a word or words—to achieve simultaneity. Like Picasso in painting, Cummings has continued to probe the syntactical barriers of language in a search for effects often yielded, and perhaps equally as often with results bewildering to the ordinary reader. Picasso said: "I do not seek—I find"; Cummings, with equal candor, might say: "I do not find—I seek." For he has constantly, devotedly, sought for the secret of emotion and movement that lies at the heart of words. This is a poet's work. It has had, and will continue to have, an incalculable impact on his contemporaries, as the experiments of Picasso have had on the painters of our time. To complete the parallel: both the painter and the poet have created their masterpieces, but perhaps have found their greatest impetus and joy in constant experimentation to push back the frontiers of language and line, poetry and paint.

An examination of Cummings's successive volumes—except the first three which were mere samplings from a large general stock—reveals a progressive growth in depth, force and invention, until single lines are almost painfully concentrated, and subtleties of texture and movement occur that sight-readers can easily overlook. An obvious comparison is suggested by the sonnet in *Xaipe* about the Canterbury pilgrims and the passage about Chaucer in "Puella Mea." More relevant, however, are the "facts" of such a poem as "no time ago," quoted earlier, and the sonnet beginning

> so many selves(so many fiends and gods
> each greedier than every)is a man
> (so easily one in another hides;
> yet man can,being all,escape from none)

which reveal growth on all levels, not excluding the poet as human
being as well as the poet as craftsman. In addition *Xaipe,* like his
other books, is one more testament of "the perfectly natural man confronting the universe." For once again Cummings has celebrated
earth and people—or, more properly, persons. There is also a general:

> (five foot five)
> neither dead
> nor alive
> (in real the rain)

a statue:

> why must itself up every of a park
>
> anus stick some quote statue unquote to
> prove that a hero equals any jerk
> who was afraid to dare to answer "no"?

the mob:

> (as
>
> the boodle's bent is the
> crowd inclined it's
> freedom from freedom
> the common man wants)

and, in the poem about Paul Rosenfeld, where an exclamation point
and parenthesis are made to express the surprise and pathos of death,
a friend:

> o
>
> the round
> little man we
> loved so isn't

no!w

a gay of a
brave and
a true of a

who have

r
olle
d i

nt

o

n

o

w(he)re

In a book of tributes to this much loved man, Allen Tate wrote:
"One Sunday he was to come to us for dinner. After we had waited
until about nine thirty we decided that he had forgotten it. My wife
thought it considerate not to remind him; so she decided not to telephone him but to invite him again in a few days; for even the appearance of discourtesy in his behavior distressed him. Two days later
Marion Cummings telephoned us from New Hampshire to ask us to
send flowers, for her and Estlin, to Paul's funeral. That was how, in
New York, in 1946, one heard about the death of one's old friend
and new neighbor." (Rosenfeld had recently moved from Irving Place
to the Village.)

3

From the mass of criticism of his work—it must fill shelves by
now—only one fact emerges with any kind of clarity: Cummings is
"different." ("Singular" no longer conveys the meaning it once had.)
To quarrel with this simple proposition has given an occupation to
many, who might otherwise have grabbled for meanings in Anacreon
or written, like Zimmerman, "On Solitude." But this, if obvious to
his critics, has not been relished by them.

In part, what has disconcerted his commentators is an unceasing preoccupation with discovery, accompanied by a seeming delight in recording everything he finds out. Of the first part of this conclusion, some words of Edmund Wilson, written in 1924, still apply: "Whatever Mr. Cummings is, he is not insulated or chilled; he is not indifferent to life. Eagerly and unconstrainedly, he takes what the world has to offer. His poetry is the expression of a temperament of a kind very rare in America—of a being who desires and enjoys, who reacts to everything that touches him with a tenderness or a mockery quite free from the inhibitions from which so much American writing is merely the anguish to escape." Of the second, it may be said that in the study of a personality such as Cummings's, the complete—if complex—record of his reactions can be useful; but in any strict estimate of his achievement it must be added that while some of his poems are merely cryptic, some mere *jeux d'esprit,* a few have led to a kind of persistent mischief by distracting from his real accomplishment.

Karl Shapiro wrote in the Harvard *Wake:* "His small shot he expended on various wops, kikes, niggers, colonels, and professors, evidently in behalf of all the putains in New York and Paris, plus the balloonman and various 'poets yeggs and thirsties.' He ended, like the leader of a finely divided minority, by becoming a snob. See the introduction to the *Collected Poems."*

Having turned again to the introduction I read, "The poems to come are for you and for me and are not for mostpeople" and "You and I are human beings;mostpeople are snobs."

Take your choice.

I propose, however, to examine one of the poems which has bothered others besides Mr. Shapiro:

> a kike is the most dangerous
> machine as yet invented
> by even yankee ingenu
> ity(out of a jew a few
> dead dollars and some twisted laws)
> it comes both prigged and canted

This poem, on its first appearance in the *Quarterly Review of Literature* and afterwards on page 46 of *Xaipe,* dampened the ardor of some of Cummings's admirers, although it was not long before a different kind of explanation than the seemingly obvious one began to appear. A writer in *Congress Weekly,* a Jewish publication, stated unequivocally: "Even a cursory examination of Exhibit 46 should prove that, far from being anti-Semitic in intent, the lines are pointedly and effectively anti anti-Semitic."

But this view was not shared by other writers in *Congress Weekly.* Among them was Stanton A. Coblentz, who began his contribution with the fearless statement: "In articles for other publications, I have expressed my opinion of E. E. Cummings as a poet." Mr. Coblentz was only too happy to have another kind of ammunition passed to him. He now wrote: "Under these circumstances, I believe that Cummings as a writer is socially as vicious as he is poetically base."

I asked Cummings: "What is the real meaning of poem 46 in *Xaipe?* Is it reaction to a particular individual?" He replied:

"I feel that a poem 'means' differently for each individual who encounters it;but which(if any)of its 'meanings' deserves to be called the 'real' one,I don't know. All I can even try to tell you is what this poem means so far as I'm concerned.

"Whereas in unpopular parlance 'a kike' equals a jew,for me 'a kike' equals an UNjew. Why? Because for me a jew is a human being;whereas 'a kike' is a machine—the product of that miscalled Americanization,alias standardization(id est dehumanization)which, from my viewpoint,makes out&out murder a relatively respectable undertaking."

4

It was Allen Tate who brought T. S. Eliot to Patchin Place—not, I have been told, a joyous occasion, for Mr. Eliot remained wrapped in his reserve, and Cummings had little opportunity to be entertaining. Atmosphere and moods changed when Mr. Tate returned after handing Eliot into a taxi, hopped on a chair, and danced an impromptu jig. In 1950, John Malcolm Brinnin brought Dylan Thomas. Mr. Brinnin has described how the meeting came about. At a bar on Christopher Street Thomas mentioned that he "had hoped to meet E. E. Cummings."

"I phoned Marion Morehouse (Mrs. Cummings), who said they would be delighted to have us come over right away," Brinnin wrote. "We walked the few blocks to Patchin Place where one apartment house holds Cummings's living quarters and his studio. Once they had overcome a brief, exploratory and mutual shyness, Dylan and Cummings seemed happily at ease and intimately sympathetic as they came upon ways to express the curiously double-edged iconoclasm that marks the work and character of each of them. As our teatime conversation ranged lightly over literary terrain, it seemed to me that some of their judgments showed the acerb, profound and confident insights of artists who in their work have defined a world within the world, and that some showed merely the conspiratorial naughtiness of gleefully clever schoolboys. Cummings's poetry, both Dylan and I knew, had for years met with determined or outraged resistance in England; often, with but a puzzled and tentative interest. Introducing this subject himself, Cummings told us of recent instances when a book of his had been returned to its English publisher by wary reviewers who suspected a literary hoax. In distinction to this reaction, Cummings was touched, I felt, to have been paid the first respect of a British poet whose work he regarded so highly. He had been so moved by Dylan's reading the previous Thursday evening, his wife told me, that he had left the auditorium to walk the streets alone for hours" *(Dylan Thomas in America)*.

Around the corner from Patchin Place, and a short walk up West Eleventh Street, was St. Vincent's Hospital where three years later Dylan Thomas would die. To the *Yale Literary Magazine,* which published a memorial issue in 1954, Cummings contributed the following:

FROM MY DOUBTLESS LIMITED POINT OF VIEW THE ONLY THING TO SAY ABOUT DYLAN THOMAS IS THAT BEING A TRUE POET HE'S ALIVE

To me he said, returning Georges Blond's *The Great Migrations:* "I knew a couple of lemmings once. Nobody could stop them. On they rushed—straight ahead—and plunged in." He paused, gesturing. "Hart Crane and Dylan Thomas."

5

In *95 Poems,* his first separate collection since *Xaipe,* he has again taken his stand on the side of Nature and in behalf of particular persons. It is a book redolent of the seasons, streaked by flights of birds, and days when to stand(alone)in some

    autumnal afternoon:
    breathing a fatal
    stillness;while

    enormous this how

    patient creature(who's
never by never robbed of
day)puts always on by always

    dream,is to

    taste
        not(beyond
        death and

        life)imaginable mysteries

Two of the birds are the "crazy jay blue," which Cummings nevertheless salutes, it being part of the scheme of things, and the chickadee:

        spirit colossal
        (& daunted by always
        nothing)you darling
        diminutive person

        jovial ego(&
        mischievous tenderly
        phoebeing alter)
        clown of an angel

        everywhere welcome
        (but chiefly at home in
        snowily nowheres
        of winter his silence)

        give me a trillionth
        part of inquisitive
        merrily humble
        your livingest courage

Both the chickadee and phoebe say "phoebe," hence the play on
alter ego. But here all comparisons end, for the phoebe is gross, the
chickadee crisp and bright-eyed; and "darling" is the correct word.
Of spring:

in time of daffodils(who know
the goal of living is to grow)
forgetting why,remember how

in time of lilacs who proclaim
the aim of waking is to dream,
remember so(forgetting seem)

in time of roses(who amaze
our now and here with paradise)
forgetting if,remember yes

in time of all sweet things beyond
whatever mind may comprehend
remember seek(forgetting find)

and in a mystery to be
(when time from time shall set us free)
forgetting me,remember me

Of the particular persons, I choose "dominic depaola" who

gives me a most tremendous hug

knowing
i feel
that

we & worlds

are
less alive
than dolls &

dream

The book also contains two poems—"Thanksgiving (1956)" and
"i am a little church(no great cathedral)"—which will be found in
the next chapter; the birthday poem "For Marion" quoted earlier,
and a sonnet which ends

i carry your heart(i carry it in my heart)

Chapter 16

THE POET AS READER

1

Public appearances by writers are not new, but the vast number of readings by contemporary poets is a modern phenomenon. What it means I leave to the sociologists to decide. They have had a long time to ponder the subject, for the vogue for eminent speakers in this country has a long history, and almost as long has been the vogue for speakers who were writers. Perhaps it is due to American love of a spectacle. But it is not so simple as all that, for nowadays the audiences at readings have read the poetry—enough of it, anyway, to feel *au courant*. It is partly spectacle, all the same.

Gerald Weales, who has made a study of the reading poets of our time in "The Poet as Player," divides them into three categories: performer, personality, and public speaker. In the first, he placed Dylan Thomas, Dame Edith Sitwell, W. H. Auden, Ogden Nash, and E. E. Cummings. In the second, Marianne Moore, Wallace Stevens, T. S. Eliot, Robert Frost, and William Carlos Williams. In the third: Louis MacNiece, Archibald MacLeish, and Stephen Spender. "If success is measured by the size of the crowds that flock to hear him, the performer is the matinee idol of the poetic circuit," Mr. Weales wrote.

Mr. Weales heard Cummings read at the Poetry Center of the
Y.M.H.A., Lexington Avenue at 92nd Street, New York City. He
said of him:

"He is an actor. He uses no gimmicks, no fanfares, no toy balloons.
He simply comes on stage, sits at a table, and reads everything carefully, intelligently, correctly. On the night that I saw Cummings, the
house was not nearly full, an indication that even at this distance
George Bernard Shaw is right. When he was a dramatic critic, Shaw
used to preface each good acting notice with the prediction that the
public, preferring shimmer to substance, would completely ignore the
actor in question. Although Cummings is a handsome man, with a
face like a sensitive truck driver, his performance is aimed at the
mind, and he cannot expect to compete with velvet and gold. The
care with which he works is apparent in the fact that he reads all the
casual introductory material which has been prepared with the precision that marks his poetry.

"On the night that I heard him, he read some of his lyrics and
some of the satirical poems, making clear the beauty of the first and
not losing a good line in the second; he read an hilarious chapter of
an unfinished novel; and he read a long scene from *Him* with such
skill that any producer who is thinking of doing the play—which
would make more sense than half the season's offerings—had better
sign Cummings now for the part of the Personage, John Rutter, the
President pro tem of the Society for the Contraception of Vice."

Cummings, who was the first poet to read at the Poetry Center,
has also read there when the house was not only full, but overflowing
to the corridors. He says the "Y" is "still the best audience in New
York."

Cummings does not like the idea of having to read in public, and
he does it for the same reason that everyone else does. He does not
like the preparation that is involved—since he is conscientious about
it—because it takes him away from his work. (The care with which
he prepares his readings may be exemplified by a tape-recording he
once made for the National Association of Educational Broadcasters.
Self-rehearsed, he arrived at NBC, where a studio engineer suggested a run-through. Cummings said he was ready to record, no run-
through was necessary. His allotted time was 29 minutes 30 seconds.
He finished reading on the thirtieth second. The engineer insisted
on buying him a drink, and in fact bought him two.) He does not

like the travel that is often involved, because it takes him away from home as well as from work. But once arrived at his destination, and once fairly launched on the platform, he is a showman to his finger tips, establishing an instant rapport with his audience which the audience gives back to him.

I think, therefore, that Mr. Weales was correct in stating "He is an actor." Cummings has, in addition to the skills for which an audience pays to hear him, the true actor's responsibility toward that audience. He has read at most of the major centers of learning. There is room for mention of only a few.

He set out for Loyola University, Chicago, in the dead of winter and arrived in a blizzard, certain that no one would come to hear him. The hall was nevertheless full, and there were standees in the back. He was so surprised that he expressed it to a Jesuit brother, who replied: "Don't you know our motto? 'Discipline above all else'?"

The second surprise occurred just as he was being introduced.

"Here I was, all ready to give my reading," he related at Patchin Place, "when at the very last minute a group of nuns trooped solemnly in and sat down in the first row, right under my nose. You can be sure I made a quick change in the program."

"What change?" asked Allen Tate.

"I had to cut out several poems I had been planning to read." The omitted poems were "a salesman is an it that stinks Excuse" and "a politician is an arse upon."

"Oh, but you needn't have, Cummings," said Tate, amused. "Those nuns can take it, you know."

"Yes, but I couldn't," was the reply. "I was well brought up."

The third surprise occurred when, to prevent a rush for autographs, two husky Jesuits virtually lifted him by the shoulders and bore him down the aisle to safety. Cummings does not autograph for strangers (indeed, the only books he ever signs are those he gives to friends).

Winfield Townley Scott, poet and one-time literary editor of the Providence *Journal*, introduced Cummings at Brown University. He told me that Cummings had liked his remarks, particularly a reference to Thoreau:

" I said we New Englanders should claim Cummings as a regional poet," Scott wrote me. "Not in the accustomed sense, but in an intellectual sense. I quoted Emerson, 'Give all to love,' and Thoreau, 'Institutions are like snowdrifts: they occur where there is a lull in

the wind.' There, I said, if I understand Cummings's poetry at all,
are the two sides of his coin: love and rebellion. He is a direct heir
and descendant of the great New Englanders; and where we have
fixed in our firmament the stars of Emerson, Thoreau, Dickinson,
and Robinson, he too belongs and will remain there."

Mr. Scott also told me that at Professor Damon's house after the
reading, Cummings, on being praised by Mrs. Damon, pointed to her
husband, and said: "I owe everything to him."

2

In November of 1955, the English Club of the University of
North Carolina, wishing to inaugurate a series of talks by "truly outstanding authors and critics," invited Cummings to Chapel Hill. His
visit there was recorded both by a student and a member of the
faculty. Dr. Roy Moose, chairman of the English Club, wrote in the
Chapel Hill *News-Leader:*

"The visit to Chapel Hill last week of poet E. E. Cummings and
his wife, sponsored jointly by the English Club and Graham Memorial, was an astounding success that few who heard Mr. Cummings
will ever forget. For during his two-day visit, the renowned poet was
full of pleasant surprises.

"It was with uneasy trepidations that Dr. Lyman Cotten and I
greeted Mr. and Mrs. Cummings at the airport, for I had previously
received from his agent a list of taboos that made the poet seem to
be a recluse. However, much to our relief, Dr. Cotten and I met a
gentle, warm-hearted poet and a charming, sophisticated wife, both
of whom were eager to discover the 'spell' of Chapel Hill, since so
many of his friends had spoken about it so often.

"The only taboo that Mr. Cummings insisted upon was that he
not be photographed. He and Mrs. Cummings just do not like photographers, although Mrs. Cummings is a famous photographer in
her own right."

Dr. Cotten and his mother entertained them at a "small cocktail
party." The next day they sent her a dozen long-stemmed roses.

On a tour of the campus with Dr. Cotten, Cummings remarked
that the University has "the most attractive campus I have visited,
including Harvard, my alma mater." In the library he was shown
a collection of his own works, on display in the lobby. "Moreover,"

wrote Dr. Moose, "during his tour Mr. Cummings dropped into Dr. Cotten's modern poetry class and read one of his own poems to the class."

The tour of the campus was observed by a sharp-eyed student, J. A. Dunn, who wrote an account of it in the *Daily Tar Heel,* the University newspaper, under the heading of "e. e. cummings: an old old soul with wit and pan-pipes":

"They passed on, chatting brightly with one another, behaving completely unlike two men who had been all over the world, had seen all kinds of strange things and people, and had highlighted their lives by reading and writing thousands and thousands of words. I considered following the pair and playing at keen-eyed-observer-of-the celebrity, but discarded the thought in favor of discretion over curiosity, and had just resumed my conversation with the squirrel when two coed friends walked by buzzing tensely amongst one another. I hailed them.

" 'Do you know who that was?' one of them asked, barely able to control her excitement.

" 'Yes,' I said, 'that was . . . '

" 'That was e. e. cummings and we've been following him all over the campus. He came to class and Dr. Cotten dismissed the class and we've followed him *everywhere.* Come on.'

"I followed obediently. As Messrs. Cotten and cummings ambled past Bingham, and went into the library, the coeds gave me two (simultaneous) resumes of their morning's gumshoeing:

" 'We followed them out of Bingham and they went across campus and marched right up the steps into y-court and nobody recognized him. Isn't that funny? And then they went across the big stretch of land in front of GM—where all the big trees are, and they stopped and looked at bushes and trees and things, and laughed, and we followed them, and then they went into the Episcopalian Chapel and stayed in there for about fifteen minutes and we sat outside and waited for them and talked about him and everything, and then when they came out we followed them through the *Arboretum* and they just talked and laughed and carried on and then we came down here. Isn't that fabulous?' I agreed that it was, indeed, fabulous, and we shimmered private-detectiveishly into the library.

"Dr. Cotten and e. e. cummings were standing beside the door to the General College reading room and examining the e. e. cummings display case. I unobtrusively examined a poster plugging dialogue sermons on 'Roadblocks to Faith' and watched out of the corner of my eye. Mr. cummings didn't act like a poet. He didn't even laugh like a poet. Just a good hearty laugh. He and Dr. Cotten had a good hearty laugh over something, left the display case and went upstairs into the less frequented sanctums of the library. The two coeds and I followed, lost them, and finally re-discovered them going down the back stairs.

" 'They went down here,' said one of Mr. cummings' two—nay, three, counting myself—admirers in a stage whisper, leaning dangerously over the banister. We went down the stairs, but they were gone. 'Isn't he just *fabulous?*' she said.

"Just exactly how fabulous mr. cummings was became much more evident that evening at his reading in Hill Hall."

Cummings read the following poems, the same ones recorded earlier for the National Association of Educational Broadcasters:

> as freedom is a breakfastfood
> except in your
> of all the blessings which to man
> no time ago
> this is a rubbish of human rind
> a salesman is an it that stinks Excuse
> a politician is an arse upon
> i sing of Olaf glad and big
> kumrads die because they're told)
> a man who had fallen among thieves
> MEMORABILIA
> what freedom's not some under's mere above
> my father moved through dooms of love

3

On February 5, 1957, David McCord, poet and executive secretary of the Harvard Fund, wrote to Cummings from 4 Wadsworth House, Cambridge:

> As chairman of the Poetry Committee of the Boston Arts Festival—of which both Archibald MacLeish and Jack

Sweeney[1] at Harvard are members—I have the honor to invite you to be the Festival Poet in June of this year. Your predecessors have been successively Robert Frost, Carl Sandburg, and Archie himself.

We hope very much that you will accept this invitation and agree if possible to one of these two dates: Sunday, June 23, as first choice, and Sunday, June 16, as second.

We ask only that you write a poem for the occasion—which need not be long—perhaps 100 lines more or less. You would have an hour or an hour and a quarter at your disposal in the evening and the balance of your part would simply be reading from your own poems, preferably with commentary. The affair takes place in the evening in the Boston Public Gardens, and the crowd is both large (6- to 8,000 or so) and generous. The public address system is excellent so that your voice will easily carry across the open-air theater.

If you accept, the Festival Committee will be more than delighted. There is an honorarium of $500 plus traveling expenses, and you would receive the Festival Medal which goes each year to the poet of our choice.

This invitation from Mr. McCord touched off a prolonged correspondence, in the course of which Cummings withdrew his consent twice, was twice prevailed upon to reconsider, reconsidered, and at length made perhaps his most triumphant appearance as a reader.

> 4 Patchin Place
> New York City
> 11
>
> February 9 1957

Dear Mr. McCord—
    thank you for a most generous greeting;
    and a much more than kind invitation,which
    arrived like the proverbial bombshell.

---

[1] John L. Sweeney, Librarian, Houghton Library, Harvard.

Might I be granted a week or ten days to
collect my socalled senses? Here's hoping
                                        —sincerely
                              E. E. Cummings
it's a fact(is it not)that nothing but an hour's reading is
expected of the "festival poet":and that in "the occasional
poem" he can say whatever he likes?

This was clairvoyance. Mr. McCord wrote back:

> Yes, an hour's reading, with such comment as you care to
> make on each poem (or on poetry in general) is all that is
> expected.
> You can choose your own subject for the occasional poem.
> I enclose what Archie MacLeish wrote last summer—
> chiefly to guide you in length. There is no tradition about
> this since his was the first of the occasional poems in a
> series of three. For my own part, I should like to think that
> a Boston or New England subject might become a tradition
> since this is a New England festival. If we should ever in-
> vite my cousin Robinson Jeffers, he would undoubtedly
> change all that!

With the receipt of this letter the original bombshell turned into
a hand grenade, which Cummings tossed back:

> many thanks for your enlightening
> second letter and the copy of Archie's
> expert opus. Studying these documents,
> I realize what a "festival poem" should
> be;something quite(as it happens)foreign
> to my own feeling. Let me only add that
> am sorry I've wasted your time,and wish
> you may have much better luck with your
> next candidate

McCord wrote:

> Won't you reconsider and agree simply to read one new
> poem of any length whatever, on any subject whatever, and
> then read from and comment on some of your published
> poems? I take all this as a personal disappointment, since

I hope I am enough of a poet to understand your own strong feeling of individuality.

Cummings now replied:

> am delighted that "a new poem"
> will suffice;partly on general
> principles;partly because I've
> two new poems and should enjoy
> reading either of them. But
> one of these poems may be published
> in a Bard College magazine called
> Quarterly Review of Literature,and
> the other in a British periodical
> entitled Encounter,before June 23rd.
> Does this possibility disqualify
> both poems? I trust not

McCord wrote:

> I am joyful and springlike after reading your letter of February 24. Peter Temple and I (he is the manager of the Boston Arts Festival) see no possible objection to the fact that your poem may be published prior to June 23. If it is published—whichever one you elect to read—we shan't say anything about it.

Mr. Temple wrote on March 7:

> With the thought that you might welcome discussing the presentation ceremonies and reading scheduled for Sunday, June 23, I am writing to say I will be in New York Thursday next, the 14th, and would be available to meet with you. Around 11:30 is preferable for me, but I can make it earlier or later. If this is convenient, would you name the place?

Cummings replied:

> March 9, 1957
>
> Dear Mr. Temple—
> thanks for your letter of March 7.
> I'll be free from 3 to 3:30 next

Thursday afternoon(the 14th)and
trust you'll find it possible to
drop in here at that time:if not,
please telephone ORegon 5-5374;
preferably about noon. Patchin
place is off West 10th Street,
between Greenwich and Sixth Avenues:
but since taxidrivers never heard
of it you'd better say "113 West
10th Street",which they may understand.
Here's hoping

　　　　　　　　　　　　　—sincerely
　　　　　　　　　　　E. E. Cummings

Mr. Temple came, and the ceremonies were discussed. Nothing
was said about a "Festival poem." But an inquiry followed, April 8:

Dear Mr. Cummings:
　　Have you decided about allowing the Boston papers to
carry the poem? If this should be agreeable, I would appreciate your sending up a copy so we may have it accurately reproduced.

　　　　　　　　　　　Sincerely yours,
　　　　　　　　　　　Peter Temple

Cummings had not yet made up his mind which of his two new
poems it was to be, and soon another inquiry arrived:

Dear Mr. Cummings:
　　Sunday, June 23, now appears the best date from our
viewpoint, and assuming it is still convenient for you, I
wonder if we can settle on it.
　　Could you also let me know your feelings on release
of the poem to the local papers as we are being pressed
with inquiries.

　　　　　　　　　　　Sincerely yours,
　　　　　　　　　　　Peter Temple

The next day, Cummings sent copies of his poem to Mr. McCord,
with the following note:

4 Patchin Place

April 30 1957

Dear Mr McCord—
  at last my choice is made. Enclosed
  are two copies of the "principal" poem.
  Would you very kindly see that one copy
  reaches Mr. Temple;who has been most
  patient? And tell him(please)that if
  any miscalled newspaper can exactly
  reproduce these 28 lines,their progenitor
  will be both astonished & delighted

                                    —sincerely
                              E. E. Cummings

He also wrote to Temple:

          Sunday June 23rd suits me well.
          Will you please reserve two
          single adjoining rooms at The
          Parker House? My wife & I
          expect to arrive early Saturday
          evening

The poem selected by Cummings as his "principal" poem for the
Boston Arts Festival reading was inspired by the Hungarian uprising
of October, 1956. The apathy of the Western powers, and particularly
that of the United States, was an additional spur. Cummings told me:
"I was so frantic and sick, I felt I would die if I couldn't do something in this situation. Then the poem came."
  This is the poem:

                    THANKSGIVING
                       (1956)

      a monstering horror swallows
      this unworld me by you
      as the god of our fathers' fathers bows
      to a which that walks like a who

      but the voice-with-a-smile of democracy
      announces night and day

"all poor little peoples that want to be free
just trust in the u s a"

suddenly uprose hungary
and she gave a terrible cry
"no slave's unlife shall murder me
for i will freely die"

she cried so high thermopylae
heard her and marathon
and all prehuman history
and finally The Un

"be quiet little hungary
and do as you are bid
a good kind bear is angary
we fear for the quo pro quid"

uncle sam shrugs his pretty
pink shoulders you know how
and he twitches a liberal titty
and lisps "i'm busy right now"

so rah-rah-rah democracy
let's all be as thankful as hell
and bury the statue of liberty
(because it begins to smell)

A long silence descended on Boston. Like Sandburg's fog, it moved
on little cat feet from the Festival offices on Newbury Street and
over the Public Gardens. And in New York, Cummings waited for
word. The word that came was not from McCord or Temple. At noon
on Tuesday, May 21, Cummings dispatched the following wire to 4
Wadsworth House, Cambridge:

RUMORS HAVE REACHED ME WHICH comma FOLLOWING
YOUR FAILURE TO ACKNOWLEDGE MY LETTER OF APRIL
THIRTEENTH ENCLOSING A POEM ENTITLED THANKS-
GIVING 1956 comma MAKE ANY CONNECTION WITH THE
BOSTON ARTS FESTIVAL COMPLETELY UNDESIRABLE
FROM MY STANDPOINT semicolon KINDLY THEREFORE

Chapter 17

HARVARD REVISITED

suddenly it lies in the air like fame.
RILKE'S "ROSE."

1

"I don't know how it all started, but it seems that everyone was in favor of seeing the return of the native. I think the lectures were useful to him, too, to lay the ghosts of his Cambridge revolt."

The speaker was John H. Finley, Jr., a donnish professor of Greek, and Master of Eliot House, who talked with familiarity and ease about modern poetry, although he thinks a text of Aeschylus sufficient to occupy him contentedly for the rest of his life. We were discussing Cummings's appointment as the Charles Eliot Norton Professor of Poetry at Harvard, in which Dr. Finley had played an important role. From talk of the appointment we turned to talk about the appointee.

"Cummings," he said, "is closer to the modern world of abstraction and physics than other poets. He knows there is no return to a primitive world and primitivist images, as in Yeats, for example. Cummings's achievement is his mind as much—if not more—as his sensibilities. That is, he grasps things quickly, much in the manner of modern scientists and physicists."

It would appear, also, that the scientist and physicist see the earth whole, with a comprehension of Nature found only as a rule in naturalists and poets. Dr. Finley did not overlook the naturalist side of Cummings, for he went from abstraction to Nature as seen through Cummings's eyes. I am especially grateful to him for telling me about the poet's view of the woodchuck, an animal that farmers dislike and shoot on sight—if their markmanship is good.

"The farmer," Cummings had told Dr. Finley, "only sees two percent of the woodchuck, comprising that part which nibbles a few leaves in his vegetable garden. He doesn't see the other ninety-eight percent, the dignified animal who lives in his own world and has his own business to attend to, which he does very well."

2

The first word about the Harvard appointment came from Paul H. Buck, University Provost, who wrote Cummings on February 18, 1952:

> On behalf of Harvard University, I have the honor to extend to you a cordial invitation to accept a one-year appointment as Charles Eliot Norton Professor of Poetry for the academic year 1952–53 with a salary of $15,000. The Norton Professor must be in residence in the University from October 1 to Christmas, and from February 1 to May 1, and is expected to deliver not less than six lectures with obligation to publish these lectures through the Harvard University Press.
>
> The Charles Eliot Norton Professorship is our most distinguished appointment for visiting scholars in the field of the humanities.
>
> If you wish more information before making your decision, I shall be happy to answer your questions. Professor John H. Finley, Jr., Chairman of the Faculty Committee on the Charles Eliot Norton Professorship, is also writing you in greater detail about the appointment.

Dr. Finley wrote, February 19:

> I can imagine no one whose presence at Harvard would rouse more widespread interest or who would be welcomed more eagerly. . . .

Enclosed with this letter is a statement of the nature and purpose of the professorship. You will see that you are free to give to the term Poetry the interpretation you wish. In practice the chair has been occupied in alternate years by literary men and in the other years by musicians and men interested in the fine arts. Gilbert Murray's "The Classical Tradition in Poetry" and T. S. Eliot's "The Use of Poetry and the Use of Criticism" were obviously of a critical and analytical nature. C. M. Bowra's lectures on the English Romantic Poets and Thornton Wilder's series of a year ago, "The American Characteristics of Classical American Literature," were rather more historical in emphasis. One could imagine lectures of many other kinds. We have hoped that some subject may have been at the back of your mind in recent years which you might welcome this impulse to work out.

The terms of the professorship require a series of not less than six lectures. Many have extended them to eight, a few to ten. These have commonly been divided between the two college terms, and have tended to fall in November and December and again in March and April. Incumbents of the professorship are always asked by one or another department to give added instruction, formal or informal, for graduates or undergraduates, during one of the two college terms, and some have enjoyed the ties with students which grow from such courses. On the other hand there exists in the terms of the professorship no obligation whatsoever, express or implied, that a man assume such an added task. The sole stipulation beyond the giving and the publishing of the lectures is that of residence in Cambridge and of some association with faculty and students throughout the year. Norton Professors have commonly been absent from Cambridge during the so-called January reading period and the period of examinations which immediately follows, and the spirit of the stipulation has been felt to be carried out if men are here from early October to Christmas and again from early February until May.

I am sorry to say I do not know whether you are married. If not, or if you would be alone, one of the college Houses will be most eager to have you as a resident member, and

E. E. CUMMINGS / THE MAGIC-MAKER

though quarters in a House would not be free of charge, they would be cheaper than those available elsewhere as well as comfortable and in natural and easy access to faculty and students. If you preferred to live outside the college, that would be entirely acceptable.

I have so far left unexpressed all the more important things: our admiration for your life and writings, our hope that the return of the native to changed scenes would be stimulating and perhaps even encouraging, and our simple eagerness to have you here. The professorship best fulfills itself if it gives a spur to a man's doing what for want of such a clear interval he might never get around to. If it can perform some such function for you, it will fulfill our highest hopes.

Cummings thought it over. On February 23 he replied from Patchin Place:

Dear Mr. Buck—

your excellent letter (magnificently
seconded by Professor Finley's) has
arrived. May I ask for a little time
to consider this most generous invitation
with the careful seriousness which it
more than merits?

perhaps you'll be so very kind as to
tell me exactly when (and if possible
where) the six lectures are delivered;
how long each lecture is presumed to last;
whether or no a lecturer may say whatever
he likes in whatever way he chooses; and
(finally) if the appointee could postpone
his appearance until October 15

please assure Professor Finley that,should
anything lead me to suppose myself capable
of accepting,it certainly would be his cordial
and complete comprehending of the undersigned's
temperament and aim
                                    —sincerely
                                    E. E. Cummings

On February 25, Mr. Buck replied:

> I received today your letter of February 23 and hasten
> to reply that you may, of course, delay your decision until
> you have had time to give it careful consideration.
>
> As for your other questions, I believe Professor Finley
> could answer them in greater detail and perhaps more ap-
> propriately than I, and so I have referred them to him.
> You will therefore hear shortly from him. I might add that,
> should you decide to accept the Chair, there is no reason
> why you could not delay your coming to Cambridge until
> October 15.

On February 26, Dr. Finley wrote Cummings again:

> Mr. Buck has referred your recent letter to me, and I
> cannot be glad enough that Cambridge beckons at least suf-
> ficiently to raise questions. Some of them are very simply
> answered.
>
> For instance, the date of your appearance in Cambridge
> seems, within certain limits, quite unimportant. Certainly
> October 15th would be quite as acceptable as October 1st.
>
> As for your freedom in choosing and treating your sub-
> ject, it is clearly limited only by federal and state laws.
> You have been invited because of our respect for your
> mind and work, and anything you choose to say is what we
> wish to hear. From your letter I was not wholly clear what
> emphasis you gave the question about freedom of choice,
> and may be concerned with manner of exposition rather than
> with idea. There seems to me here much scope for fresh-
> ness and individuality. Mr. Copland has hit upon the novel
> scheme this year of talking himself rather generally about
> certain specific musical aims or problems and then at the
> conclusion of his lecture having a small concert, some-
> times with a singer or two, occasionally with three or four
> instruments. These concerts, as I understand them, do not
> specifically illustrate points made by him but have only a
> general relationship to his earlier argument. My reason for
> bringing up Mr. Copland's practice is simply to make clear
> that interesting departures from the conventional proce-
> dure of lectures are more than welcome. What such a de-

parture might be in your case I of course do not know. I can imagine a far more analytical and detailed treatment of certain poems, your own or those of others, than has been common hitherto. Conversely a more philosophic and speculative attack on the nature of poetry would seem more than possible. Special understanding might be evoked and communicated by reading poetry, with appropriate comment. One could conceive a scheme not unlike Mr. Copland's, by which certain general points were made first and these then followed simply by reading. . . .

As for the question of at least six formal appearances and where these would take place, we seem to have comparatively little freedom both under the terms of the gift and through tradition. The terms call for certain announced Norton lectures, which have become widely known throughout the college and the community. It seems obvious that they have become the most valued recurrent event at Harvard, when men appear who are not commonly here. They have been held either at the New Lecture Hall or at Sanders Theatre, the latter being slightly larger (though it does not seem so) and having somewhat more interest as a room.

The last letter in the series was brief:

4 Patchin Place
New York City

March 11, 1952

Dear Mr Buck—

I've decided to accept the appointment. Thank you for giving me so much time

—sincerely
E. E. Cummings

On May 5, 1952, the Harvard *Crimson* headlined the appointment. With the story was a photograph of Cummings wearing a beret. The same photograph appeared with another *Crimson* story, on October 3. This one announced:

NORTON PROF. CUMMINGS
WILL NOT TEACH COURSE

"E. E. Cummings, '15, this year's Charles Eliot Norton Professor of Poetry," it read, "will be in Cambridge sometime next week, but unlike the majority of his 18 predecessors in this post, he will not teach a course in the University.

"John H. Finley, '25, Eliot Professor of Greek Literature, said yesterday that Cummings, eminent American poet and painter, will be in town well before the first six Charles Eliot Norton Lectures, scheduled for October 28. According to Finley, Cummings was in Cambridge last week to rent an apartment, but then returned to New Hampshire.

"Explaining Cummings's failure to teach a course, Professor Finley said yesterday, 'I don't think that he is interested in the academic process. He is a poet, not a scholar, and he does not intend to make a pretense at being one.'

" 'A poet by definition is not a scholar,' Finley said, 'with the exception of a few, such as T. S. Eliot.' "

Cummings rented a house at 6 Wyman Road, Cambridge, where he and his wife lived during the time he held the Norton professorship. He told me that the reason he inquired about the October 15 date—in his letter to Mr. Buck—was that he wanted to be in New Hampshire "when the trees turned red," for him a never-missed event. The first lecture was delivered to "a packed Sanders Theatre audience" the night of October 28. By the third lecture it was standing room only. The *Crimson* reported on November 26:

CROWD JAMS SANDERS TO HEAR LAST
NORTON TALK TILL SPRING TERM

"A locked door and 'No More Admittances—Hall Filled' turned away over 50 students from the last E. E. Cummings lecture last night," said the *Crimson* story. "For twenty minutes the crowd pounded and fumed outside Sanders Theatre."

Between the third and fourth lectures—the latter delivered on February 16—Cummings and his wife left Cambridge for Patchin Place. The last lecture was delivered on March 16, after which the Cummingses left Cambridge for good, returning to New York only to prepare for their sojourn in New Hampshire.

The Charles Eliot Norton Lectures 1952–1953 were published by Harvard University Press, 1953, under the title *i: Six Nonlectures*. The book bears the dedication "For John Finley." The jacket photo-

graph was made by Marion Morehouse. It is a superb portrait of
Cummings, tanned from his summer in New Hampshire, in an open
white shirt, the bronzed neck powerfully cylindrical, the face full, the
eyes, as in life, thoughtful and piercing. He was then fifty-eight
years old.

The lectures were written during the summer of 1952. The pre-
dominantly autobiographical tone was the suggestion of a graduate
student, Norman Friedman, now Professor of English at Queens
College. Friedman told Cummings that nothing would be more
interesting to his audiences than hearing from him about the world
he grew up in, and the other formative influences of his life. This
suggestion, together with Professor Finley's letter about Copland,
provided the basic form for the six talks. In them Cummings set out
to review his whole life, from his birth in Cambridge to the time he
delivered the lectures there, taking in New York, Paris, two wars, and
several skirmishes on the way. The book is also a little anthology of his
work, prose as well as poetry, and the poems of others, some of them
surprising in this context: Wordsworth, Keats, Shelley, Nashe, Chaucer, Swinburne, Robert Burns, Charles d'Orléans, Dante, Donne,
Walter von der Volgelweide, and several ballads. Rossetti was not
included.

Commenting on his selections, Alfred Kazin wrote in *The New
Yorker:*

"[Cummings] has always made a point of defying the Philistines,
but at Harvard he stood up against our terrible century armed only
with his memories and the Golden Treasury."

But as this is precisely what Cummings did would it not have been
more to the point to examine what he accomplished by it? I prefer to
think that Cummings was stating that in a time of disorder like
ours, the artist is the guardian of order, and that even a world in
transformation is held up by pillars of the past. Mr. Kazin's review
was long and magnificent, but it was not about *i: Six Nonlectures.* "In
the new American scriptures, fathers don't count," he declared, after
quoting Cummings's letter to Paul Rosenfeld about his father. I confess I am ignorant of what the "new American scriptures" consist,
but I take it this is the new American criticism: "one reads a book
like this with disappointment at hearing so many familiar jokes told
over again, while the poet escapes into a fairyland of his fathers and

points with a shudder to all who are not, equally with him, his father's son."

3

Cummings's *Collected Poems* of 1938, as pointed out earlier, had been merely a selection, and three volumes had followed it—in 1940, 1944 and 1950. It was therefore gratifying to his followers when, in 1954, Harcourt, Brace published a large volume—468 pages —which contained all of Cummings's poetry then in book form, from *Tulips and Chimneys* (1923) through *Xaipe* (1950). The volume was called *Poems 1923–1954*. As no poems written after 1950 were included the title was, to say the least, ambiguous. It was not Cummings's title. He wrote Bernice Baumgarten, of Brandt and Brandt, his literary agents, March 11, 1954:

"Am sure that what I intended to suggest was a volume entitled, not COMPLETE POEMS, but POEMS 1923–1950; & comprising
  1) an index of first lines
  2) the full text of each of the following books
      as originally published:
      Tulips and Chimneys
      & (AND)
      XLI Poems
      is 5
      vv (viva)
      No Thanks
—selections from which constitute poems 1–293 of Collected Poems
  3) introduction & poems 294–315 of Collected Poems
  4) the full text of each of the following books as orig-
      inally published:
      50 Poems
      One Times One
      XAIPE
—nothing less & nothing more: *not,* for example, my contributions to Eight Harvard Poets, certain (if not all) of which may be found in books above mentioned; e.g. 'it may not always be so: and i say' which is Collected Poems 43 (from Tulips and Chimneys) & 'this

is the garden: colours come and go' which is Collected Poems 115 (from XLI Poems)

At all events, & whatever my earlier letter suggested, I wish to make perfectly clear that the preceding paragraph expresses my present wishes with regard to any collection of my poems published in the immediate future."

Cummings's letter was forwarded to Robert Giroux, editor-in-chief of Harcourt, Brace, who replied to Miss Baumgarten, March 16:

> Your letter of March 12th which we discussed on the phone yesterday, arrived this morning. This is simply by way of acknowledging it and to tell you that we are in complete agreement with Mr. Cummings's ideas regarding the contents. The eight poems in *Eight Harvard Poets* all turn up in somewhat different typographical form in the later books, so we have nothing to complain about. As for the index of first lines, we have actually started to compile this. I hope you will let me know when I can see Cummings and talk it over.

Meanwhile, contracts were drawn up. On June 8 Miss Baumgarten wrote Mr. Giroux:

> Marion Cummings wanted to discuss several points in the contracts with her lawyer, Alfred Rice, who is as you probably know Hemingway's lawyer as well. Mr. Rice has suggested several changes and because it seems simpler I have typed them into the copies you sent me although I believe the agreements will have to be redrawn.

Work on the book had already started, and for a time it even looked as though it might be ready for publication on Cummings's birthday. By midsummer the immense labor of proof-reading was well advanced. In charge of this phase of the operation was Catherine Carver of the Harcourt, Brace staff. The operation was involved, and required extraordinary patience and care. On August 11 Miss Carver wrote to Cummings in New Hampshire:

"I send you herewith revised proofs of pages 1–174, along with your set of marked pages. You will notice a few corrections still to be made, but on the whole I think they have followed your spacing changes faithfully."

Cummings had written in the top righthand corner of a page of corrections:

> in general—I want as
> much space(empty) as
> possible BETWEEN poems;
> when two poems, or one poem
> & a part of another poem,
> occur on the same page:but it
> 's an interesting fact
> that some poems,when juxta
> posed,tend to intermingle
> more than do others;hence
> I can make no rule,&
> "lift" or "lower" poems
> as seems best(visually)

One or two corrections may be cited for the light they throw on his attitude toward his work:

> 241 poem "XXVI" is what I'd call a *picture poem*—cf VII(p393) & 20(p440)—which loses its significance if runover. Consequently I've moved it to p 241 & renumbered it "XXV";following it with "XXVI"(formerly XXV). Here the space-between-poems is peculiarly important;so let's have as much as possible—i.e. start XXV at top of page & lower three lines of XXVI as far as possible.
>
> . . . . .
>
> 393 here again is a *picture poem*(cf p 141);so I've given it a chance to show itself. Start it at top of page, & put as much space as possible between it & poem VIII
>
> . . . . .
>
> 440 *picture poem* 20—see note on proof

Cummings continued to send in corrections, and to ask for corrected pages. He also wired:

> PLEASE CORRECT PAGE 243 POEM 29 STOP THE SECOND WORD OF THE FIRST LINE SHOULD BE A NOT THE STOP

THUS THE FIRST LINE SHOULD READ QUOTE IN A MIDDLE
OF A ROOM UNQUOTE

Western Union was somewhat baffled, and repeated "SHOULD BE A
NOT THE." This was on August 25; the same day he wrote Miss Carver: "I like the titlepage VERY MUCH. The dedication is ok as set. In
the typographically excellent Contents—& you certainly deserve a
diamond croix-de-guerre for typing it or them—please make these
additional corrections (besides those already marked in redink)."
On August 27 he wired again:

PAGE 261 POEM 52 PLEASE INSERT A CLOSING PARENTHE-
SIS AFTER THE WORD LEAF AT THE END OF THE EIGHTH
LINE

The same day he wrote Miss Carver:

> thank you for ordering the correction
> mentioned in my first telegram;& trust
> you received my 2nd wire,sent today
> am returning(with luxurious ease—thanks
> to your large envelope)corrected pages
> between 260 & the end;also pp. 42–43,218
> –219,& 256–257. Please have the following
> recorrections made & the resurrected pages
> sent me
>   p 42) restore the original setting of
>   "Bur   s"
>   304) lower poem 42
>   closeup parenthesis—line 9
>   387) insert "(One Times One)" under
>   "1 x 1"
>   411) "mayflowers:
>
>   quite"
>   442) lower poem 25 as far as possible
>   & distribute the extra space
>   evenly between the poems
>
> I await these recorrected pages;also the
> pages previously recorrected,also pp 242
> –243;also(as per my second wire)260–261—

> with the corrected 8th line of poem LIII,
> reading "acute from root to leaf)"
>
> may I sugest that in the Contents we don't
> need "Seventy-one Poems (after "XAIPE"?
> Seem to remember that the publisher(Oxford)
> was responsible for this addendum

By September there were clean pages, and Cummings realized with a start that the title of the book, which he had admired, was not what he had had in mind. He protested to Miss Baumgarten. As a result, on September 20 Mr. Giroux wrote Cummings in New Hampshire:

> I am very sorry that there is a misunderstanding between us about the dates and the title. It appeared "1923–1954" in the original contract. Since you changed it from *The Poems of E. E. Cummings: 1923–1954* to Poems 1923–1954, it appears that way in the present contract. It also appears in the catalogue copy which we sent you, and on the title-page proof which you approved. We therefore thought that it had your OK and, when Catherine Carver received (as we thought) your OK'd final revisions on September 7th, I released the book for the press. We were extremely distressed to learn on September 10th that you took exception to the dates and we hope that you will understand that we acted in good faith.
>
> If you feel that the dates, 1923–1954, imply that there are poems later than 1950 in the book, I can only answer that the very full table of contents, and the blurb, belie this. . . . What we have always meant by the 1954 in the title, and assumed you agreed with, was the date of *this* book. . . .

To this Cummings replied on September 26:

> re the misunderstanding about "1950":
> if our non(even more than usual)hero
> signed a contract reading "1954",it's
> obvious that noone's at fault but
> himself

Although bound copies were ready by Cummings's birthday, October 14, review copies had not been distributed in time to make that day the date of publication. Instead, October 25 was chosen; on that day, Catherine Carver dispatched the following telegram to Patchin Place:

HARCOURT BRACE IN GENERAL AND BOB GIROUX GERALD
GROSS AND I IN PARTICULAR WISH YOU A HAPPY PUBLICA-
TION DAY

On October 31, Randall Jarrell reviewed *Poems 1923–1954* in the New York *Times Book Review*. He wrote:
"This formidable collection is going to get much praise and several prizes, and will be for many readers a veritable feast: all this year and next, people will be rising from the book stuffed, their ribs sore with laughter, their wits sharpened with typographical puzzles, their eyes shining with big lyric tears. 'Good old Cummings!' they'll say. 'There's nobody like him.'

"And I will nod: it's so. And then I will sit there dumbly, a stranger at a feast which, to me, is not a feast at all but a picnic— a picnic which goes on for yard after yard, mile after mile, of hot dogs, rat cheese, soda crackers, boiled ham curled into imitation rose petals, Valentines, jokes and favors from the Jokes and Magic Shop, warm chain-store beer. Here and there, I have to admit—I'm eager to admit—one comes on real wildflowers, the realest and brightest of chipmunks, a portable phonograph playing a wonderful popular song, a gold lock of a drunk girl's hair; and the sun sets behind the picnic, and the moon rises before it, like things from the Iliad or things from a nickel postcard."

This, I take it, is the new American scriptures. His review concludes (in the manner of the new American criticism):
"What I like least about Cummings's poems is their pride in Cummings and their contempt for most other people; the difference between the I and you of the poems, and other people, is the poems' favorite subject. All of his work thanks God that he is not as other men."

The great achievement represented by the volume under review went disregarded so the reviewer could turn a phrase or two. It remained for the editors of the *Book Review* to quote from Cummings's work. In "Nonlecture One" Cummings said at Harvard:

"During my six fifteen minute poetry readings, I shall only try to read poetry as well as I don't know how. If you object 'but why not criticize as well?' I shall quote very briefly from a wonderful book, whose acquaintance I first made through a wonderful friend named Hildegarde Watson—a book whose English title is Letters To A Young Poet, and whose author is the German Poet Rainer Maria Rilke:

> Works of art are of an infinite loneliness and with nothing
> to be so little reached as with criticism. Only love can grasp
> and hold and fairly judge them.

In my proud and humble opinion, those two sentences are worth all the soi-disant criticism of the arts which has ever existed or will ever exist."

Later, in reply to a letter from a high school editor who asked for his "advice to teenagers who would try to try writing poetry," Cummings wrote "A Poet's Advice," which appeared in the Ottawa Hills (Grand Rapids, Michigan) High School *Spectator* of October 26, 1955:

> A poet is somebody who feels,and who expresses his feel-
> ings through words.
>
> This may sound easy. It isn't.
>
> A lot of people think or believe or know they feel—but
> that's thinking or believing or knowing;not feeling. And
> poetry is feeling—not knowing or believing or thinking.
>
> Almost anybody can learn to think or believe or know,
> but not a single human being can be taught to feel. Why?
> Because whenever you think or you believe or you know,
> you're a lot of other people:but the moment you feel,
> you're nobody-but-yourself.
>
> To be nobody-but-yourself—in a world which is doing
> its best,night and day,to make you everybody else—means
> to fight the hardest battle which any human being can
> fight;and never stop fighting.
>
> As for expressing nobody-but-yourself in words, that
> means working just a little harder than anybody who isn't
> a poet can possibly imagine. Why? Because nothing is quite
> as easy as using words like somebody else. We all of us

do exactly this nearly all of the time—and whenever we do it,we're not poets.

If, at the end of your first ten or fifteen years of fighting and working and feeling,you find you've written one line of one poem, you'll be very lucky indeed.

And so my advice to all young people who wish to become poets is:do something easy,like learning how to blow up the world—unless you're not only willing,but glad,to feel and work and fight till you die.

Does this sound dismal? It isn't.

It's the most wonderful life on earth.

Or so I feel.

Index of Persons and Places